Put a positive skew on GCSE Stats with CGP!

This CGP book explains everything you'll need to know for Edexcel 9-1 GCSE Statistics — forming a hypothesis, gathering data, interpreting your results... the lot! It covers Higher and Foundation Levels, with all the Higher topics clearly marked.

We've even included a free Online Edition of the whole book to read on the go. Super.

How to access your free Online Edition

This book includes a free Online Edition to read on your PC, Mac or tablet. To access it, just go to **cgpbooks.co.uk/extras** and enter this code...

4272 8270 0159 9106

By the way, this code only works for one person. If somebody else has used this book before you, they might have already claimed the Online Edition.

CGP — still the best! ☺

Our sole aim here at CGP is to produce the highest quality books — carefully written, immaculately presented and dangerously close to being funny.

Then we work our socks off to get them out to you — at the cheapest possible prices.

Contents

Published by CGP

Editors:
Will Garrison, Tom Miles, Alison Palin, Rosa Roberts, David Ryan, Caley Simpson

Contributors:
Andy Ballard, Sally Gill, Janet West

Data used to produce the Method of Transport table on page 31 Copyright: table CT0015EW: Method of Travel to Work, Census 2011, © Crown copyright, Office for National Statistics licensed under the Open Government Licence v.3.0. http://www.nationalarchives.gov.uk/doc/open-government-licence/version/3/

Data used to produce the RPI Price of Bread table on page 65 from the Office for National Statistics and contains public sector information licensed under the Open Government Licence v3.0 http://www.nationalarchives.gov.uk/doc/open-government-licence/version/3/

Data used to produce the Change in CPI Data table on page 66 from the Office for National Statistics and contains public sector information licensed under the Open Government Licence v3.0 http://www.nationalarchives.gov.uk/doc/open-government-licence/version/3/

ISBN: 978 1 78294 949 7

With thanks to Mona Allen and Glenn Rogers for the proofreading.
With thanks to Emily Smith for the copyright research.

Clipart from Corel®
Printed by Elanders Ltd, Newcastle upon Tyne

Based on the classic CGP style created by Richard Parsons.

Planning an Investigation

Statistics is all about <u>data</u> — you've got to <u>collect</u> it, <u>process</u> it and <u>interpret</u> it. But before you can get on with any of that, you need to know precisely what you're <u>investigating</u>. That's where a <u>hypothesis</u> comes in...

An Investigation starts with a Hypothesis

> A HYPOTHESIS is a <u>statement</u> that might be <u>true</u> or <u>false</u>, but you haven't got enough <u>evidence</u> to support it either way yet. A hypothesis must be <u>testable</u>.

 A tourist board wants to investigate whether more people go to a particular beach when the weather is warm. Suggest a suitable hypothesis for the tourist board to test.

You'd expect more people to go to the beach when it's warmer, so a <u>testable hypothesis</u> could be:
'<u>The higher the temperature, the more people go to the beach.</u>'

Once you've chosen a <u>hypothesis</u>, you should <u>plan</u> your investigation to <u>test</u> it. That means planning how you'll <u>collect</u> and <u>analyse</u> suitable <u>data</u>, and how you'll use it to draw <u>conclusions</u> about your hypothesis.

An Investigation has Several Stages

When <u>planning</u> an investigation, you should consider the <u>five stages</u> of the <u>statistical enquiry cycle</u> (see the example below) and plan what you'll do at each stage. In the exam you might be asked to give <u>examples</u> of things to include in a plan and to <u>explain</u> why they're <u>appropriate</u>.

 A tourist board is planning to investigate the popularity of a particular beach. Their hypothesis is 'the higher the temperature, the more people go to the beach'. Give five examples of other details they should include in their plan, and say why each is appropriate.

> **1.**   <u>Planning</u> — choose your hypothesis, what data to collect and how to record and use it

E.g. Measure air temperature at the beach to the <u>nearest degree</u> and observe the number of people there every Saturday at the <u>same time of day</u> for a <u>year</u>, so that data is recorded for <u>all seasons</u> and is <u>consistent</u>.

> **2.**   <u>Collecting data</u> — choose data sources and collection methods, identifying any constraints

E.g. Collect your own data (<u>primary data</u>). This should be <u>reliable</u> because you can <u>control</u> how the data is collected (e.g. you can record the temperature at the same time each day).

Constraints are <u>limitations</u> due to availability and reliability of data, practicalities of methods, etc. (see p.3).

> **3.**   <u>Processing and presenting data</u> — choose diagrams and measures, considering use of technology

E.g. Put the data in a <u>spreadsheet</u>, so that a scatter diagram and calculations can be produced <u>easily</u> and <u>accurately</u>.

> **4.**   <u>Interpreting results</u> — plan analysis in order to draw conclusions and make predictions

E.g. Interpret a <u>scatter diagram</u> to see if there's a <u>relationship</u> between temperature and number of people.

> **5.**   <u>Communicating results clearly and evaluating methods</u> — being aware of the target audience

E.g. Describe what the scatter diagram shows to suit the <u>target audience</u> — this will be a <u>clear</u> visual representation of the results.

<u>Evaluating</u> could involve planning <u>more analysis</u> — e.g. looking at the summer months separately.

Most people hate novelty ringtones — a detestable hypothesis...

Knowing the stages of the statistical enquiry cycle is pretty important, so read the page again, then try this question.

1) A researcher plans to investigate whether children can solve a logic puzzle faster than adults.
   a) Suggest a suitable hypothesis for the researcher to test.
   b) Using your hypothesis, explain three other details they could include in their investigation plan.

Planning an Investigation

This page is all about <u>problems</u> — problems to consider while <u>planning</u>, how planning can <u>reduce</u> problems and how it's a problem that I can't hold down a relationship. OK, the last one isn't on there — but enjoy the rest.

Think About Constraints at the Planning Stage

When you're planning where to get data from and how to collect it, you need to <u>identify constraints</u> (i.e. things that <u>limit</u> your choice of data sources and collection methods).

You should consider the following <u>constraints</u> when <u>planning</u> your investigation:

1) <u>Time</u> — you might be under pressure to do an investigation within a certain <u>time limit</u>.

2) <u>Costs</u> — there could be a <u>budget</u> or you might just want to <u>minimise spending</u>.
   Generally, the <u>longer</u> an investigation takes, the <u>more expensive</u> it becomes.
   You need to think about costs of <u>travel</u>, <u>equipment</u> you'll need, etc.

3) <u>Ethical issues</u> — make sure your research <u>doesn't cause</u> any <u>harm</u> or <u>distress</u> to anyone involved.
   Some hypotheses might be <u>unethical</u> (i.e. wrong) to actually test.

4) <u>Confidentiality</u> — some information might be considered <u>sensitive</u> (e.g. incomes and health).
   People might prefer to be <u>anonymous</u> (i.e. have their identity hidden).

5) <u>Convenience</u> — a hypothesis could be <u>difficult</u> or <u>impossible</u> to test.
   You should think about the most convenient way to <u>access</u> the data you need.

Together these constraints will affect <u>where</u> you get data from — e.g. whether you use <u>primary</u> or <u>secondary</u> data (see p.9) and the <u>method</u> you use to collect it (see Section Two).

Identify one problem that might occur with each of the following investigations:
a) A scientist wants to find out how a chemical affects organisms in a river.
b) A company wants to test the durability of the laptops that it makes.
c) A council wants to know the incomes of residents in a town.

a) E.g. The chemical could <u>harm</u> plants and animals, so testing it on them would be <u>unethical</u>.
b) E.g. This would be <u>expensive</u>, because you'd probably end up with lots of broken laptops.
c) E.g. A person's income is <u>sensitive</u>, so it could be <u>hard</u> to get <u>accurate data</u> (they might lie or refuse to answer).

Good Planning Helps Reduce Problems

Often problems can crop up as you're doing an investigation, but some can be <u>avoided</u> with good planning:

- You can <u>prevent</u> problems by doing a <u>pilot study</u> first (see p.19). E.g. if people struggle to answer parts of a pilot questionnaire, you can improve those questions for the real thing. You might also be able to deal with <u>unexpected outcomes</u> from a pilot study — e.g. make changes to your investigation.

- Choose a <u>data-collection method</u> to <u>suit the situation</u>. E.g. if it's <u>difficult to identify</u> the <u>whole population</u> (see p.10), you can choose a <u>sampling method</u> that works without a full list of everyone. Or, if a full experiment is <u>impractical</u>, you could use <u>simulation</u> instead (see p.25).

- For <u>questionnaires</u> there are ways to reduce <u>non-response</u> and <u>incomplete responses</u> (see p.18).

- The <u>random response technique</u> can get more accurate answers to <u>sensitive questions</u> (see p.19).

Failing to plan an investigation is planning to fail...

...Your GCSE Stats exam. So you'd better have a peruse over this page again, before trying this question.

1) Identify one constraint with each of the following investigations:
   a) Measuring how a group of primary school children respond to watching a super scary film.
   b) A company wants to know how many of their workers have had a mental illness.
   c) Misha needs to make a report on the weather in a town by the end of the week.
   d) Polly wants to find out the favourite animal of members of the royal family.

Types of Data

Here at CGP we cater for all data tastes. For the carnivores amongst you, I'd recommend the data served raw.

Raw Data is Unprocessed

RAW DATA is unprocessed.	1) Raw data <u>hasn't</u> been <u>processed</u> (edited) in <u>any</u> way.
	2) For example, a <u>list</u> of your friends' favourite colours or a <u>spreadsheet</u> of temperatures sent by a space probe.

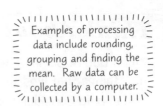
Examples of processing data include rounding, grouping and finding the mean. Raw data can be collected by a computer.

Data can be Quantitative or Qualitative

QUANTITATIVE DATA measures <u>quantities</u>.	1) <u>Quantitative data</u> is anything that you can measure with a <u>number</u>.
	2) For example, <u>heights</u> of people, the <u>time taken</u> to complete a task or the <u>mass</u> of puppies.
	3) Quantitative data tends to be <u>easier to analyse</u> than qualitative data.

QUALITATIVE DATA is <u>descriptive</u>.	1) <u>Qualitative data</u> is data that uses <u>words</u> to describe it — it doesn't use any numbers.
	2) For example, <u>gender</u>, eye <u>colour</u> or how <u>nice</u> a curry is.
	3) Qualitative data is quite often <u>subjective</u> (it depends on people's opinions) — e.g. are someone's eyes hazel or brown?
	4) So this sort of data is usually <u>harder to analyse</u> than quantitative data.

Quantitative Data is Either Discrete or Continuous

DISCRETE DATA is data that can be measured <u>exactly</u>.

1) If your data is something that's <u>countable</u> in whole numbers or can only take certain <u>individual values</u>, it's called <u>discrete data</u>.

2) Things like the <u>number of points</u> scored in a game, the <u>number of people</u> going into a shop on a Saturday and the <u>number of pages</u> in this revision guide are all examples of discrete data.

CONTINUOUS DATA is data that can take <u>any value</u> in an interval.

1) If your data is something that could <u>always</u> be <u>more accurately measured</u>, it's continuous data.

2) <u>Height</u> is an example of continuous data. E.g. a height that measures 297 mm to the nearest mm could actually take <u>any value</u> in the interval 296.5 mm to 297.5 mm. But you'd get a <u>more accurate</u> height if you measured to the nearest 0.1 mm or 0.01 mm or 0.001 mm or 0.0001 mm, etc...

3) Other things like the <u>weight</u> of a pumpkin, the <u>age</u> of a chicken and the <u>length</u> of a carrot are continuous data.

EXAMPLE: A darts player records the score of nine darts. Which two words best describe the data: raw, processed, qualitative, discrete, continuous?

<u>Raw</u> and <u>discrete</u> — the data is <u>unprocessed</u> and the score of each dart is a <u>countable</u> number.

Measuring how loud lions are — roar data...

Learn the different types of data on this page, then have a crack at the question below.

1) State whether the data below is   i) raw or processed,   ii) qualitative, discrete or continuous:
   a) The number of spectators at a rugby match, rounded to the nearest 100.
   b) A list of the different colours of pebbles on a beach.
   c) The fastest daily wind speeds, recorded by a weather station.

Types of Data

Time to look at something that's cold-blooded and might have scales — no not a reptile, it's more data.

You Can Put Data onto Different Scales

CATEGORICAL SCALES

Categorical scales give names or numbers to classes of qualitative data so the data can be more easily processed. The numbers are only used for labelling the classes — they don't have any other meaning.

E.g. You could split the data from a survey on eye colour into the classes 'blue', 'brown' and 'other'. Or you could describe people with blue eyes as class 1, brown eyes as class 2 and other as class 3.

ORDINAL SCALES

Ordinal (or rank) scales give numbers to the classes, which can be ordered in a meaningful way.

E.g. A survey could ask people to rank three celebrities in order of popularity by labelling them 1 (most popular), 2 or 3 (least popular). The numbers let you rank the celebs in order but don't give any information about how much more popular the celebrity at 1 is than those at 2 or 3.

Bivariate Data — Measuring Two Variables

Bivariate data is data that is made up of two (bi-) variables (-variate). A variable is anything that can be measured that may change.

1) In this set of data, each student had two variables recorded — shoe size and weight.

2) Bivariate data can be qualitative or quantitative — here shoe size is discrete and weight is continuous.

3) It can also be grouped (see p.7) or ungrouped — both of these variables are ungrouped.

4) For bivariate data, the variables are often called the 'explanatory' variable and 'response' variable — see p.22 for more on these.

Student A has size 3 feet and weighs 56 kg.

Student	A	B	C	D	E	F
Shoe size	3	11	7	7	5	6
Weight (kg)	56	77	60	56	54	68

Bivariate data consists of pairs of data values — i.e. there's a pair of values for each student.

Multivariate Data — More Than Two Variables

Multivariate data is data that is made up of more than two variables.

1) Here each student has four variables recorded — shoe size, weight, height and eye colour.

2) Like bivariate data, the variables can be qualitative or quantitative and also grouped or ungrouped.

3) There are different combinations of variables to compare — e.g. weight and eye colour, or all four variables.

Student A is also 151 cm tall and has brown (B) eyes.

Student	A	B	C	D	E	F
Shoe size	3	11	7	7	5	6
Weight (kg)	56	77	60	56	54	68
Height (cm)	151	181	163	158	159	172
Eye colour	B	G	B	B	Bl	G

Sorry, I can't date 'er — she's just not my type...

Nothing too complicated here — just a few more definitions to learn. Once you've got 'em, try this question:

1) The table below shows race position and jersey colour for the ten fastest cyclists in a race:

Cyclist	A	B	C	D	E	F	G	H	I	J
Race position	5	3	8	6	4	9	1	2	10	7
Jersey colour	Red	Black	White	Red	Yellow	Yellow	Green	White	Red	White

a) State which variable uses an ordinal scale.
b) Is the data bivariate or multivariate? [Higher only]

Higher

Higher

Simplifying Data

Tabular presentation of convoluted data is burdensome, methinks — perchance 'tis preferable to make plain henceforth. In other words, data in <u>complicated tables</u> might need <u>simplifying</u>. Gadzooks!

Simplifying Tables Makes Them Easier to Analyse

1) <u>Simplifying</u> a table can make it easier to pick out <u>useful information</u> and <u>spot patterns</u> in the data.

2) However, when you <u>simplify</u> tables of data, you're likely to end up with <u>less detail</u> in the new table than you started with (not surprising really). This means <u>important information</u> can be <u>lost</u>.

3) This table shows the numbers of different species of butterfly in the Marshy-Lea conservation area per year. The table has <u>lots</u> of data in it so it's <u>hard</u> to spot <u>trends</u> (patterns) in the data.

Species of Butterfly	2003	2004	2005	2006	2007
A	112	82	98	72	61
B	52	30	41	28	25
C	63	57	52	45	41
D	14	17	23	25	27
E	22	18	20	19	4

You can Simplify by Combining Categories

You can combine categories by <u>totalling</u> the data — this helps you spot <u>general trends</u>.

EXAMPLE:

a) Simplify the Marshy-Lea butterfly table above, by totalling the data for each year.

b) State whether the original or simplified table would be most suitable for the situations below. Give a reason for each answer.
   i) Presenting the trend in butterfly numbers to some primary school children.
   ii) Analysing the population of species D.

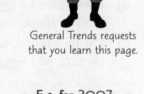

General Trends requests that you learn this page.

a) <u>Adding up</u> the data for each year gives the simplified table:

Year	2003	2004	2005	2006	2007
Total No. of Butterflies	263	204	234	189	158

E.g. for <u>2007</u>:
61 + 25 + 41 + 27 + 4
= <u>158 butterflies</u>

b) i) <u>Simplified table</u> — the extra information might be confusing for the <u>target audience</u> (primary school children).

   ii) <u>Original table</u> — there's <u>no information</u> about species D in the simplified table.

The simplified table shows that the <u>overall trend</u> is that the total number of butterflies is <u>decreasing</u>. However, some trends are <u>masked</u> — e.g. the number of species D butterflies is actually increasing slightly each year. You can read more about trends and other ways to interpret tables on page 31.

When I wear socks and sandals it's hard to spot any trends...

There's nothing too challenging on this page, but make sure you understand the consequences of simplifying data.

1) The table below shows the film ratings of a group of cinema-goers and the types of ticket they bought:

		Very bad	Bad	Good	Very good
Ticket Type	Child	2	5	11	15
	Adult	8	14	19	13
	Concession	7	0	1	5

a) Simplify the table by totalling the data for each rating category.
b) Explain one advantage and one disadvantage of simplifying the table in this way.

Grouping Data

It's often a good idea to put numerical data into groups. For example, if you asked 100 people their age, you'd have loads of different answers — it would make sense to group the data.

You can Split your Data into Classes

? Cutlery Category

1) The data you collect can be left ungrouped and processed directly.

2) But if there's lots of it or it's spread out over a large range you can make it more manageable by grouping it into different classes.

3) When you do this, it's important that you define the classes well so none of them overlap — this means that each bit of data can be put into only one class.

(1) The range of a class is called a class interval. Sometimes a class interval is shown with a hyphen (e.g. 40 – 59), and sometimes with inequality signs (e.g. $40 \leq x < 60$).

Score on a maths test	0 – 19	20 – 39	40 – 59	60 – 79	80 – 99
Number of people	6	13	14	8	9

Notice that the classes don't overlap — each score can be put into only one class. There are gaps between the classes because the data is discrete.

(2) The values at the top and bottom of the classes are called the upper and lower class boundaries (or class limits).

(3) The class width is the difference between the lower boundary of one group and the lower boundary of the next group. E.g. this class width is 80 – 60 = 20.

Grouping Data has Pros and Cons

PROS

1) Grouping puts the data into a form that's easy to read and process.

2) You can see patterns and compare the different classes.

CONS

1) You lose some of the accuracy of the data because you don't know what the exact data values are any more.

2) This means that calculations (such as the mean) are only estimates and diagrams can be misleading.

EXAMPLE: The IQ scores of 40 people are recorded in the table below.

IQ score	70 – 94	95 – 109	109 – 125	126 – 150
Number of people	4	17	14	5

a) Correct one of the class intervals so that there aren't any overlaps.
b) Find the class width of the 70 – 94 class.
c) Lewis wants to find the highest and lowest IQ scores. Explain whether he can use the table to find these values.

The classes here have different widths.

a) A score of 109 can go into two classes, so change 109 – 125 to 110 – 125 (or 95 – 109 to 95 – 108).

b) Class width = (lower boundary of 95 – 109) – (lower boundary of 70 – 94) = 95 – 70 = 25

c) The table doesn't show the exact values of the data, so Lewis could only estimate the highest and lowest scores — e.g. the highest IQ score could be anything from 126 to 150 (which is quite a big range).

Class boundaries overlapped when I met the Queen...

Be careful when making your own classes — remember, each data value should be able to go into only one class.

1) In a supermarket, 80 shoppers spend between £18 and £107 (to the nearest whole pound).
   a) Suggest suitable class intervals for grouping the data into classes of equal width.
   b) Give one disadvantage of grouping the data into these class intervals.

Grouping Data

Continuous data can take <u>any value</u> in a range, so there should be <u>no gaps</u> between the class intervals.
<u>Inequality signs</u> are used to make sure classes don't overlap — e.g. $0 \leq x < 5$, $5 \leq x < 10$, etc.

Choose Class Widths That are Suitable for the Data

Sometimes it's more <u>suitable</u> to have <u>unequal</u> class widths. Generally, you should choose <u>narrower</u> classes when there are <u>lots</u> of data values <u>close together</u>, and <u>wider</u> classes when values are more <u>spread out</u>.

EXAMPLE: The tables below show the temperature at which some workers drink their cup of tea. Both tables represent the same data. Compare the suitability of the class widths in each table.

①

Temperature (x °C)	Frequency
$20 < x \leq 30$	1
$30 < x \leq 40$	0
$40 < x \leq 50$	2
$50 < x \leq 60$	4
$60 < x \leq 70$	11
$70 < x \leq 80$	4

1) Table 2 combines the <u>first three classes</u> in Table 1 into one <u>wider</u> class. This makes the table <u>neater</u>, but you <u>lose information</u> — e.g. you don't know that there isn't any data between 30 °C and 40 °C.

2) A <u>large proportion</u> of the data is between <u>60 °C and 70 °C</u>, so it's a good idea to split it into <u>narrower</u> classes. Table 2 shows that more cups of tea were drunk at $60 < x \leq 65$ °C than at $65 < x \leq 70$ °C.

②

Temperature (x °C)	Frequency
$20 < x \leq 50$	3
$50 < x \leq 60$	4
$60 < x \leq 65$	8
$65 < x \leq 70$	3
$70 < x \leq 80$	4

Be Careful when Rounding Continuous Data

You need to be <u>careful</u> if you <u>round</u> data values <u>before</u> grouping the data.
Sometimes a <u>rounded value</u> might sneak into a different class and <u>distort</u> the data.

EXAMPLE: A 100 m sprinter runs the following practice times (t, in seconds):
11.56... 10.47... 9.98... 10.94... 11.89... 10.81... 11.77... 10.20... 11.91... 10.03...

a) Record the data in groups with a class width of 0.5 seconds.
b) Give one disadvantage of grouping in this way.
c) The sprinter decides to round the times to the nearest 0.1 seconds, before grouping the data. Explain how this could distort the data.

a) The <u>quickest</u> time is 9.98..., so the first class could be $9.5 < t \leq 10$.
The <u>slowest</u> time is 11.91..., so the final class will be $11.5 < t \leq 12$.
Completing the other classes gives the table:

Time (t seconds)	Frequency
$9.5 < t \leq 10$	1
$10 < t \leq 10.5$	3
$10.5 < t \leq 11$	2
$11 < t \leq 11.5$	0
$11.5 < t \leq 12$	4

b) The original <u>detail</u> has been <u>lost</u> — you no longer know the fastest time of 9.98... s, only that it's between 9.5 and 10 s (for all you know the sprinter might have beaten the world record time).

c) The time of <u>10.03 s</u> would be rounded down to <u>10.0 s</u> and recorded in the <u>wrong class</u> — i.e. in the $9.5 < t \leq 10$ class, instead of the $10 < t \leq 10.5$ class.

Over the Christmas period my figure is continuously rounding...

Make sure you can choose suitable class widths and can handle continuous data before trying this question.

1) The following times were recorded, in seconds, in the world championship snail racing competition:
   15.25, 15.04, 15.73, 16.42, 16.94, 15.85, 16.96, 15.02, 15.89, 16.53, 16.74, 15.94
   a) Round the times to the nearest 0.1 seconds, and group them in a table, with six equal classes between 14 and 17 seconds.
   b) Give one way that your table is misleading.
   c) Describe one disadvantage that doubling the class width would have.

Contestant 13 was disqualified due to a technicality.

Section One — Planning Data Collection

Data Sources

You need to collect data to provide evidence for or against your hypothesis. You can get your data from two different types of source — primary or secondary. Both types have their advantages and disadvantages.

You can use Primary Data...

PRIMARY DATA is data you have collected yourself.

1) There are lots of ways to gather primary data — e.g. questionnaires, interviews, experiments, observations, etc. You can find out all about these methods in Section Two.

2) The data you collect is usually raw data — i.e. it hasn't been processed.

PROS
- You can gather data that directly relates to and tests your hypothesis.
- You have complete control over your method of collection — so you know how reliable the data is.

CONS
- Some methods have problems with reliability — e.g. people might lie on a questionnaire.
- It can often cost a lot of time and money.
- It might be difficult or even impossible to collect your own data — e.g. from celebs.

...Or Secondary Data

SECONDARY DATA is data someone else has collected.

1) Sources of secondary data include — newspapers, magazines, websites, databases, historical records and the government's Office for National Statistics (ONS).

2) Secondary data has often already been processed — e.g. it could be presented as a graph or table.

3) When using secondary data, it's important to acknowledge your source.

PROS
- It can be easier to get hold of.
- You can gather data quickly and cheaply (sometimes for free).
- Data sets are often bigger than you could collect on your own.

CONS
- It might be in the wrong format or rounded.
- It could be difficult to find data that matches your hypothesis exactly — e.g. it might be out of date or there might not be any relevant data available.
- You don't know how accurate the data is — it might be biased or collected poorly.

You Might have to Spot Problems with Data Sources

EXAMPLE: A student uses data from a newspaper article to investigate the following hypothesis:
'Race horses are faster today than they were 20 years ago'.

a) Give two problems the student might have when using data from the newspaper.

b) Explain why the student needs to collect secondary rather than primary data.

a) E.g. The newspaper is trying to make an interesting story, so the data may be biased. The student is unlikely to know the reliability of the data.

b) It would be impossible to collect primary data for horses from 20 years ago.

Secondary data always needs to be treated with care — you need to check how accurate it is, make sure it represents the correct population and isn't biased.

Red or brown — it's time to choose your sauce...

When explaining the pros and cons of a data source, try to relate your answer to the context of the question.

1) Kiran plans to collect primary data to test the hypothesis:
   'Students in Year 10 get more pocket money than students in Year 7'.
   a) Suggest one problem Kiran might have in collecting her data.
   b) Explain why Kiran has chosen to collect primary data.

Populations and Sampling

When doing a statistical investigation you should identify what the population is.
Then you can decide how you're going to find out about it.

Population — The Group You Want to Find Out About

1) For any statistical project, you need to find out information about a group of people or things.
   This group is called the population. Examples of populations are:
   - All the pupils in a school.
   - All the 16-year-olds in the UK.
   - All the boxes of cereal produced by a factory.
   - All the newts living in a pond.

2) To investigate your hypothesis you can collect data from the whole population
   (a census, see below) or part of the population (from a sample, see next page).

Clean yourself, not cupboards
Cockroaches are a population too
Respect our 'roach rights

A Census Investigates Every Member of the Population

When you collect data about every member of a population, it's called a census.

1) If you want to carry out a census you need to carefully define your population. This means knowing
   exactly who or what's in the population, so you can be sure you've got data from every member.

2) It's easier to carry out a census on a small population because there are fewer members to survey.
   E.g. if you're finding out how long it takes every student in a class to get to school in the morning,
   the population is all the students in the class, so it's easy to just go and ask each of them.

3) There's a national census that counts all of the people in the UK every 10 years.
   A big questionnaire is sent to each household asking all sorts of questions about the people
   in the household. The government uses the data collected to plan services (e.g. healthcare)
   and developments (like housing and schools).

PROS
A census takes into account the whole population,
so the data you get will be accurate.

CONS
- For big populations it can be really hard or even impossible to do a census
  — it might take too long, cost too much, or be impractical.
- You might not be able to define the whole population, or access all the members.
- A census isn't an option when items are being used up or damaged by the investigation.

EXAMPLE: Explain why a census wouldn't be used in the following investigations:
a) A battery manufacturer wants to find out how long their batteries last.
b) A marine conservation group wants to find out the weight of sharks in the sea.

a) To carry out a census, the battery manufacturer needs to test
   every single battery. This would be impractical because all the
   batteries would be used up and there wouldn't be any left to sell.

b) It would be very difficult to define the whole population of
   sharks in the sea, and impossible to weigh them all.

'How is your health in general?
What passports do you hold?'

How does the government know so much — they sense us...

This page is nice and straightforward — once you've got your head around it have a go at this:

1) For the following statistical projects say what the population is and if it would be suitable to carry out a census:
   a) A business finding out the income of people who live on a certain street.
   b) A student finding out how much time 16-year-olds in the UK spend watching TV every day.
   c) A scientist finding out the size of grains of sand on a beach.
   d) The government finding out the full names of everyone in the UK.

Populations and Sampling

If investigating every member of the population is too difficult, you can just investigate some of them...

Sampling — a Cheap and Easy Alternative to a Census

1) Choosing <u>some</u> members of a population is called <u>sampling</u>
   — investigating a sample is a much <u>easier</u> way of finding out about a population.

2) You can use the data you collect to make <u>estimates</u> and <u>draw conclusions</u> about the <u>whole population</u>.

3) E.g. Pete needs to find out about the heights of trees in a <u>forest</u> for his biology project. Measuring every tree would take ages, so he measures a <u>sample of 50 trees</u> to represent the whole population.

PROS	Sampling is a lot <u>quicker</u>, <u>cheaper</u> and often <u>more practical</u> than doing a census of the entire population.	**CONS**	Samples <u>don't</u> give you information about <u>every member</u> of the population so the data can be <u>less accurate</u> and may be <u>biased</u>.

Make a Sample Frame from the Population

1) Before you can choose a sample from a population you need to make a <u>list</u> or <u>map</u> of <u>all the members</u> of the population — this is called a <u>sample frame</u>.

2) It's easiest to do this with a <u>small well-defined population</u> because:
   • if it's <u>small</u> it's easier to <u>list everything</u>.
   • if it's <u>well-defined</u> you know exactly what needs to be included.

**EXAMPLE:** A student is trying to find out the average Key Stage 2 SATs score for Maths in England in 2017. State the population and sample frame for this investigation.

The <u>population</u> would be all students in England who took the Key Stage 2 Maths SAT in 2017.
The <u>sample frame</u> would be a <u>list</u> of all students who took the Key Stage 2 Maths SAT in 2017.

Be Careful — Sample Data Must be Representative

1) It's <u>important</u> to make sure that a sample <u>fairly represents</u> the <u>whole population</u>. This means any <u>conclusions</u> you draw from the data in the sample can be <u>applied</u> to the whole population.

2) A <u>biased</u> sample is one that <u>doesn't fairly represent</u> the <u>whole population</u>. To avoid bias you need to:
   • Sample from the <u>correct population</u>. This means only choosing items from the <u>sample frame</u> and making sure that no items are <u>missing</u> from the sample frame.
   • Select your sample at <u>random</u> (see next page).

3) A <u>bigger sample</u> is <u>better</u> because it's more likely to be <u>representative</u>. It'll provide <u>more reliable data</u> — but it might be <u>less practical</u> to collect.

4) Even if <u>two samples</u> from a population are both sensibly chosen, the data (and any statistics you calculate) won't be exactly the same because the <u>samples are different</u>. This is called the <u>variability between samples</u>.

**EXAMPLE:** A study of the incomes of people in a town collects data from a sample of 10 households on one street. Explain whether this is a sensible sample.

The sample <u>isn't sensible</u> because the sample size is <u>too small</u> — the incomes of 10 households can't fairly represent the incomes of a whole town's population, which could be thousands.

All the people live in the <u>same street</u>, so the sample is only representative of that street and not the whole town.

When getting a sample — size matters...

...so that it's more representative. Learn the stuff on this page and then have a go at these fab questions:

1) A doctor's surgery wants to know the ages of registered patients. State the sample frame.

2) Pablo is investigating what music pupils at his school like to listen to. He chooses a Year 7 class as his sample. Explain whether his sample is likely to be representative of the population.

Random Sampling

Sampling is a good thing — but you can't just go round choosing the items you like the look of. There are several different methods for choosing samples on the next few pages.

Random Sampling Chooses Items at Random

1) In a random sample every person or item in a population has an equal chance of being chosen.
2) You need a full list of the population, so everyone has the same chance of being included.

PROS	CONS
Every member of the population has an equal chance of being selected, so it's completely unbiased and the sample should represent the population.	• It's not always practical or convenient — e.g. if the population is spread over a large area, the researcher will have to travel a lot. • It might be impossible to list the whole population or to access everyone.

Simple Random Sampling uses Random Numbers

1) Simple random sampling is a method for choosing a random sample.
2) It's easiest when you have a small, well-defined population.
3) To select the sample you need to use random numbers. Here's how you do it:

> 1) Assign a number to every member in the sample frame.
> 2) Use a computer, calculator, random number table/list, dice or cards to create a list of random numbers.
> 3) Finally, match the numbers of the members in the sample frame to the numbers on the random list to create the sample.

Dmitry wasn't so keen on the random thought generator.

EXAMPLE: Describe how you would use simple random sampling to select a sample of 30 students from a population of 900 students, using the random number table below.

1) Get a list of all the students (a sample frame) and assign the numbers 1 to 900 to the students.

2) Use the random number table to get a list of 30 different random numbers between 1 and 900. You need to make your method of choosing numbers from the table clear and stick to it.

- To get numbers between 1 and 900 you could choose to use the last three digits of each number and read across the table — e.g. the first number would be 712.

- If you come to a number that's outside your range (e.g. 936) or a repeated number (e.g. 712) you just ignore it.

- Keep going until you have 30 numbers: 712, 839, 210, ... 797, 044, 510.

0712	7839	6210	0335	1691	7748
5509	1784	7362	2731	1725	4283
9936	8012	3502	7523	3450	3718
6021	1344	9275	3281	2914	5002
1712	7787	3243	3262	3718	4452
5166	4797	1044	4510	2272	4971
1244	1397	4425	8677	0560	1986

3) Then match the 30 random numbers from the table with the list of students to get your sample.

Getting random numbers from a table will take a while — it'd be quicker to use a computer or calculator if you can.

Be good this year to get in Santa's sample frame...

Make sure you know how to use random numbers to select a random sample. Then try these...

1) You want to find out the average amount of pocket money received by students in your school. Describe how you would get a random sample of 40 from a population of 748 students.

2) The children in a class are numbered 1 to 28. Select a random sample of 9 children from the class using the random number table above. Explain your method clearly.

Section One — Planning Data Collection

Stratified Sampling

If the population splits into nice groups, it might be better to use <u>stratified sampling</u>.

Stratified Sampling uses Proportional Representation

1) Sometimes the population is made up of <u>groups</u> or <u>categories</u> — e.g. age groups or gender.

2) A <u>stratified sample</u> gives the different groups in the sample an amount of <u>representation</u> that's <u>proportional</u> to how big they are in the population — this means big groups get more representation and small groups get less.

3) This is useful when people in the <u>different groups</u> are likely to give <u>different results</u> — e.g. younger and older people might have different opinions of a film, so they need to be represented fairly.

PROS
- If you have <u>easy to define categories</u> in the population (e.g. males and females), this is likely to give you a <u>representative sample</u>.
- You can <u>compare results</u> from <u>different groups</u>.

CONS
It isn't useful when there <u>aren't</u> any <u>obvious categories</u> or when the categories are <u>hard</u> to <u>define</u>. It can be <u>expensive</u> because of the extra detail involved.

Here's the <u>method</u> for choosing a <u>stratified sample</u>:

1) Split the population into different <u>categories</u>.

2) Calculate the <u>number to sample</u> from each category, using: $\dfrac{\text{number in category}}{\text{total number}} \times \text{sample size}$

3) Use <u>random sampling</u> to choose the sample members from each category.

EXAMPLE: At Eastfield School there are 400 students in Year 10, 400 students in Year 11 and 200 students in Year 12. Describe how you could use stratified sampling to choose a sample of 50 students from the 1000 students in Years 10 to 12.

1) The population of 1000 students can be split into <u>three categories</u> — Years 10, 11 and 12.

2) Use: $\dfrac{\text{number in year group}}{\text{total number}} \times \text{sample size}$ ⟶ Year 10: (400 / 1000) × 50 = <u>20</u>, Year 11: (400 / 1000) × 50 = <u>20</u>, Year 12: (200 / 1000) × 50 = <u>10</u>

3) Use <u>random sampling</u> to choose <u>20 students</u> from <u>Year 10</u>, <u>20</u> from <u>Year 11</u> and <u>10</u> from <u>Year 12</u>.

You Can Stratify by More Than One Category

EXAMPLE: The table shows the distribution of students at Eastfield School by year group and gender. In a sample of 50 students, stratified by year group and gender, how many boys and girls from each year should be chosen?

	Boys	Girls	Total
Year 10	179	221	400
Year 11	196	204	400
Year 12	119	81	200

Year 10: (179 / 1000) × 50 = 8.95 and (221 / 1000) × 50 = 11.05. Rounding gives <u>9 boys</u> and <u>11 girls</u>.
Year 11: (196 / 1000) × 50 = 9.8 and (204 / 1000) × 50 = 10.2. Rounding gives <u>10 boys</u> and <u>10 girls</u>.
Year 12: (119 / 1000) × 50 = 5.95 and (81 / 1000) × 50 = 4.05. Rounding gives <u>6 boys</u> and <u>4 girls</u>.
<u>Check</u> that the rounded values add up to the sample size: 9 + 11 + 10 + 10 + 6 + 4 = <u>50 students</u> (all good).

My population has no groups — I can't get no stratifaction...

Remember that the proportion in the sample must be the same as in the population. Then have a go at this:

1) A data company investigates the voting habits in a town with 1500 adults. 600 of them earn less than £20 000, 750 earn between £20 000 and £40 000 (inclusive) and 150 earn more than £40 000.
   a) Explain whether stratified sampling would be suitable or not for this investigation.
   b) In a sample of 100 adults, stratified by income, how many adults from each income bracket should be chosen?

Systematic and Cluster Sampling

What's that I hear? You want more sampling methods? Well try these two beauties for size.

Systematic Sampling — Choosing Every n^{th} Item

1) You can use systematic sampling to generate your sample when the population is very large.
2) It works by choosing a random starting point and then taking a sample at regular intervals afterwards.
3) It's particularly good if you want a method to choose items for quality control checks on a mass production line because you can set the machines up so they sample every n^{th} item.

PROS Systematic sampling should produce an unbiased sample and can be carried out by machine.

CONS The nth item chosen might coincide with a pattern — e.g. if every tenth gizmo produced by a machine is faulty and you sample every tenth gizmo for quality control, your sample will either be completely faulty or completely without faults — either way, your sample will be biased.

EXAMPLE: A machine makes 10 000 computer chips a day. Describe how you would create a systematic sample of 100 computer chips on any day.

1) First you need to number all the computer chips 1 to 10 000.
2) Next divide the population size by your sample size — 10 000 ÷ 100 = 100 and then choose a random start number between 1 and 100 — e.g. 53.
3) Your sample would start with the 53rd computer chip on the list, and then every 100th one after that until you have 100 computer chips. So the sample would be the 53rd, 153rd, 253rd, 353rd... etc.

You could use a random number table or calculator for this bit.

Cluster Sampling Randomly Samples Groups

1) Sometimes, in a large population, you can pick out smaller groups called clusters — they're often based on criteria like location, e.g. towns within a county.
2) Cluster sampling is where a random sample of clusters is chosen, and then every member in those clusters is included in your sample.
3) The closer the distribution of members within the cluster is to the whole population, the less bias there will be in the sample.
4) For this type of sampling you only need a list of the clusters and the members in the sampled clusters.

PROS It's fairly convenient — it can save a lot on travel time when the population is spread over a large area.

CONS It's easy to get a biased sample though — e.g. people living in the same postal district could have similar incomes or employment. Or if the sampled clusters are similar to each other, you might get a biased sample.

EXAMPLE: A town council wants to know people's opinions on green energy. The town splits into 16 streets. Describe how to use cluster sampling to choose a sample of people from the town.

Each street in the town is a cluster, so choose a random sample of, say, 3 of the 16 streets.
Then everyone who lives in those streets makes up your sample.

Cluster sampling — trying those nutty bits in your cereal...

Make sure you can explain how systematic and cluster sampling work, then have a go at these questions:

1) A bakery makes biscuits in batches of 150. Describe how you would create a systematic sample of 30 biscuits from a batch.
2) A restaurant chain wants to get some customer feedback. They plan to randomly select one of their eight restaurants and survey the customers there. Give one advantage and one disadvantage of this sampling method.

Quota, Opportunity and Judgement Sampling

Sorry but I've crammed three sampling methods onto this page. But they <u>are</u> the last ones — honest...

Quota Sampling — Sample Until Quotas are Met

1) The population is divided up into <u>groups</u> — the groups could be based on <u>age</u>, <u>gender</u>, etc.

2) Then an interviewer is told to interview a <u>certain number</u> of people from each group
   — e.g. 20 men and 20 women over the age of 40, 15 men and 15 women under 40.

3) This method of sampling is often used in <u>interviews</u> carried out on high streets, and the
   final choice of the sample members is down to the interviewer — so it's <u>not random</u>.

PROS	CONS
It's <u>quick</u> to use, gives <u>representation</u> to different groups, and any member of the sample can be <u>replaced</u> by one with the same characteristics. It can be done if you have <u>no sample frame</u> (list of the population).	It can easily be <u>biased</u>, though — the sample chosen often depends on the <u>interviewer</u>. Also, the people who <u>refuse</u> to take part may all have similar points of view on the topic being surveyed.

Opportunity Sampling is Convenient

1) <u>Opportunity</u> (or <u>convenience</u>) <u>sampling</u> is where a sample is taken from a section
   of the population present at <u>one particular place and time</u>.

2) The sample is chosen for ease and <u>convenience</u> so it's <u>not random</u>.

3) For example, if you wanted to find out how much shoppers were spending but <u>only</u> asked people who
   walked past where you were standing, on one day and at one time, it would be convenience sampling.

PROS	CONS
It's easy to take the sample at a <u>time</u> and <u>place</u> that suits the <u>interviewer</u>. And you <u>don't</u> need a <u>sample frame</u>.	There's <u>no attempt</u> to make the sample <u>representative</u> of the population being surveyed — so it can be <u>very biased</u>.

EXAMPLE: A student wants to find out if people think the school tuck shop provides good value for money. She asks the first 20 people in the queue for the tuck shop at break time. State what type of sampling this is and explain why this isn't a representative sample.

This is <u>opportunity sampling</u>. Any students who don't shop at the tuck shop are <u>excluded</u> from giving their views. People who strongly think the tuck shop is bad value for money probably won't shop there, so the sample will be <u>biased</u> towards people with a <u>positive</u> opinion.

Judgement Sampling Aims to be Representative

1) The researcher uses their <u>judgement</u> to <u>choose</u> a sample that they think <u>represents the population</u>.

2) This can be useful when investigating something that is <u>obscure</u> or <u>very specific</u>, because the researcher
   may be able to choose a <u>more representative</u> sample than other sampling methods could.

3) E.g. A fashion brand is developing a new collection and wants feedback from people who wear similar
   items. Their researcher <u>chooses</u> people from the town centre to interview based on what they're wearing.

PROS	CONS
It can be <u>quick</u> to do and sometimes might be the <u>only</u> suitable method to use.	The researcher could be <u>unreliable</u> — they should have <u>good judgement</u> and <u>knowledge</u> of the population. It's <u>non-random</u> so can be <u>very biased</u>.

Judgement sample — only ask people with terrible dress sense...

I'd like to say do this question when you get the opportunity, or at your convenience, but do it now — now I say...

1) Explain whether the sampling methods below are quota, opportunity or judgement sampling:
   a) A researcher samples 200 people on the high street of a town at 10 am on a Monday morning.
   b) Paul surveys 30 blue-eyed people, 50 brown-eyed people, and 20 green-eyed people on his high street.
   c) A teacher chooses students to interview for research into the popularity of after-school clubs.

Revision Summary for Section One

Well, that wraps up <u>Section One</u> — there was loads of useful stuff in there, so it's time to see what you know.

- Try these questions and <u>tick off each one</u> when you <u>get it right</u>.
- When you've done <u>all the questions</u> for a topic and are <u>completely happy</u> with it, tick off the topic.

Planning an Investigation (p.2-3) ☑

1) Define "hypothesis". ☑
2) Describe the five stages of the statistical enquiry cycle. ☑
3) For each constraint below, give an example of an investigation where it might apply:
   a) ethical issues,   b) confidentiality,   c) convenience. ☑
4) Give one reason for carrying out a pilot study. ☑

Types of Data (p.4-9) ☑

5) What is raw data? ☑
6) Define qualitative and quantitative data. ☑
7) What is the difference between discrete and continuous data? Give one example of each. ☑
8) Give a definition and an example for the following: a) categorical scale,   b) ordinal scale. ☑
9) Define the following types of data: a) bivariate data,   b) multivariate data. [Higher only] ☑
10) Give one reason why you might want to simplify a table. ☑
11) Explain one disadvantage of totalling the data in a table. ☑
12) For grouped data, what are: a) class intervals?   b) upper and lower class boundaries? ☑
13) Give one advantage and one disadvantage of grouping data. ☑
14) Explain why you should be careful when grouping rounded continuous data. ☑
15) What is primary data? Give one pro and one con of primary data. ☑
16) What is secondary data? Give one pro and one con of secondary data. ☑
17) Describe a situation where using secondary data is more suitable than using primary data. ☑

Populations and Sampling (p.10-15) ☑

18) Define the following words: a) population,   b) census. ☑
19) Give an example of a population that it wouldn't be practical to take a census of. ☑
20) What is: a) sampling,   b) a sample frame? ☑
21) Describe two causes of bias when you're selecting a sample. ☑
22) Describe how to select a simple random sample of 25 from a population of 5000. ☑
23) What is a stratified sample? Give a method for selecting one. ☑
24) Describe how to select a systematic sample of 25 from a population of 5000. ☑
25) Give one advantage and one disadvantage of cluster sampling. ☑
26) Give one advantage and one disadvantage of quota sampling. ☑
27) Explain one way an opportunity sample might not be representative of the population. ☑
28) Describe a situation where you might choose to use judgement sampling. ☑

Questionnaires

Section Two is all about the various methods you can use to collect data. First up, it's the questionnaire — which is just a written list of questions. Sounds simple enough, but there's lots of stuff to consider.

Questions are Open or Closed

1) Closed questions have a fixed number of possible answers — e.g. yes/no or tick box questions. The good thing about closed questions is that you can easily process the data collected. Also, if the question is well designed, the responses won't be ambiguous at all. But, the answers are limited to the options given. Opinion scales give a statement and the respondent is asked to use a scale to say how strongly they agree or disagree with it — e.g. strongly disagree/disagree/neutral/agree/strongly agree.

> 1) Are you under 18 years of age?
> 2) Tick the mode of transport that you use to get to school.
> Bus ☐   Car ☐   Bike ☐
> Walking ☐   Other ☐

2) Open questions allow any answers. ⟶ | What is your favourite TV programme? |

They're particularly good for letting someone say exactly what they think. But the problem is that you might end up with such a wide range of answers that the data is really hard to process.

Design your Questionnaire Carefully

1) MAKE SURE YOUR QUESTIONS ARE RELEVANT

The data from the questionnaire should provide evidence either for or against your hypothesis.

2) QUESTIONS SHOULD BE CLEAR, BRIEF AND EASY TO UNDERSTAND

You might want to write your own answers to check questions are OK.

3) ALLOW FOR ALL POSSIBLE ANSWERS TO YOUR QUESTIONS

This is important if you're using a closed question — add an "other" category or e.g. "more than 10". If your answer options are ranges of data values, make sure that none of them overlap.

4) QUESTIONS SHOULDN'T BE LEADING OR BIASED

Leading or biased questions are ones that suggest what answer is wanted.
For example: "Do you agree that thrash metal is really good music?"
The problem with this question is that it could make the interviewee feel pressurised into saying 'yes'. A better question would be "What type of music do you prefer to listen to?"

5) QUESTIONS SHOULD BE UNAMBIGUOUS

Here's an example: "Do you play computer games a lot?"
This question could be interpreted differently by people. One person could answer yes, while another who plays the same amount could answer no. A better question would be "How many hours do you play computer games per week?" because it isn't open to different interpretations.

6) PEOPLE MAY NOT ANSWER QUESTIONS TRUTHFULLY

This is often because the question is sensitive and people are embarrassed about the answer — e.g. "What is your age?". You can get round this by using groups and closed questions, so they don't have to answer with their exact age (or you could have a "Prefer not to say" option).

Do you agree that penguins are better than seagulls?

I think we're all agreed on that one... Right, have a go at this question about, er, questions...

1) Give one criticism of each of these questions and write an improved version of each.
   a) Do you agree that maths is the most important subject taught in schools?
   b) Do you watch a lot of television?
   c) What is your favourite drink? Answer A, B or C.   A) Tea   B) Milk   C) Coffee

Questionnaires

Questionnaires are often the go-to method for collecting data, but they ain't all sunshine and rainbows...

Learn the Pros and Cons of Questionnaires

PROS
- Questionnaires are quick and cheap to make.
- Well-written ones shouldn't be biased.
- Respondents aren't under pressure, so their answers are likely to be truthful.
- There are lots of ways to distribute them to large numbers (see below).

CONS
- The distribution of questionnaires can lead to bias, depending on the method.
- They're easy to ignore, so there could be lots of non-responses (see below).
- Questions might not be understood by the respondent.

There are also advantages and disadvantages for the method used to distribute a questionnaire.
- HAND IT OUT — the target population gets the questionnaire, but it can be very time-consuming.
- PUT IT ONLINE — data is recorded and collected easily, but people without internet access are excluded.
- SEND IT IN THE POST/BY EMAIL — these are wide-reaching, but you're not sure who is responding to it.
- ASK PEOPLE TO COLLECT IT — easy to do, but people with strong views are more likely to take one.

Non-Response is a Big Problem

1) Non-response is when people in the sample don't respond to the questionnaire.
2) It could be for many reasons but it's often because people can't be bothered to answer the questions.

> Response rate is the number of responses to the questionnaire divided by the number sent out.

3) Here are some things you can do to improve the response rate:
   - Use clear questions that are easy to answer — you can test them with a pilot study (see p.19).
   - Follow up people who don't respond to your questionnaire — this could be impractical if you have a large sample size or they're spread over a large area.
   - Provide an incentive for them to answer — e.g. enter them into a prize draw.
   - Collect each of the questionnaires yourself — this way you'll get most or all of the responses, but is very time-consuming and not practical if the sample is across a large area.

You Might Get Some Incomplete Responses

1) Incomplete responses are when people respond to the questionnaire, but don't answer every question.
2) The missing answers could be random or for a particular question (e.g. if it's a sensitive question).
3) To reduce the number of missing answers use clear questions and be careful with sensitive questions.
4) There are several ways to deal with incomplete responses:
   - Discard all responses that are incomplete — this might be OK when you have lots of responses, but you might be removing certain parts of the population, which could lead to biased results.
   - Follow up people to fill in the missing answers.
   - Replace the missing answer by making an educated guess or substituting a value such as the mean. But be careful — this could have a big effect on the data if you have lots of incomplete responses.
   - You might even want to analyse incomplete responses to find any causes.

Who wants to do a questionnaire...

... is the (not so exciting) quiz spin-off. Make sure you learn the whole page and then try this question...

1) Rajan plans to distribute his questionnaire about public transport by handing out copies in his town centre.
   a) Give one advantage and one disadvantage of Rajan's plan for collecting data.
   b) Suggest one way Rajan could reduce the number of non-responses.

Questionnaires

This last page about questionnaires (finally!) covers <u>pilot studies</u> and <u>sensitive questions</u>.

Test your Questionnaire with a Pilot Study

A <u>pilot study</u> is where you test the questionnaire on a <u>small group</u> of people first.
There are a few <u>advantages</u> of doing this:

1) It should help you spot any questions that are <u>unclear</u> or <u>ambiguous</u>. Fixing poor questions should help to <u>increase</u> the <u>response rate</u> and decrease <u>incomplete responses</u>.

2) There might be an <u>unexpected outcome</u> — e.g. the answers might give evidence to refine your hypothesis or to change something about your investigation.

3) Any <u>problems</u> with the questionnaire are <u>easier</u> and <u>less costly</u> to fix before doing the full study.

4) You can <u>check</u> that your <u>methods</u> of <u>distribution</u> and <u>collection</u> work and can <u>estimate</u> the <u>time</u> and <u>costs</u> of doing the full study.

After doing your pilot study, make sure you keep a <u>record</u> of any problems that came up and the <u>changes</u> that you made to put them right. You might even decide to do <u>more</u> pilot studies.

Sensitive Questions Might be Answered Untruthfully

1) You might want to ask <u>sensitive questions</u> that some people <u>feel uncomfortable</u> answering.

2) As a result, people might <u>not answer truthfully</u> or may simply <u>ignore</u> the question.
This could <u>distort</u> the data and lead to <u>incomplete responses</u>.

3) Sensitive questions are often about <u>personal information</u>, such as people's <u>health</u> and <u>finances</u> — for example, "Do you have any health problems?" and "How much money do you make in a year?".

Use Random Response for Sensitive Questions

You can still get <u>accurate data</u> from sensitive questions by using the <u>random response technique</u>. This uses a <u>random event</u> to make sure that people who answer the question remain <u>anonymous</u> — which makes them <u>more likely</u> to answer it <u>truthfully</u>.

EXAMPLE: Explain how you could get accurate responses to the question "Have you committed a crime in the last 12 months?" using the random response technique.

Write the question like this:

> Toss a coin. If it lands on heads, tick 'yes'. If it lands on tails, please answer this question.
> Have you committed a crime in the last 12 months?   Yes ☐   No ☐

If 100 people are surveyed you'd expect <u>roughly 50</u> to toss <u>heads</u> and <u>roughly 50</u> to toss <u>tails</u>. So if there are <u>60 ticks</u> in the 'yes' boxes, it suggests about <u>10</u> of the <u>50</u> people who have tossed tails have committed a crime in the past 12 months. That's 20%, so it's likely that about <u>20 people</u> in the sample of 100 have committed a crime in the past 12 months. The <u>bigger your sample</u>, the <u>more accurate</u> the results will be.

Higher

Claiming that exam questions are too sensitive won't work...

...You'll still have to answer them all. Now give this question a go — note that part b) is Higher Level only.

1) Olga writes a questionnaire to investigate the driving habits of road users in her town.
   a) Give one reason why she might decide to do a pilot study.
   b) Olga sends the questionnaire to a sample of people and gets 328 responses. One of the questions is:
      "Toss a coin. If it lands on heads, answer 'yes'. If it lands on tails, please answer this question.
      Have you used a mobile phone when driving in the last three months?"
      203 people answer 'yes'. Estimate the proportion of people in the sample who have used
      a mobile phone when driving in the last three months.

Interviews

Questionnaires aren't the only way to get primary data — you can use interviews too. Fantabulous.

In Interviews You Question Each Person Individually

1) In interviews, you speak one-to-one with each person in your sample.

2) An interview could involve lots of specific questions from a questionnaire, which you complete for the interviewee, or it could just be a list of topics that you want to find out their opinions on.

3) You can carry out interviews face-to-face — where you ask someone the questions in person. You can also do them over the telephone (a phone survey) or the internet.

4) Interviews have some advantages and disadvantages when compared to questionnaires:

ADVANTAGES

1) You can ask more COMPLEX QUESTIONS in an interview.
If someone doesn't understand the question, you're there to explain what it means.

2) Face-to-face interviews usually have a HIGHER RESPONSE RATE.
If you're asking a person questions, it's a lot harder for them to ignore you than a piece of paper.

3) You know the RIGHT PERSON answered the questions.
If a questionnaire is sent out in the post it's possible for anyone to fill it in.

4) You can FOLLOW UP ANSWERS to questions if you think more information is needed.

DISADVANTAGES

1) Face-to-face interviews can take A LONG TIME to carry out.
Each interviewer can talk to only one person at a time, so it would take ages for large samples. Questionnaires can all be filled in at the same time.

2) Interviewing can be EXPENSIVE.
You might have to employ interviewers or travel large distances.

3) It's hard to get answers from a GEOGRAPHICALLY SPREAD OUT sample.
If a sample included people living across a large area, an interviewer would have a lot of travelling to do (unless you do a phone survey or use the internet).

4) The interviewees are more likely to LIE.
People might not want to answer sensitive questions in a face-to-face interview.

5) The answers could be recorded in a BIASED way.
This could be by accident if the interviewer isn't very well trained, or deliberate if the interviewer has strong views on a subject.

Question 154:
Do you prefer dogs or antelopes?

EXAMPLE: Two netball clubs are both investigating the health of their members.
Club A does interviews with every member of the club.
Club B sends a questionnaire to every member of the club.
Give two reasons why the method used by Club B could be more appropriate.

1) E.g. The interviews might be expensive — the club might want to employ a specialist to make sure that everyone is interviewed without bias and in a sensitive manner.

2) E.g. People are more likely to be untruthful about their health in an interview. They would feel more comfortable answering an anonymous questionnaire.

I didn't expect the Spanish Inquisition...

Nobody ever does... Anyway, make sure you learn all of this page before answering this question.

1) Anna is investigating people's opinions about using technology. She considers using interviews or questionnaires. Give two reasons why interviews might be more appropriate than questionnaires.

Observation and Reference Sources

Here I'm going to bowl you a googly and mix collecting <u>primary</u> and <u>secondary data</u> on the same page.

Observation Involves Counting or Measuring

When you <u>monitor</u> something you can <u>obtain</u> the <u>data</u> by <u>counting</u> or <u>measuring it</u>.

1) <u>Counting</u> — a lot of <u>discrete data</u> can be collected just by counting,
   e.g. counting the number of cars that pass a particular point.

2) <u>Measuring</u> — you can collect <u>continuous data</u> by measuring it,
   e.g. measuring the time it takes to eat a doughnut.

> An observation could be a simple survey or a more complex experiment (see p.22).

But continuous data <u>can't ever be measured exactly</u> so...
- You have to decide on a suitable <u>level of precision</u>. E.g. you'd probably measure someone's mass to the nearest 1 kg, or maybe the nearest 0.1 kg, and their height to the nearest cm.
- There's <u>always some error</u> associated with every measurement. The amount of error can <u>vary by half the unit</u> you're measuring to either way. E.g. if a cake weighs 540 g to the nearest 10 g, it could actually weigh between 535 g and 545 g.

Think About How to Record Your Data

You record data using a <u>data collection sheet</u>. This should be <u>designed</u> carefully depending on the <u>type of data</u> you're collecting and how you want to <u>analyse it</u>.

EXAMPLE: A newsagent's shop wants to collect data on its sales of two comics — The Meano and The Spandy. Design a data collection sheet they could use to record sales of the comics for 1 week.

You can record this data using a <u>tally chart</u>. You put a mark in the correct <u>row</u> in the <u>tally column</u> every time a comic is sold and then <u>add up</u> all the tallies in the <u>frequency column</u>.

Comic	Tally	Frequency
The Meano		
The Spandy		

Use Reference Sources Carefully

1) <u>Reference sources</u> are <u>secondary</u> sources of information — e.g. found online, or in published books or articles.

2) When using reference data you should <u>acknowledge its source</u> (i.e. where it came from). For example, for data found on the internet you should state the website you got it from.

3) You also need to consider the <u>reliability of the source</u> of the data — it could be <u>biased</u>. For example, data from the government's Office for National Statistics is usually more reliable than data from a newspaper (which could be biased towards a certain viewpoint).

4) Other problems with reference data can include it being <u>out of date</u>, processed in the <u>wrong format</u> or some data could be <u>incomplete/missing</u> (see p.26).

---

1 sheep, 2 sheep, 3 sheep, 4 sheep — zzzzzzzzzz...

Sorry, I must have nodded off. Make sure you learn the whole page and then have a go at these questions.

1) Draw a data collection sheet for counting the number of chickens that cross the road each day in a week.

2) Hans is investigating the number of endangered orangutans in the world. He gets his data from the internet. Give two disadvantages for Hans of using the internet as his data source.

Experiments

Here's the first of three pages on <u>experiments</u> — so lots for you to look forward to. First you need to know what experiments measure and be able to identify the different variables involved.

You Need to Identify Your Variables Clearly

A <u>variable</u> is anything that can be measured that may <u>change</u>, e.g. temperature or time. Experiments measure how <u>one variable</u> changes when you <u>change another variable</u>.

> The '**EXPLANATORY**' variable is the variable you are in <u>control of</u>.
> The '**RESPONSE**' variable is the variable you <u>measure</u> —
> it changes as a result of changing the explanatory variable.

The <u>explanatory</u> variable is called the <u>independent</u> variable, and the <u>response</u> variable is called the <u>dependent</u> variable.

You should <u>identify</u> the <u>explanatory</u> and <u>response</u> variables, so you can <u>keep everything else constant</u>.

On a graph you plot the explanatory variable on the x-axis (horizontal) and the response variable on the y-axis (vertical).

EXAMPLE: A walker wants to investigate the relationship between walking speed and heart rate. The walker measures his heart rate for different walking speeds. Identify the explanatory variable and the response variable.

The <u>explanatory</u> variable is his <u>walking speed</u>, because he controls that.
The <u>response</u> variable is his <u>heart rate</u>, because that's the variable he's measuring.

Heart rate doesn't affect walking speed, so it can't be the explanatory variable.

<u>Before</u> doing an experiment you might consider doing a <u>pre-test</u>. This is a <u>trial run</u> of the experiment, so you can spot any <u>problems</u> that might crop up. For experiments that use <u>lots of subjects</u>, you could do a pre-test on a <u>smaller scale</u>.

Keep All the Other Variables Constant

> **EXTRANEOUS VARIABLES** are any other variables (so <u>not</u> the explanatory or response variables) that could affect the experiment.

1) It's important to keep any extraneous variables <u>constant</u>, so they <u>don't influence</u> the response variable.

2) This means any change in the response variable <u>must</u> be due to changes in the explanatory variable.

EXAMPLE: Suggest three extraneous variables that might affect the results of the walker's experiment above. Explain each of your answers.

1) <u>Walking surface and gradient</u> — all walking needs to be done on the same surface (e.g. tarmac, gravel, grass, etc.) and at the same gradient because these will affect how much effort the walking takes.

2) <u>Weather conditions</u> — changes in weather and wind direction can affect how difficult it is to walk.

3) <u>Tiredness</u> — the walker's pulse rate should be back at rest rate before each trial. This means he's always starting from the same "zero" point.

In the real world it's <u>not always possible</u> to control <u>all</u> extraneous variables, but you should know what they are, so you don't draw the <u>wrong conclusions</u>.

Is Friends on TV? — the response is never variable...

...it's always yes. But that means you've probably seen it, so it's OK to miss it and answer this question.

1) A scientist is investigating the hypothesis that "younger people sleep for longer than older people".
   a) State what the explanatory and response variables are in this experiment.
   b) Give three extraneous variables that might affect the experiment.
      Explain how they could lead you to give the wrong conclusion.

Experiments — Lab, Field and Natural

It's about time you met the three amigos of experiment types — <u>laboratory</u>, <u>field</u> and <u>natural</u>.

Laboratory Experiments Give You A Lot of Control

1) In a <u>lab</u> (or similar environment) the explanatory and extraneous <u>variables</u> can be strictly <u>controlled</u>.

2) The <u>RELIABILITY</u> of an experiment is the extent to which <u>repeating</u> it will give <u>similar results</u>. Laboratory experiments are <u>very reliable</u>, because of the amount of control that you have.

3) The <u>VALIDITY</u> of an experiment is the extent to which it <u>measures</u> what it's <u>supposed to</u> measure. You can be fairly confident that any changes in the response variable are <u>only</u> due to changes in the explanatory variable, so the <u>data</u> from laboratory experiments should be <u>valid</u>.

 **EXAMPLE:** Explain why you would use a laboratory experiment to investigate how reaction times are affected by age.

The researcher can <u>control</u> the <u>ages</u> of the participants, can make sure the test is done in the <u>same way</u> each time and can <u>measure</u> the <u>times accurately</u>. They can <u>control extraneous variables</u>, such as background distractions, or what the participants have to eat or drink before the test.

A disadvantage of lab experiments is that people may not behave naturally, e.g. due to nerves or feeling under pressure.

Field Experiments are Carried out in the Real World

1) <u>Field experiments</u> are done in a <u>real-life environment</u>.

2) They're useful if you want to know how something behaves in the <u>real world</u> rather than a lab, or when doing the experiment in a <u>lab is impractical</u>.

3) The researcher controls the explanatory variable, but has <u>less control</u> over extraneous variables, so there's <u>lower reliability</u> and <u>validity</u>.

 **EXAMPLE:** Rita is studying whether children are more likely to play with toys of certain colours. Give one advantage and one disadvantage of doing this study as a field experiment.

<u>Advantage</u> — children could feel less stressed in their everyday surroundings, so results might be more <u>accurate</u>.
<u>Disadvantage</u> — Rita <u>can't control</u> extraneous variables, such as the behaviour of other children.

Natural Experiments Give You Very Little Control

1) Sometimes it can be very <u>difficult to control</u> the explanatory variable in a real-world experiment.

2) In a <u>natural experiment</u> you <u>don't change</u> the values of the <u>explanatory</u> variable — you just look at how <u>existing values</u> affect the response variable.

3) Since you have <u>very little control</u> over any variables, <u>reliability</u> and <u>validity</u> are <u>very low</u>.

 **EXAMPLE:**
a) Explain why a researcher would use a natural experiment to test the hypothesis: "Being overweight increases the chances of developing heart disease".
b) Briefly describe how they could design the experiment.

a) Because it would be <u>unethical</u> to 'feed people up' to certain weights and then investigate if this increases their chances of getting heart disease.

b) The researcher could choose people of <u>different weights</u> and <u>monitor</u> their health over a long period of time.

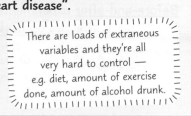
There are loads of extraneous variables and they're all very hard to control — e.g. diet, amount of exercise done, amount of alcohol drunk.

The lab, the field and au naturale...

Learn the advantages of each type of experiment, then use your experimental knowledge to answer this question.

1) Suggest the best type of experimental design (lab, field or natural) to test these hypotheses:
   a) The temperature of water affects the amount of sugar that can be dissolved in it.
   b) Bad weather conditions affect children's behaviour.
   c) Vitamin C supplements reduce the number of colds suffered in a year.

More on Experiments

If you're doing an experiment it's often good to compare <u>two groups</u>, so you can see if anything has <u>changed</u>.

Control Groups are Compared to Experimental Groups

1) Often an experiment involves investigating the effect of <u>one variable</u> on a sample from a population (e.g. the effect of a drug on a group of people).

2) When planning an experiment you can <u>randomly</u> assign members of the sample into <u>two groups</u>.

3) The <u>EXPERIMENTAL GROUP</u> is <u>treated</u> (e.g. given the drug) but the <u>CONTROL GROUP isn't</u>.

4) The control group is used as a <u>reference</u> — it lets you say with <u>more certainty</u> that any change you see in the experimental group is <u>due to the explanatory variable</u>, not just down to chance.

5) All the <u>extraneous variables</u> should be kept <u>constant</u>, so the <u>only</u> difference is the explanatory variable.

EXAMPLE: Tim has 10 strawberry plants and wants to investigate how using fertiliser affects the fruit of a plant. Explain how he could do this using a control group.

1) Randomly assign <u>5 plants</u> (half the sample) to pots that contain <u>soil only</u> (this is the <u>control</u> group) and the other <u>5 plants</u> to pots that contain <u>soil and fertiliser</u> (this is the <u>experimental</u> group).

2) All <u>extraneous variables</u> need to be <u>controlled</u> — e.g. the two groups need to be kept at the same temperature, get the same amount of light and the same amount of water.

3) Since the <u>only difference</u> between the groups is whether they had <u>fertiliser</u> or not, any differences in the size, colour or taste of the fruit should be due to the fertiliser.

Matched Pairs — Make them as Similar as Possible

1) <u>Matched pairs</u> uses a control group, but first the sample members are <u>put into pairs</u> that are as <u>similar</u> as possible. E.g. people could be paired up based on their height, weight, gender, intelligence etc.

2) Then <u>one member</u> from each pair is <u>randomly</u> assigned to the <u>control</u> or the <u>experimental</u> group.

3) For example, in a drugs trial people might be paired up based on their <u>age</u>. Both the control and the experimental groups will have a <u>mix of ages</u>, but this mix will be the <u>same</u> because the groups were made from matched pairs. This helps to <u>reduce variability</u> caused by age (an <u>extraneous</u> variable) and therefore <u>increases</u> the <u>reliability</u> of the experiment.

4) Just like above, any other <u>extraneous variables</u> are kept <u>constant</u> (as far as possible).

5) Then the <u>experimental</u> group is <u>treated</u> and the <u>control</u> is <u>not</u>. The response variable is then recorded.

6) Since the two groups are similar, any differences in the response variable are <u>likely</u> to be due to the different treatment — so the experiment's <u>validity</u> is <u>increased</u>.

Before-and-After — Test the Same Group Twice

<u>Before-and-after</u> experiments test the <u>same group</u> of people (or things) <u>before</u> and <u>after</u> an event to see how the group is affected by it. Like control groups and matched pairs, you try to keep all but one factor <u>constant</u>.

EXAMPLE: A company runs courses on improving your memory and wants to test a new system. Describe how the company would design the test.

A group of people would be given a <u>memory test</u>. After training in the new system, the <u>same group</u> of people would be given a <u>similar test again</u>. If the system works, the results of the second test will be better than the first.

Control groups — untreated and unloved — ahhhhhh...

Yes, control groups never get to have any fun. But you can by reading the page again and then trying this question.

1) Sharon wants to carry out an experiment to test the effect of light levels on a plant. She has two young pansies, grown from cuttings from the same plant. She puts one in a greenhouse and the other in a dark cellar. What is wrong with this experiment?

Simulation

Instead of going out and collecting your data, you can <u>generate</u> it based on information you know (intriguing).

Simulate Real Data by using Random Numbers

A <u>simulation</u> is a <u>prediction</u> of what might happen in a situation, based on some <u>previous data</u> or <u>known</u> <u>probabilities</u>. This is useful when collecting the real data would be <u>time-consuming</u>, <u>expensive</u> or <u>impractical</u>. To simulate data, use <u>random numbers</u> — e.g. from random number tables, dice, a calculator or computer.

EXAMPLE: A boxed toy randomly contains one of four characters, A, B, C or D. Use random numbers to simulate how many of the toys need to be bought before all four characters are collected.

1) <u>Choose a suitable method</u> for getting random numbers — e.g. a random number table.

2) <u>Assign numbers to the data</u>. Assign the numbers 1-100 to the different characters.
Each character is equally likely to be picked, so use the numbers
<u>01-25 for A</u>, <u>26-50 for B</u>, <u>51-75 for C</u> and <u>76-100 for D</u>.

3) <u>Generate two-digit random numbers</u>, using the random number table, until you have a number matching <u>all four</u> characters.
Here you could use the last two digits from each number in the table (use OO as 100). Start in the top left corner and read across each row.

Example of a random number table.

73**87**	47**36**	80**00**	63**76**
28**21**	31**28**	35**53**	6383

4) <u>Match the random numbers</u> to the correct character.
The numbers 87, 36, OO, 76, 21, 28 and 53 <u>represent</u>
D, B, D, D, A, B and C. So this simulation predicts that
<u>7 toys</u> need to be bought before all four characters are collected.

> To get a more reliable estimation you could repeat the simulation lots of times (possibly using a computer) and then calculate the mean number of toys bought before all are collected.

There are Different Ways to Get Random Numbers...

1) <u>Calculators</u> can generate <u>random numbers</u>. Your calculator might have a 'Ran#' function that generates a <u>random decimal</u> between 0 and 1 (e.g. 0.693 or 0.581). It might also have a 'RanInt' function that you can use to <u>set limits</u> — e.g. RanInt(1, 13) chooses a random whole number between 1 and 13.

> Make sure you know how your calculator works.

2) <u>Computers</u> are useful for generating <u>large amounts</u> of random numbers <u>quickly</u>, in the interval you want — e.g. a spreadsheet can generate 100 random numbers between 1 and 100.

3) A trusty <u>dice</u> is good for <u>six</u> random numbers and you can also use a deck of <u>cards</u>.

EXAMPLE: Over one month, a shopkeeper monitors the flavour of ice cream her customers buy. She finds that half of her customers choose vanilla, a third choose chocolate and a sixth choose mint. Explain how you could simulate the choice of ice cream for the next five customers.

1) <u>Choose a suitable method</u> for getting random numbers — you could use a fair dice in this case because it's easy to assign the outcomes to the numbers 1 to 6.

2) <u>Assign numbers to the data</u>. $\frac{1}{2}$ of 6 is 3 so use three numbers for <u>vanilla</u>, e.g. <u>1, 2 and 3</u>,
$\frac{1}{3}$ of 6 is 2 so use two numbers for <u>chocolate</u>, e.g. <u>4 and 5</u>, $\frac{1}{6}$ of 6 is 1 so use one number for <u>mint</u>, e.g. <u>6</u>.

3) <u>Generate five random numbers</u> by rolling the dice 5 times.

4) <u>Match the random numbers</u> to the flavour of ice cream.
E.g. the next five customers could be: 2 = <u>vanilla</u>, 4 = <u>chocolate</u>, 1 = <u>vanilla</u>, 6 = <u>mint</u>, 5 = <u>chocolate</u>.

You won't get a yellow card for diving into this page...

Make sure you know the four steps for simulating data before having a go at this question.

1) A box contains milk, white and dark chocolates. There is an equal chance of picking either a white or a dark chocolate. The probability of picking a milk chocolate is four times that of picking a white chocolate. Given that a chocolate is randomly selected then replaced, explain how you could simulate the next three selections.

Problems with Collected Data

Collected data may end up in a bit of a <u>mess</u>, especially if it's been recorded by <u>lots of different</u> people.

You Need to Spot Problems with Recorded Data

1) Some values might be <u>outliers</u> — values that seem out of place with the rest of the data. These could be accurate but <u>extreme</u> values, or <u>incorrectly recorded</u> — e.g. the height of 4.72 m is certainly <u>inaccurate</u>.

2) There could be <u>missing data</u> values — e.g. this eye colour is missing.

3) It might be given in the <u>wrong format</u> — e.g. the data for the 4th person is in the <u>wrong order</u> and some eye colours have been written as one letter instead of the word.

4) There might be <u>units</u> or <u>other symbols</u> in the data (particularly in spreadsheets) and <u>different units</u> may have been used (e.g. m and cm).

Eye colour	Height
Blue	4.72 m
	162 cm
Brown	1.49
1.80 m	Brown
G	157
B	1.73 m

Data is Cleaned by Fixing Problems

When there are problems with <u>raw data</u>, it should be '<u>cleaned</u>' before it is <u>processed</u>.

> **CLEANING DATA** means <u>fixing</u> problems — by <u>removing/correcting inaccuracies</u> and <u>missing data</u>, dealing with genuine <u>outliers</u>, putting data in the <u>same format</u> and <u>removing units/symbols</u>.

You might decide to <u>remove outliers</u> or use analysis that's unaffected by extreme values, but this could lead to inaccurate conclusions Another option is to try to <u>record</u> that data <u>again</u>, but this can be <u>difficult</u> and <u>time-consuming</u>.

EXAMPLE:

Kevin thinks that older students spend more money on their lunch than younger students. He carries out a census of the 1000 students at his school by asking them to fill in an online database with how much they spent on their lunch that day. The first few entries are shown in the table.

a) Explain three ways that Kevin could clean the data.
b) Give two problems with the method Kevin has used to collect the data.

Age	Money spent on lunch
13	1.80
14	£0
14	£2.05
Eleven	195p
15	
46	£5.25
Fourteen	168p

Cleaning the data gives:

Age	Money spent on lunch (£)
13	1.80
14	2.05
11	1.95
14	1.68

a) 1) Put the data in the <u>same format</u> by showing all ages as a <u>number</u> and all the money spent in <u>pounds</u>.

2) <u>Remove</u> the £ and p <u>symbols</u> from the money spent column.

3) <u>Remove outliers</u> (e.g. get rid of the person aged 46 or 'correct' it to 16 — it could be incorrectly recorded), <u>missing values</u> and any <u>zeros</u> (a zero could <u>distort</u> the data since the student didn't buy lunch).

b) 1) Some students might take a packed lunch, leading to <u>missing data</u>. So a <u>census</u> probably <u>isn't</u> a <u>suitable</u> way to collect data.

2) The amount students spent on their lunch that day might <u>not reflect</u> how much they spend on <u>other days</u>.

> Other problems include: students not responding, students filling in the database incorrectly/inconsistently or not having access to the internet.

First rule of the Stats Kitchen...

...Always clean raw data before processing. Double-check you know how to clean data and then try this question.

1) A group of students record how long it takes them to finish a short puzzle. The data is shown below.

Gender	103 s	Boy	Girl		F	Female	M
Time taken	Male	2 mins	137 s	178 s	53	1 min 9 s	0

Give two reasons why the data should be cleaned.

Revision Summary for Section Two

It's time to collect your wits (and maybe some data) and have a go at this block of Section Two questions.
- Try these questions and <u>tick off each one</u> when you <u>get it right</u>.
- When you've done <u>all the questions</u> for a topic and are <u>completely happy</u> with it, tick off the topic.

Questionnaires and Interviews (p.17-20) ☑

1)   What is the difference between open and closed questions?

2)   List three things you need to bear in mind when designing each question in a questionnaire.

3)   Give one advantage and one disadvantage of using a questionnaire to collect data.

4)   What's meant by a non-response to a questionnaire?
     Give two ways you can reduce the problem.

5)   What's meant by an incomplete response to a questionnaire?
     Give two ways you could deal with an incomplete response.

6)   What's the best way to test the quality of a questionnaire once you've written it?

7)   Explain why the following question might be answered untruthfully:
     "Have you dropped litter in public over the last month?"

8)   Describe the method of random response questioning. [Higher only]

9)   Give three advantages and three disadvantages of carrying out face-to-face interviews
     rather than asking your sample members to fill out a paper questionnaire.

Observation, Reference Sources and Experiments (p.21-24) ☐

10) Give two examples of collecting data through observation.

11) Describe a data collection sheet you could use to record the colour of cars
     that travel down a stretch of road, in the next five minutes.

12) Give two things you should think about when choosing a reference source for your data.

13) Explain the terms "explanatory variable" and "response variable"
     in the context of statistical experiments.

14) Why do you need to keep extraneous variables constant during experiments?

15) a) Name the three types of experiment.
     b) Give one example of each type of experiment.
     c) Comment on the reliability and validity of each type of experiment.

16) What is a control group? [Higher only]

17) What are matched pairs? [Higher only]

Simulation and Problems with Collected Data (p.25-26) ☑

18) Explain what data simulation is and when it might be useful.

19) A magician has successfully performed a trick 86 times and failed to perform it 14 times.
     Describe how you could use random numbers to simulate the outcome of the trick
     the next 5 times he performs it.

20) State two problems you might come across with recorded data.

21) Explain what is meant by cleaning data and give two examples of it.

Frequency Tables

Ahhhh, I love the smell of a new section. It's like that new car smell — fresh and clean and slightly odd.
This one is about <u>representing</u> your data. First up is <u>frequency tables</u> — they make data easier to analyse.

Raw Data Can be Organised into a Frequency Table

The word <u>FREQUENCY</u> means <u>how many</u>, so a <u>FREQUENCY TABLE</u> is just a table that shows <u>how many</u>
of <u>each value</u> or <u>category</u> there are. Here are some more things you need to know about frequency tables:

> 1) Frequency tables usually have three columns (or three rows).
> 2) The <u>first column</u> (or row) just gives the <u>VALUES</u> or <u>NAMES</u> of the different pieces of data
>   (e.g. 1 goal, 2 goals, etc.)
> 3) The <u>second column</u> (or row) shows a mark for each piece of data — this is the <u>TALLY</u>.
> 4) The <u>third column</u> (or row) is the <u>FREQUENCY</u>, which you get by <u>adding up</u> the tally marks.
> 5) You can draw a frequency table for data you've collected, or to <u>record</u> the data <u>straight into</u>.
> 6) An advantage of frequency tables is that they show the <u>actual data values</u>
>   — so <u>calculations</u> (e.g. the mean and median) using the table will be <u>exact</u>.

You Need to Know How to Draw a Frequency Table

EXAMPLE: A hockey team lists the number of goals they score in each match of a season.
Draw a frequency table for the data: 1, 2, 0, 3, 2, 1, 0, 2, 3, 2, 2, 1, 2, 0, 1, 5

Start by drawing a table with 3 columns — label them "<u>no. of goals</u>", "<u>tally</u>" and "<u>frequency</u>".
Then follow these steps:

(1) <u>Fill in</u> all the <u>values</u> or <u>names</u>
of the data — here it's
number of goals.
You need to cover the
<u>whole range</u> of data, 0-5.
Start with 0 in the first row.

No. of Goals	Tally	Frequency
0	III	3
1	IIII	4
2	IHI I	6
3	II	2
4		0
5	I	1

(3) <u>Add up</u> the tally marks in each
row to find the <u>frequency</u>.

*It's a good idea to cross off your data
as you go, e.g. X, X, Ø, 3... so you don't
miss one or count one twice.*

*You saw a frequency table as a
data collection sheet on page 21.*

(2) Draw a little <u>tally mark</u> in the correct row to represent each piece
of data. Tallies are bunched together in <u>fives</u>, e.g. IHI = 5.

<u>Don't</u> try to speed things up by <u>missing out</u> the <u>tallying</u> stage — you're more likely to make <u>mistakes</u>.

You Can Interpret Data from a Frequency Table

You can use the frequency table above to find out <u>two important things</u> from the data:

*See p.52 for how to
find averages from
frequency tables.*

1) <u>The total number of matches played</u> — <u>add up</u> all the numbers in the
<u>frequency</u> column. $3 + 4 + 6 + 2 + 1 = 16$, so <u>16 matches</u> were played in total.

2) <u>The total number of goals scored</u> — <u>multiply</u> the <u>number of goals</u> by the <u>frequency</u> and
<u>add up</u> all the answers — $(0 \times 3) + (1 \times 4) + (2 \times 6) + (3 \times 2) + (4 \times 0) + (5 \times 1)$
$= 0 + 4 + 12 + 6 + 0 + 5 = 27$, so <u>27 goals</u> were scored in total.

The frequency of bad jokes in these books is appalling...

Make sure you know how to draw and interpret a frequency table, before testing yourself with this snazzy question:
1) Sadio records the number of coins in his pocket at the end of each day in June.
Construct a frequency table to show the results.
5, 4, 3, 2, 3, 4, 4, 2, 0, 3, 4, 5, 4, 1, 3, 4, 2, 3, 2, 4, 3, 1, 2, 2, 3, 4, 2, 3, 5, 4.

Grouped Frequency Tables

Grouped frequency tables split data into... yes, you've guessed it, groups. The name kinda gives it away.

Class Intervals Should Never Overlap

1) GROUPED FREQUENCY TABLES are useful when you have a large range of data, because you don't need to draw a row/column for each value. You've already seen examples of them on pages 7-8.

2) The data is split into groups using class intervals — which should never overlap. Class intervals are different depending on the type of data you have — discrete data has gaps between classes (e.g. 1-5, 6-10) and continuous data has no gaps (e.g. $1 \leq x < 5$, $5 \leq x < 10$ — see below).

3) The first and last classes can be left open-ended — so the first class has no lower limit and the last class has no upper limit. This is useful when there are only a few values at either end of the data.

4) Grouping the data into classes makes it easier to understand and analyse, but it's less accurate as you don't know the exact values — so calculations are only estimates.

 **EXAMPLE:** The manager of a TV shop records the prices of 15 televisions that are sold one Saturday. Draw a frequency table for her data: £449, £250, £479, £499, £549, £525, £534, £1099, £650, £600, £589, £650, £599, £230, £689

1) Look at the data — the prices are discrete (they're exact pounds) and range from £230 to £1099.

2) Choose some sensible class intervals — to show this data in hundreds, you'd need nine class intervals and four of those intervals would be empty. So use an open-ended class for the first and last group.

3) Record the data — be careful to avoid overlaps (and there'll be gaps between the different classes).

Cost of TV (£)	less than 400	400–499	500–599	600–699	700 and over
Tally	||	|||	|||||	||||		
Frequency	2	3	5	4	1

Use Inequalities for Continuous Data

For continuous data, you don't want gaps between classes, so use inequalities to define your class intervals.

 **EXAMPLE:** Adam measured the heights of 12 plants in a biology experiment to the nearest 0.1 cm. Draw a frequency table for his data: 6.2, 1.3, 5.0, 7.2, 3.1, 8.8, 13.7, 7.1, 4.9, 19.6, 10.0, 15.0

1) Look at the data — the heights are continuous, so your frequency table should be grouped with no gaps.

2) Choose some sensible class intervals — the data ranges from 1.3 to 19.6, so go up in fives from 0 to 20.

3) Use inequalities to write the intervals and record the data — note that 5.0 (for example) goes into the second group and anything less than 5.0 goes into the first group.

Height (cm)	$0 \leq h < 5$	$5 \leq h < 10$	$10 \leq h < 15$	$15 \leq h < 20$
Tally	|||	|||||	||	||
Frequency	3	5	2	2

The rounding of continuous data can distort it (see p.8). The rounded height 10.0 cm above goes into the $10 \leq h < 15$ class, but the actual height could belong in the $5 \leq h < 10$ class (e.g. if it was 9.98 cm).

Class intervals — the part of school I enjoyed the most...

Once you've learnt how to group both discrete and continuous data into class intervals, have a go at this question:

1) Using the plant data above, complete a grouped frequency table using the following class intervals:

$0 < h \leq 4$ $4 < h \leq 8$ $8 < h \leq 12$ $12 < h \leq 16$ $16 < h \leq 20$

Two-Way Tables

Get ready for some more <u>data</u> and yet more <u>tables</u>. The fun continues...

Two-Way Tables are Used to Summarise Bivariate Data

1) <u>Bivariate data</u> measures <u>two variables</u> (see page 5), often to investigate <u>links</u> between them.
2) The two variables both describe the same thing, such as a person, an animal, a country, etc.
   E.g. age in years and height in cm of a person, or birth rate and average life expectancy of a country.
3) A <u>two-way table</u> is a good way of organising bivariate data — one variable is shown
   <u>vertically</u> (i.e. in the columns) and the other <u>horizontally</u> (i.e. in the rows).
4) Two-way tables often show <u>row and column totals</u> — these can help you find <u>missing values</u>.

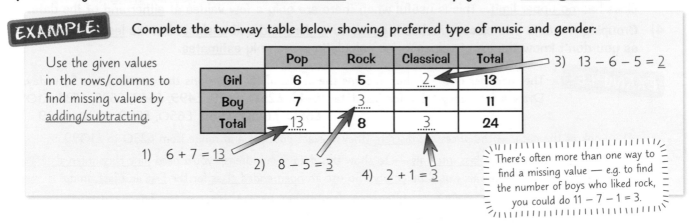

EXAMPLE: Complete the two-way table below showing preferred type of music and gender:

Use the given values in the rows/columns to find missing values by <u>adding/subtracting</u>.

	Pop	Rock	Classical	Total
Girl	6	5	2	13
Boy	7	3	1	11
Total	13	8	3	24

1) $6 + 7 = \underline{13}$
2) $8 - 5 = \underline{3}$
3) $13 - 6 - 5 = \underline{2}$
4) $2 + 1 = \underline{3}$

There's often more than one way to find a missing value — e.g. to find the number of boys who liked rock, you could do $11 - 7 - 1 = 3$.

You Need to be Able to Read Two-Way Tables

You might be given a completed two-way table and asked questions about <u>reading</u> and <u>interpreting</u> it.

EXAMPLE: An ecologist draws the following two-way table to show the weights and lengths of newts in a local pond:

The two variables are <u>weight in grams</u> and <u>length in millimetres</u>.

Length (mm)	Weight (g)		
	$10 \leq w < 40$	$40 \leq w < 70$	$70 \leq w < 100$
$50 \leq l < 70$	7	4	0
$70 \leq l < 90$	3	8	4
$90 \leq l < 120$	0	2	10

a) **How many newts weigh between 10 and 40 g?**

The <u>total</u> of the 1st column gives all the newts weighing between 10 and 40 g.
So you need to add up all the numbers: $7 + 3 + 0 = \underline{10 \text{ newts}}$.

b) **How many newts are between 90 and 120 mm long, and weigh between 70 and 100 g?**

Follow the row for $90 \leq l < 120$ mm across to where it meets the
column for $70 \leq w < 100$ g and that's your answer — <u>10 newts</u>.

Strangest part of a waitressing job — to weigh tables...

Once you're sure you know how to read data from a two-way table, answer these questions:

1) Complete the two-way table showing gender and test result.
2) Using the table above showing weights and lengths of newts, find:
   a) the number of newts that are between 70 and 90 mm long,
   b) the number of newts that weigh between 70 and 100 g,
   c) the number of newts that were measured altogether.

	Boy	Girl	Total
Pass	13		24
Fail		4	
Total	16		

Interpreting Tables

You'll be glad to hear that this is the last page on tables — this time it's all about <u>interpreting</u> them.

Interpreting Tables is Just Finding Information

1) You might be given a table (possibly with <u>real-world data</u>) and asked to <u>read</u> or <u>interpret</u> it.
2) Tables can be produced using a <u>spreadsheet</u> or some other <u>statistical software</u>. These are extremely useful for <u>sorting</u> and <u>processing</u> large amounts of data easily and presenting <u>summary statistics</u>.
3) You need to be comfortable doing the following things with a table of data:

- <u>Identifying</u> a value or category <u>directly</u> — e.g. the highest or lowest values for a category.
- Using the table to find a <u>total</u> or calculate a <u>percentage</u>.
- <u>Describing a trend</u> (i.e. a pattern) in the data — this is usually saying whether it's <u>upwards</u> (<u>increasing</u>) or <u>downwards</u> (<u>decreasing</u>) over time. Trends are <u>general</u> — it's OK for the odd value to not fit the trend, but the overall pattern should be upwards or downwards.
- <u>Explaining</u> why part of the table might be <u>inconsistent</u> — e.g. the total of a column might actually be different from its sum because values have been <u>rounded</u>.

EXAMPLE:

The table below shows the percentage of people using different methods of travelling to work across different regions of England in 2011.

a) Which region had the largest percentage of people travelling to work on foot?
b) What percentage of people in the East travelled to work by car?
c) The percentages for each region don't add up to 100%. Explain why.
d) Describe the trend for the different methods of travelling in all of the regions.
e) Jim says 'More people travel to work by bus in Yorkshire than in the North West'. Give a reason why Jim might be wrong.

'Just dropping by the office.'

Region	Method of Transport		
	Car	Bus	Foot
North West	65.4%	8.1%	10.2%
Yorkshire	64.4%	8.4%	10.9%
East	63.3%	3.7%	9.1%
South West	63.8%	4.6%	12.2%

(Source: adapted from data from the Office for National Statistics)

a) Follow the column for <u>foot</u> down to the <u>largest percentage</u>, then follow this row along to find the region — <u>South West</u>.

b) Follow the row for <u>East</u> across to where it meets the column for <u>car</u> — <u>63.3%</u>.

c) The percentages for each region add up to <u>less than 100%</u> — e.g. for the East: 63.3 + 3.7 + 9.1 = 76.1%. The table only shows <u>some of the methods</u> — other people might cycle, get the train or parachute to work.

d) <u>Look at the data</u> in each column to spot any <u>trends</u> — all the regions follow a similar pattern. For each region the <u>car</u> is (by far) the <u>most popular</u> method of transport, followed by on <u>foot</u> then the <u>bus</u>.

e) The table <u>doesn't say how many people</u> are in each region. Saying 'A <u>higher proportion</u> of people travel to work by bus in Yorkshire than in the North West' would be a better (and more accurate) statement.

Les tables ont quatre jambes...

Once you're happy with finding information from a table of data, have a go at the question below:

1) The table below shows the profit of a small business, by each of its three branches, from 2014 to 2018.

Profit (£1000s)	2014	2015	2016	2017	2018
Wickersley	21.6	21.9	21.8	22.3	23.4
Maltby	51.5	50.2	48.1	48.3	44.8
Rawmarsh	32.1	31.3	28.2	28.2	26.7
Total profit	105.2	103.3	98.1	98.8	94.9

a) Find the percentage of the total profit that came from Maltby in 2015.
b) Describe the overall trend of the total profit from 2014 to 2018.
c) Give a possible reason why profits in the 2015 column don't exactly add up to the total profit shown.

Bar Charts

It's a good idea to represent qualitative or discrete data as <u>pictograms</u> or <u>bar charts</u>.

Pictograms use Pictures to Represent Data

In a <u>pictogram</u>, a <u>symbol</u> is used to show a particular <u>number of items</u> — e.g. ★ = 4 books.
This means a fraction of a symbol represents a fraction of the number of items — e.g. ⬧ = 2 books.
Pictograms are a <u>simple</u> way to show data and are usually drawn in a <u>table</u> with a <u>key</u>.

EXAMPLE: In a survey, Peter asked the pupils in his school what their favourite colour was.
The results are shown in the pictogram below.

a) How many pupils liked blue best?
b) 15 pupils said their favourite colour was yellow. Complete the pictogram.
c) How many more pupils chose green than chose red?

a) Number of stick men in the blue row = 2.5.
2.5 × 10 = <u>25 pupils</u> liked blue best.

b) First, use the <u>key</u> to work out how many stick men
you need. 1 stick man = 10 pupils, so 15 ÷ 10 = <u>1.5 stick men</u>.
Then <u>draw</u> the stick men in the correct row.

c) Number of pupils that chose red = 3 × 10 = 30 pupils.
Number of pupils that chose green = 5 × 10 = 50 pupils.
50 − 30 = <u>20 more pupils</u> chose green than chose red.

🚶 = 10 pupils

Purple	🚶🚶🚶
Blue	🚶🚶⬧
Yellow	🚶⬧
Red	🚶🚶🚶
Green	🚶🚶🚶🚶🚶

Multiple Bar Charts Can be Used to Compare Data Sets

1) <u>Simple bar charts</u> show <u>frequencies</u> of data values or names in a data set — the <u>frequency</u> is
plotted up the <u>side</u> and the <u>data labels</u> along the <u>bottom</u>.

2) <u>Multiple bar charts</u> show <u>two or more</u> sets of data at
once so it's easy to <u>compare</u> them. Each category
has two or more bars — one for each data set.

The multiple bar chart on the right shows the
same data as above, but it's split into two sets
— <u>boys</u> and <u>girls</u>.

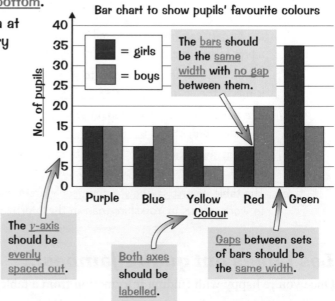

Bar chart to show pupils' favourite colours

The <u>bars</u> should
be the <u>same</u>
<u>width</u> with <u>no gap</u>
between them.

The <u>y-axis</u>
should be
<u>evenly</u>
<u>spaced out</u>.

<u>Both axes</u>
should be
<u>labelled</u>.

<u>Gaps</u> between sets
of bars should be
the <u>same width</u>.

EXAMPLE: Use the bar chart on the right
to answer the following questions:

a) What was the most popular
colour amongst the boys?
b) How many more girls
than boys like green?

a) The highest blue bar is for <u>red</u>.

b) 35 girls like green and 15 boys like green.
35 − 15 = <u>20 more girls</u>.

Pictograms — the one time you get away with drawing stick men...

Have a recap of how to draw and interpret these charts,
then answer the following question:

1) The pictogram on the right shows the number of
books withdrawn from a library during a week.
a) On which day was the smallest number of books withdrawn?
b) How many books were withdrawn in total?

⬤ = 40 books

Monday	⬤⬤⬤
Tuesday	◹
Wednesday	⬤⬤◖
Thursday	⬤⬤⬤
Friday	⬤

Bar Charts

This page has more bar charts for <u>qualitative</u> and <u>discrete</u> data than you can shake a ~~stick~~ bar at.

Composite Bar Charts show Categories in the Data

1) A <u>composite bar chart</u> has <u>single</u> bars, split into <u>sections</u>. The sections show <u>frequencies</u> for the different <u>categories</u> that make up the whole bar.

2) It's easy to read off <u>total frequencies</u> (the heights of the bars), and it's <u>simpler</u> to look at than data in a big table. However, if there are <u>lots of categories</u> it can be <u>difficult</u> to compare them.

The composite bar chart below shows the number of men, women and children visiting a country show.

 Use the bar chart on the right to answer the following questions:

a) On which day was the country show busiest?

b) On which days were there more children than women?

a) Look at the total number of people shown by the height of the bars. <u>Saturday</u> was busiest — it's the highest bar.

b) Look for days with longer green bars than pink bars:
<u>Saturday</u> — 90 children and 70 women, and <u>Sunday</u> — 80 children and 50 women.

Make sure you read the axis carefully — it goes up in 20s, so half a row is 10.

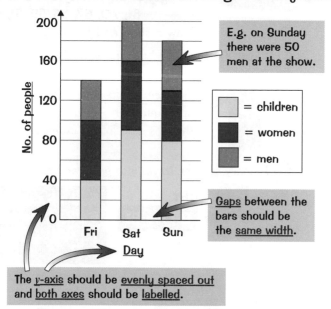

E.g. on Sunday there were 50 men at the show.

= children
= women
= men

<u>Gaps</u> between the bars should be the <u>same width</u>.

The <u>y-axis</u> should be <u>evenly spaced out</u> and <u>both axes</u> should be <u>labelled</u>.

Composite Bar Charts might show Percentages

The bar chart might show <u>percentages</u>, with the size of the whole bar representing <u>100%</u>. This is useful for showing <u>proportions</u> clearly, but you don't know the <u>exact data values</u> (such as the total frequencies).

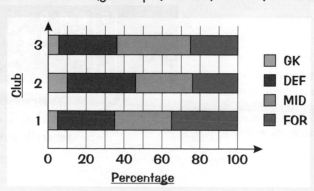 The bar chart below shows the proportion of football players in different positions (goalkeeper, defence, midfield, forward) for three different football clubs.

a) In which position did Club 2 have the fewest players?

b) Which club had the highest proportion of midfielders?

c) Which club had the same proportion of defenders and midfielders?

a) Look for Club 2's narrowest bar — <u>Goalkeeper</u>.

b) Look for the widest bar for midfield — <u>Club 3</u>.

c) Look for a club where the defence and midfield bars are the same width — <u>Club 1</u>.

Bar charts aren't the musical tastes of sheep...

Woah, have another gander over this page, then test yourself with this delightful question:

1) Use the results from the "boring team names" quiz to draw a composite bar chart showing how the teams scored in each round.

Team	Green	Blue	Red	Yellow
Points — 1st round	24	15	20	25
Points — 2nd round	16	15	22	20

Stem and Leaf Diagrams

Don't panic. <u>Stem and leaf diagrams</u> are another way to <u>show</u> and <u>compare data</u>. But they have nothing to do with biology at all — none, not a hint, not an iota, nowt, zip, nada, not a sausage...

Stem and Leaf Diagrams Show Shapes of Distributions

<u>Stem and leaf diagrams</u> split numerical data into two parts, called a <u>stem</u> (e.g. the tens digit) and <u>leaves</u> (e.g. the ones digit). You always need to include a <u>key</u> to show what the information means. The leaves must be <u>in order</u>, so it's easy to find values such as the <u>median</u> and <u>mode</u> (see second example).

 **EXAMPLE:**

The ages of the members of a 'seniors' yoga class are listed below.
81, 70, 67, 56, 59, 51, 64, 73, 62, 71, 64, 64
Draw a stem and leaf diagram of this data.

(1) First decide on the 'stem' for your diagram.

The stem is often the <u>first digit</u> of the numbers — so we'll use the <u>tens</u> digit in this example.

(2) Add the <u>ones digit</u> of each number <u>one by one</u> from the list. <u>Don't miss any out</u>. These are the '<u>leaves</u>'.

```
5 | 6 9 1
6 | 7 4 2 4 4
7 | 0 3 1
8 | 1
```

(3) Finally <u>sort</u> the leaves into <u>order</u> and add a <u>key</u>.

KEY
```
8 | 1 = 81
```

```
5 | 1 6 9
6 | 2 4 4 4 7
7 | 0 1 3
8 | 1
```

To read a number, you read the <u>stem first</u> and <u>then the leaf</u> — so the top line is 51, 56 and 59.

The diagram shows you the <u>shape</u> of the data — most of it is towards the lower end of the distribution and it peaks in the 60s.

You can Compare Two Sets of Data Back-to-Back

A <u>second set</u> of data can be added <u>back-to-back</u> to the first stem and leaf diagram, e.g. another yoga class. This keeps the data for each set <u>separate</u> but lets you <u>easily compare them</u>.

EXAMPLE:

Use the stem and leaf diagram to find:
a) the modal age of yoga class 1,
b) the median age of yoga class 2,
c) the range of ages for each yoga class.

KEY FOR CLASS 2
```
4 | 8 = 84
```

KEY FOR CLASS 1
```
8 | 1 = 81
```

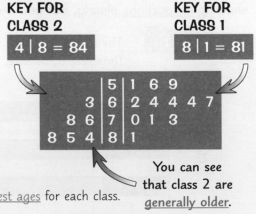

a) The <u>modal</u> (most common) age of class 1 is <u>64 years</u> — the 4s being side by side sort of stand out.

b) The <u>median</u> age of class 2 is halfway between the third and fourth values — it's easy to read these values off the diagram as the ages are already presented in ascending order.
Median = (78 + 84) ÷ 2 = <u>81 years</u>.

c) The <u>range</u> is simple — you can easily see the <u>smallest</u> and <u>largest ages</u> for each class.
Class 1: range = 81 − 51 = <u>30 years</u>
Class 2: range = 88 − 63 = <u>25 years</u>

You can see that class 2 are <u>generally older</u>.

Stem and leaf diagrams — branching into new types of analysis...

These are pretty straightforward — if you think you've got the hang of them, try answering this question...

1) The commuting distances of various people to two cities (in miles) are given below:
City 1: 26, 23, 18, 39, 13, 27, 12, 28, 18, 36, 14, 41   City 2: 16, 27, 32, 44, 18, 33, 26, 42, 28, 32, 37, 32

   a) Draw a stem and leaf diagram to show all the data.   c) What are the ranges of each set of data?
   b) What are the modal distances for each city?   d) To which city do people generally travel further?

Population Pyramids and Choropleth Maps

A couple more graphing methods on this page — one involves <u>bar charts</u> and the other <u>crayons</u>...

Population Pyramids are made of Bar Charts

1) <u>Population pyramids</u> are made from two <u>bar charts</u> that are back-to-back, so you can <u>compare</u> the data they show.

2) They're used to show the <u>numbers</u> or <u>proportion</u> in each <u>age range</u> for <u>two groups</u> within a population — e.g. men and women or Towns A and B.

3) As always, you need to be able to <u>interpret</u> them...

> If you draw a population pyramid you always put the groups on the y-axis and the population on the x-axis.

EXAMPLE: Below is a population pyramid for the country Barland. Are there more men or women in the 10-19 age group?

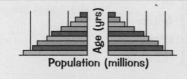

① First look for the 10-19 age group for men — the number in this group is <u>2.9 million</u>.

② There are <u>3 million</u> women in the 10-19 age group. So there are <u>more women</u> than men in the 10-19 age group.

4) The <u>shape</u> of the pyramid can tell you different things about the <u>distribution</u> of the population.

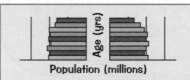

A "<u>PYRAMID</u>" shape shows there is a <u>higher proportion</u> of <u>younger</u> people than <u>older</u> people — this suggests the population has a <u>high birth rate</u>, <u>high death rate</u> and a <u>short life expectancy</u>.

A "<u>BARREL</u>" shape shows that the <u>proportion</u> of <u>younger</u> and <u>older</u> people is about <u>equal</u> — this suggests the population has <u>declining birth</u> and <u>death rates</u> and an <u>increasing life expectancy</u>.

An "<u>INVERTED PYRAMID</u>" shows there is a <u>higher proportion</u> of <u>older</u> people than <u>younger</u> people — this suggests the population has a <u>very low birth rate</u>, <u>low death rate</u> and <u>long life expectancy</u>.

Choropleth Maps use Shading, Hatched Lines or Dots

1) <u>Choropleth maps</u> split a geographic <u>area</u> into <u>regions</u>. Each <u>region</u> of the map is <u>shaded</u> (with a <u>colour</u> or a <u>pattern</u>) depending on the <u>value</u> of the data (e.g. the number of people in a region).

2) Each map comes with a <u>key</u> that tells you what each type of shading <u>means</u>.

3) E.g. A choropleth map could show the number of Stone Age tools found in different parts of a field — the field could be split into <u>squares</u>, which are <u>coloured</u> to show the number of tools in that part.

EXAMPLE: The choropleth map shows the distribution of flowers in a garden. Which part of the garden has the most flowers? Explain your reasoning.

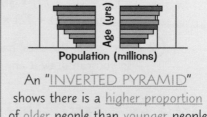

- Most flowers are in the <u>centre</u> of the garden.
- Use the <u>key</u> to explain your answer — squares in the centre are <u>darker</u>, which represents a <u>higher number</u> of flowers.

Choropleth maps — colouring by numbers...

I do love a good bit of colouring in. Make sure you can interpret both types of diagram and then try this:

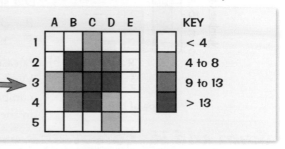

1) Describe two differences between the population of these two towns.

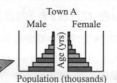

Section Three — Representing Data

Pie Charts

I'm sure you wondered when <u>pie charts</u> would pop up — well, here they are. Enjoy.

Pie Charts Show Proportions

1) <u>Pie charts</u> show how data is <u>divided</u> into <u>categories</u>. The <u>size</u> of each <u>sector</u> shows the <u>proportion</u> of the total data in that <u>category</u>.

> *Pie charts are good for showing qualitative data.*

2) To <u>draw</u> a pie chart, use the method below:

> 1) Calculate the <u>angle</u> for each <u>sector</u>: Angle = $\dfrac{\text{Number in category}}{\text{Total number}} \times 360°$
>
> 2) <u>Draw a circle</u> — it might have to be a <u>specific size</u> or you might be <u>given a circle</u> to use.
>
> 3) <u>Accurately draw the sectors</u> — it might help to start with a <u>vertical line</u> and measure <u>clockwise</u>.
>
> 4) <u>Label the sectors</u> — with a <u>key</u> or by writing on the sectors (if there's room).

> *You should check that your angles add up to 360°.*

EXAMPLE: Readers of Pastry Digest magazine voted on their favourite type of pie. 24 people said pi, 20 said apple, 18 said steak and 10 said humble. Draw a pie chart to show this data.

① <u>Total</u> number of votes = 24 + 20 + 18 + 10 = 72
Pi = (24 ÷ 72) × 360° = <u>120°</u>
Apple = (20 ÷ 72) × 360° = <u>100°</u>
Steak = (18 ÷ 72) × 360° = <u>90°</u>
Humble = (10 ÷ 72) × 360° = <u>50°</u>

② The <u>size</u> of the circle hasn't been given, so you can draw it any size you like.

③ <u>Draw</u> the sectors with the angles you found — e.g. this measures 120°.

KEY
- ☐ Pi
- ☐ Apple
- ☐ Steak
- ☐ Humble

④ <u>Label</u> the sectors with a <u>key</u>.

You Can Compare Pie Charts to Other Diagrams

1) Pie charts are useful because they show <u>proportions clearly</u>. You might need to <u>compare</u> them to some other diagrams (e.g. a table or a bar chart).

2) When <u>interpreting</u> pie charts it's important to remember that they show <u>proportions, not numbers</u>.

3) If you know <u>one value</u>, then you can work <u>backwards</u> to <u>extract</u> values for the <u>other categories</u>.

EXAMPLE: Kala collects data about the different types of bird she sees in her garden for an hour in the morning and an hour in the afternoon. She uses statistical software to represent data from the morning as a bar chart and data from the afternoon as a pie chart.

a) Give a reason why she might choose each of these diagrams.

b) In the afternoon, Kala sees 20 birds in the garden. Did she see more robins in the morning or afternoon?

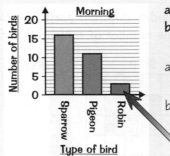

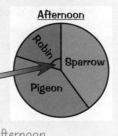

a) <u>Bar chart</u> — it shows the <u>number</u> of birds <u>clearly</u>.
<u>Pie chart</u> — it shows <u>proportions clearly</u>.

b) Measure the <u>angle</u> for robins in the afternoon: <u>72°</u>
Working backwards from the formula above gives:
number of robins = (72° ÷ 360°) × 20 = <u>4 robins</u>
In the morning she saw <u>3 robins</u>, so she saw more in the <u>afternoon</u>.

Spot the pie chart that looks like an arcade game character...

Check that you know how to draw, interpret and ogle pie charts before trying this question:

1) a) Use the bar chart showing the types of bird in the morning to draw a pie chart with a radius of 2.5 cm.

   b) In the afternoon, Kala saw 20 birds in the garden. How many pigeons did she see?

Comparative Pie Charts

On this page, it's buy one, get one free on all pie charts — and by 'free' I mean you've got to do some work for it. Note: this special offer only applies to Higher students.

Comparative Pie Charts use Areas

1) If you want to <u>compare</u> two pie charts you make their <u>areas proportional</u> to the populations they represent — e.g. a chart representing <u>twice</u> the <u>number</u> of people should have <u>twice</u> the <u>area</u>.

2) This means that you use the <u>same area</u> for each <u>unit</u> of data (i.e. 1 person or item).

3) To find the <u>radius</u> of a second pie chart given the radius of the first pie chart you need to:
   - Work out the <u>area</u> for <u>one unit of data</u> using: <u>area of first pie chart</u> (πr^2) ÷ <u>number of items</u>.
   - <u>Multiply</u> the area for <u>one unit</u> of data by the <u>total</u> number of items for the second pie chart.
   - Then rearrange <u>area = πr^2</u> to find r for the <u>second</u> pie chart.

EXAMPLE: A restaurant owner asked his weekend customers to fill in a survey rating the service. The pie chart with radius 1.4 cm shows the results from the 120 people who filled in the survey on Saturday. On Sunday, 163 people thought the service was good, but 82 people thought it was bad. Find the radius of the pie chart for the ratings on Sunday and draw it.

Saturday

(pie chart: radius = 1.4 cm, sectors Bad and Good)

1) First of all, work out the <u>area</u> used to represent <u>each unit of data</u> in <u>Saturday's</u> pie chart. Saturday's pie chart has a radius of 1.4 cm and represents 120 people.

   area for <u>120 people</u> = πr^2 = $1.4^2\pi$ = <u>6.157... cm²</u>,
   so area for <u>1 person</u> = 6.157... ÷ 120 = <u>0.051... cm²</u>

Sunday

(pie chart: radius = 2 cm, sectors Bad and Good)

2) Use this to work out the <u>radius</u> of the comparative pie chart for <u>Sunday</u>:
   Sunday's survey had 163 + 82 = <u>245 people</u>. 1 person = 0.051... cm²,
   so area for <u>245 people</u> = 245 × 0.051... = <u>12.571... cm²</u>.

   Area = πr^2, so radius = $\sqrt{(\text{area} / \pi)}$ = $\sqrt{12.571... / \pi}$ = <u>2.0 cm</u> (to 1 d.p.)

3) To draw the comparative pie chart for <u>Sunday</u>, work out its angles:
   <u>Good</u> = (163/245) × 360° = <u>240°</u> (to the nearest degree)
   <u>Bad</u> = (82/245) × 360° = <u>120°</u> (to the nearest degree)

<u>Comparing</u> the two pie charts above, you can see that more people said the service was bad on Sunday (because it has a <u>larger area</u>), even though "bad" is a <u>smaller proportion</u> of the pie chart than on Saturday.

Larger Area Means More Data

Having <u>two</u> related pie charts is useful because you can <u>compare</u> both <u>proportions</u> and <u>numbers</u>.

EXAMPLE: The comparative pie charts show profit in 2017 and predicted profit in 2027 for the types of product sold by a company.

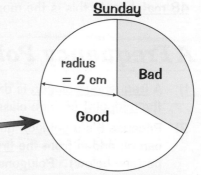

☐ = Films
■ = Games
☐ = Toys
☐ = Other

a) Which type of product makes the largest profit in both years?
   <u>Films</u> — it has the <u>largest sector</u> in both years.

b) The sizes of the angles for both pie charts are the same. Compare the profit for toys in 2017 and in 2027.
   The profit for toys is predicted to be <u>higher in 2027</u>, because the yellow sector in 2027 has a <u>larger area</u> than in 2017.

Two pies are always better than one...

Go over comparative pie charts, then have a bash at this:

1) Draw comparative pie charts for the data in the table. Use a radius of 2 cm for Plumson.

Cups of coffee sold by two coffee shops	Large	Medium	Small
Coffee Group Place	82	62	62
Plumson	11	13	21

Vertical Line Charts and Frequency Polygons

There are a couple more diagrams for you to learn here — one for <u>discrete data</u> and one for <u>continuous data</u>.

A Vertical Line Chart is Like a Bar Chart but with Lines

<u>Vertical line charts</u> (or <u>bar line charts</u>) show <u>frequency distributions</u> for <u>discrete</u> data. They're like bar charts (see p.32-33), but use <u>thin lines</u> instead of bars.

There's more on distributions in Section Seven.

EXAMPLE: Boxes of matches claim to have an average content of 48 matches. George counts the exact number of matches in each of 10 boxes and records his results in the frequency table below. Draw a vertical line chart of the results.

Here's <u>how</u> you draw a vertical line chart:

Matches	46	47	48	49	50
Frequency	0	2	5	2	1

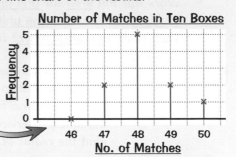

Number of Matches in Ten Boxes

1) Look at the table and work out the <u>axes</u>:
   y-axis: frequency — O to 5, x-axis: no. of matches — 46 to 50.

2) Mark the correct <u>frequency</u> above each number of matches and then <u>draw</u> a <u>straight line</u> from the x-axis to each of the marks.

You can <u>read off</u> data from a vertical line chart (like with a bar chart). For the example above, <u>5 boxes had 48 matches</u> — this is the mode. You can see that the distribution is fairly <u>symmetrical</u> about the <u>mode</u>.

A Frequency Polygon Uses the Midpoint of Each Class

1) A <u>frequency polygon</u> is drawn from <u>continuous data</u> in a <u>grouped frequency table</u>. To draw one, you plot the <u>midpoint</u> of each class (on the x-axis) against the corresponding <u>frequency</u> (on the y-axis).

2) Because it's a <u>polygon</u> you use <u>straight lines</u> (not curves) to join these points together. <u>Straight lines</u> can be added from the <u>first</u> and <u>last</u> points to the <u>x-axis</u> where the next (imaginary) class midpoint would be (see below). Polygons with these extra lines are called "<u>closed</u>" — "<u>open</u>" polygons don't have them.

3) The <u>shape</u> of the frequency polygon shows the <u>distribution</u> of the data.

EXAMPLE: This frequency table shows the heights of 12 plants in a biology experiment. Draw an open frequency polygon using this data.

Height (cm)	$0 \leq h < 5$	$5 \leq h < 10$	$10 \leq h < 15$	$15 \leq h < 20$
Frequency	3	5	2	2

1) Work out the <u>midpoint</u> of each class — e.g. $(O + 5) \div 2 = \underline{2.5}$:

Height (cm)	$0 \leq h < 5$	$5 \leq h < 10$	$10 \leq h < 15$	$15 \leq h < 20$
Midpoint	2.5	7.5	12.5	17.5
Frequency	3	5	2	2

2) Then <u>plot</u> the frequency polygon — plot the midpoint of each class against its corresponding frequency. Because it's a <u>polygon</u> (rather than a curve), join the points with <u>straight lines</u>.

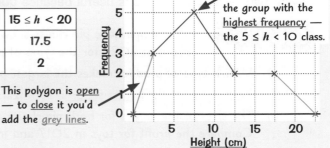

The highest point is the group with the <u>highest frequency</u> — the $5 \leq h < 10$ class.

This polygon is <u>open</u> — to <u>close</u> it you'd add the <u>grey lines</u>.

What do you call a missing parrot — Polygon...

This page isn't too tricky, but make sure you go over it again. Then use the table to answer this question:

1) The distances thrown in a shot put competition are shown below. Draw a closed frequency polygon for the data.

Distance (m)	$10 < d \leq 12$	$12 < d \leq 14$	$14 < d \leq 16$	$16 < d \leq 18$	$18 < d \leq 20$
Frequency	4	7	15	9	3

Cumulative Frequency Diagrams

Cumulative frequency diagrams can be drawn for <u>discrete</u> and <u>continuous data</u> — here's an example of each.

Cumulative Frequency Step Polygons look like Steps

The <u>CUMULATIVE FREQUENCY</u> is a running total of the frequencies — the <u>total</u> number <u>less than or equal to</u> each value.

A <u>cumulative frequency step polygon</u> is used for <u>discrete</u> data — you use <u>horizontal lines</u> between the points as the data isn't continuous.

EXAMPLE: Draw a cumulative frequency step polygon for the matches data from page 38.

1) Add a <u>cumulative frequency row</u> to the table.

Matches	46	47	48	49	50
Frequency	0	2	5	2	1
Cumulative Frequency	0	0 + 2 = 2	2 + 5 = 7	7 + 2 = 9	9 + 1 = 10

2) <u>Draw axes</u> — cumulative frequency on the y-axis and number of matches on the x-axis.

3) Draw the step graph. Plot the <u>cumulative frequency</u>, draw a <u>horizontal line</u> to the next value along and draw a <u>vertical line</u> to the next point.

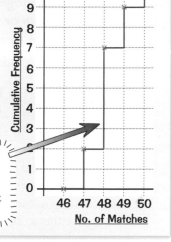

The height of each step is the same as the frequency for its corresponding value — e.g. this step shows that 5 boxes had 48 matches.

A Cumulative Frequency Chart Uses the Highest Value

<u>Continuous</u> data can be shown on a <u>cumulative frequency chart</u>. You plot the <u>cumulative frequency</u> against the <u>highest value</u> in each <u>class</u> — because the values are <u>less than</u> (or equal to) the <u>highest value</u>.

EXAMPLE: a) Draw a cumulative frequency chart for the plants' height data from page 38.

1) Add a <u>cumulative frequency row</u> to the table.

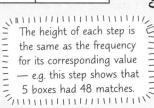

Height (cm)	$0 \le h < 5$	$5 \le h < 10$	$10 \le h < 15$	$15 \le h < 20$
Frequency	3	5	2	2
Cumulative frequency	3	3 + 5 = 8	8 + 2 = 10	10 + 2 = 12

2) Then <u>plot</u> the cumulative frequencies at their corresponding <u>upper class boundaries</u>. You can also plot one more point on the graph to show that no plants were less than 0 cm tall.

3) Join the points with <u>straight lines</u> or a <u>smooth curve</u> — either is fine for continuous data.

Cumulative frequency charts can be used to find the interquartile range — see p.56.

b) **Estimate the number of plants with a height less than 12.5 cm.**

Draw a <u>vertical line</u> from 12.5 on the x-axis and read off the corresponding cumulative frequency — <u>9 plants</u>.

My running total for putting off revision is massive...

When drawing a polygon you always use straight lines, but for a chart you can use either curved or straight lines.

1) Draw a cumulative frequency chart using the table on the right showing the ages of people living in a village.

Age (yrs)	$0 \le y < 20$	$20 \le y < 40$	$40 \le y < 60$	$60 \le y < 80$	$80 \le y < 100$
Frequency	40	50	50	30	20

Histograms

Histograms are a neat way to show <u>continuous</u> data. When the classes are <u>equal</u>, everything is peachy.

Histograms Can Have Equal Class Widths

1) <u>Histograms</u> display <u>continuous data</u> from a <u>grouped frequency table</u>. On this page, the <u>class widths</u> of the groups are <u>all equal</u>.

2) To <u>draw</u> a histogram for data with equal class widths, put <u>frequency</u> on the y-axis and a <u>suitable scale</u> for your data on the x-axis — then draw a <u>bar</u> for each <u>class</u>.

3) They look a lot like <u>bar charts</u>, but there's one key <u>difference</u> — there are <u>no gaps</u> between the bars. This is because the scale on the <u>x-axis is continuous</u> and each class ends at the start of the next one.

4) You can use histograms to identify the class with the <u>highest</u> or <u>lowest</u> frequency, <u>estimate</u> the frequency above or below a certain value and comment on the <u>distribution</u> of the data (see p.42).

5) You might need to <u>complete</u> a grouped frequency table from a histogram — you'll be given the frequency of <u>one class</u>, which you use to label the <u>y-axis</u> on the histogram and <u>read off</u> the values.

> The y-axis can also be labelled 'frequency density' — see next page.

EXAMPLE: The heights of students in Class C are shown in the histogram.
a) Use the histogram to complete the frequency table below.
b) Estimate the number of students shorter than 155 cm.

> The squiggle on the histogram shows that some of the x-axis is missing.

a) The first bar is 5 units tall and has a frequency of 20, so <u>1 unit</u> = 20 ÷ 5 = <u>4 students</u>. Use this to complete the y-axis and then <u>read off</u> the frequencies to complete the table.

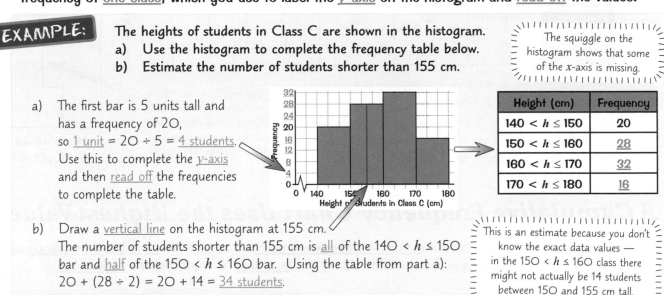
Height of Students in Class C (cm)

Height (cm)	Frequency
$140 < h \le 150$	20
$150 < h \le 160$	<u>28</u>
$160 < h \le 170$	<u>32</u>
$170 < h \le 180$	<u>16</u>

b) Draw a <u>vertical line</u> on the histogram at 155 cm. The number of students shorter than 155 cm is <u>all</u> of the $140 < h \le 150$ bar and <u>half</u> of the $150 < h \le 160$ bar. Using the table from part a): 20 + (28 ÷ 2) = 20 + 14 = <u>34 students</u>.

> This is an estimate because you don't know the exact data values — in the $150 < h \le 160$ class there might not actually be 14 students between 150 and 155 cm tall.

Histograms are Similar to Frequency Polygons

1) To draw a frequency polygon from a histogram (with <u>equal class widths</u>), plot points at the <u>midpoint</u> of each class and the <u>top</u> of the bar. Then join the points with <u>straight lines</u>.

2) To draw a histogram from a frequency polygon, draw <u>bars</u> using the points as the <u>top</u> and <u>midpoint</u> of each bar — and make sure that all your bars have the <u>same class width</u>.

The <u>histogram</u> is shown by the <u>blue bars</u> and the <u>frequency polygon</u> is shown by the <u>red line</u>.

Each <u>blue bar</u> and <u>red point</u> are the <u>same height</u>.

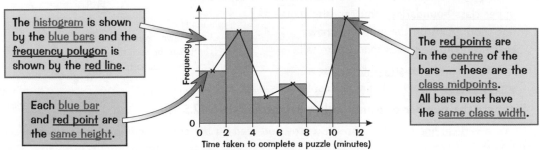
Time taken to complete a puzzle (minutes)

The <u>red points</u> are in the <u>centre</u> of the bars — these are the <u>class midpoints</u>. All bars must have the <u>same class width</u>.

Histograms — a good old-fashioned diagram...

The key skills to take away from this page are how to draw and interpret histograms with equal class widths.

1) In the histogram for the puzzle data above, the bar from 0 to 2 minutes represents 4 people.
   a) Use the histogram to create a grouped frequency table.
   b) Estimate the number of people that took longer than 5 minutes to complete the puzzle.

Histograms

You've seen that all class widths can be equal, but here some classes are more equal than others.
That's right — histograms can have <u>unequal</u> class widths as well.

Calculate Frequency Density for Unequal Class Widths

Drawing histograms for data with <u>unequal</u> class widths is trickier — you need to remember:
- <u>Frequency</u> is represented by the <u>AREA</u> of the bars instead of the <u>height</u>.
- <u>Frequency density</u> (NOT frequency) goes on the <u>y-axis</u>.

1) To work out the <u>heights</u> of the bars you need to calculate the <u>frequency density</u> for each data class:

FREQUENCY DENSITY = FREQUENCY ÷ CLASS WIDTH

2) Then, draw the axes with <u>frequency density</u> on the <u>y-axis</u> and the <u>variable values</u> on the <u>x-axis</u>.

3) Now draw <u>bars</u> for each class — the <u>height</u> is the <u>frequency density</u> and the <u>width</u> is the <u>class width</u>.

EXAMPLE: Use the table below to draw a histogram.

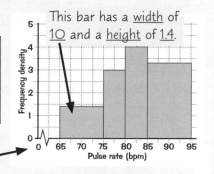

This bar has a <u>width</u> of <u>10</u> and a <u>height</u> of <u>1.4</u>.

Pulse rate (bpm)	$65 \leq p < 75$	$75 \leq p < 80$	$80 \leq p < 85$	$85 \leq p < 95$
Frequency	14	15	20	33
Class width	75 – 65 = <u>10</u>	80 – 75 = <u>5</u>	85 – 80 = <u>5</u>	95 – 85 = <u>10</u>
Frequency density	14 ÷ 10 = <u>1.4</u>	15 ÷ 5 = <u>3</u>	20 ÷ 5 = <u>4</u>	33 ÷ 10 = <u>3.3</u>

① Add a <u>class width</u> and <u>frequency density row</u> (using the formula above).

② Then draw the <u>axes</u> and the <u>bars</u>.

Note that <u>frequency density</u> takes <u>class width</u> into account — e.g. the first two bars above have a <u>similar frequency</u> (14 and 15), but the class width of the first bar is <u>wider</u>, so the bar is <u>shorter</u>.

You can use Histograms to Estimate Frequencies

To <u>estimate</u> the <u>frequency</u> for a given interval of values you just <u>rearrange</u> the formula to get:

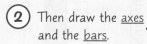

Frequency = Frequency Density × Class Width

Be careful when calculating <u>class widths</u> — the interval might <u>start</u> and/or <u>end midway</u> through a class.

EXAMPLE: The histogram below shows the heights of sunflowers entered into a local competition. Estimate how many sunflowers were between 170 and 179 cm tall.

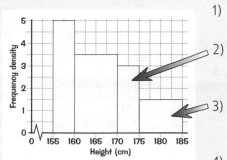

1) The <u>3rd</u> and <u>4th</u> bars cover the height range 170-179 cm, so break the calculation into <u>two chunks</u> and use the formula for each.

2) For the third bar:
Class width = 175 – 170 = <u>5</u> and frequency density = <u>3</u>.
So frequency = 5 × 3 = <u>15</u>.

3) For (part of) the fourth bar:
Class width remaining = 179 – 175 = <u>4</u> and frequency density = <u>1.5</u>.
So frequency = 4 × 1.5 = <u>6</u>.

4) Add the frequencies together: 15 + 6 = <u>21 sunflowers</u>.

You can use two histograms to <u>compare data sets</u>. However, you should make sure that the <u>frequency density scale</u> and the <u>class intervals</u> are the <u>same</u> on both histograms for a good comparison.

My brain frequently feels very dense...

Make sure you know that formula for frequency density off by heart. Then, you know the drill...

1) Using the histogram above, estimate the number of sunflowers between 155 and 162 cm tall.

The Shape of a Distribution

You've seen diagrams that show the shape of a <u>distribution</u>. This page shows you how to <u>describe</u> that shape.

Frequency Distributions have Different Shapes

You need to know the <u>names</u> and <u>shapes</u> of different frequency distributions shown by histograms (p.40-41).

① <u>Symmetrical Distribution</u>

Mode = Median = Mean

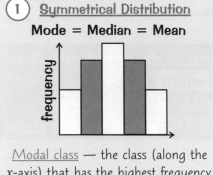

<u>Modal class</u> — the class (along the *x*-axis) that has the highest frequency.

② <u>Bimodal Distribution</u>

Two modes

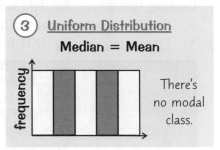

③ <u>Uniform Distribution</u>

Median = Mean

There's no modal class.

The distributions apply to histograms with equal class widths.

④ <u>Positive Skew</u>

Mode < Median < Mean

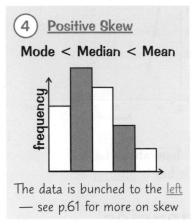

The data is bunched to the <u>left</u> — see p.61 for more on skew

⑤ <u>Negative Skew</u>

Mode > Median > Mean

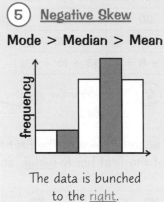

The data is bunched to the <u>right</u>.

EXAMPLE: The histogram shows the heights of a random sample of women.
a) Comment on the shape of the distribution.
b) What is the modal class?

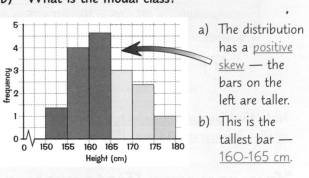

a) The distribution has a <u>positive skew</u> — the bars on the left are taller.
b) This is the tallest bar — <u>160-165 cm</u>.

Distributions Can be Shown on Different Diagrams

<u>Stem and leaf diagrams</u> (p.34), <u>vertical line charts</u> (p.38) and <u>frequency polygons</u> (p.38) all show the shape of a distribution. You can <u>compare distributions</u> by drawing two data sets on the same diagram.

EXAMPLE: The frequency polygon shows employee salaries for workers in two companies, Caps and Socs.
a) Compare the distributions of the two companies' salaries.
b) Which company has the modal class £30 000-£40 000?

a) The distribution for <u>Caps</u> is <u>positively skewed</u> (most of the data is bunched to the left), whereas for <u>Socs</u> it's <u>fairly uniform</u>.

b) The class £30 000-£40 000 is the highest class midpoint of the red line, so it's the modal class for <u>Socs</u>.

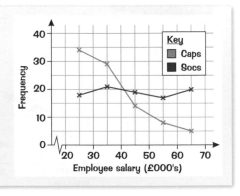

Police officers follow a uniform distribution...

It can be easy to get positive and negative skew mixed up, so have another read over this page. Then it's time to conquer your fears with this creepy question:

1) The frequency polygon on the right shows the lengths of two species of spider, A and B, collected in a park by a scientist.
   a) Compare the distributions of the lengths of the two species.
   b) Which species of spider is longer? Give a reason for your answer.

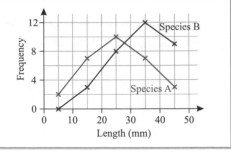

Scatter Diagrams

Scatter diagrams show two variables on the same graph and show you if they're related — clever things.

Scatter Diagrams are used for Bivariate Data

Scatter diagrams are useful when you've got two different variables that you want to compare. You plot the explanatory variable on the x-axis and the response variable on the y-axis. See page 5 for more about bivariate data and page 22 for definitions of the variables.

EXAMPLE: The data below was collected to investigate how high the water level of a river rises when it rains different amounts. Use the data to draw a scatter diagram.

Rainfall (mm)	Height of river (m)
10	0.7
40	0.8
120	1.0
130	1.2
190	1.3
260	1.9

1. First, label the axes — rainfall is the explanatory variable that goes on the x-axis and height of river is the response variable that goes on the y-axis.

2. Then choose a suitable scale for each axis. The scale doesn't have to be the same on both axes so pick one that makes it easy to mark on the points — e.g. 0 to 300 mm for rainfall and 0 to 2 m for height of river.

3. Finally, carefully plot the data points — (10, 0.7), (40, 0.8), (120, 1.0), (130, 1.2), (190, 1.3) and (260, 1.9). Make sure that you don't join the points.

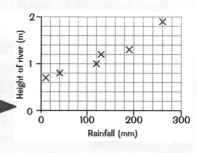

Draw a Line of Best Fit if there is a Relationship

1) If the points lie roughly on a straight line there's a linear relationship between the variables — and you can draw a line of best fit through them.

2) This should be a straight line passing as close to as many points as possible with roughly equal numbers of points on both sides.

3) The connection between the variables is called correlation. The slope of the line of best fit tells you what type of correlation it is:

There's more information on correlation, drawing lines of best fit and interpreting scatter diagrams on p.72-74.

POSITIVE Correlation means one variable INCREASES as the other INCREASES.

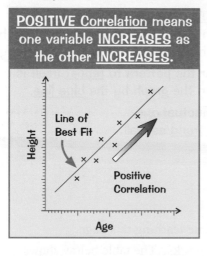

NEGATIVE Correlation means one variable DECREASES as the other INCREASES.

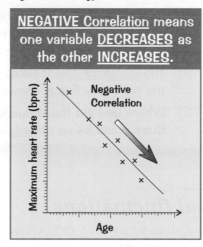

ZERO Correlation means the points are TOO SCATTERED about to draw a line of best fit.

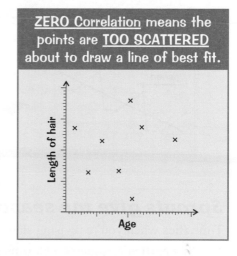

The bivariate data's coming — everybody scatter...

...but before you do, learn the page and answer this question. Arghhhhhhhh...

1) a) Use this data to draw and label a scatter diagram.
   b) Draw a line of best fit through the data.
   c) What type of correlation does the data show?

Average temperature °C	15	21	16	27	8	14	19
Number of cold drinks sold	15	29	19	38	4	16	24

Time Series Graphs

The graphs below were drawn by an <u>evil genius</u> — she just loves to spend her nights <u>plotting</u>.

Time Series are plotted with Time on the x-Axis

A <u>line graph</u> plots some <u>ordered points</u> and joins them with a <u>straight line</u> — you need to know about a certain type of line graph called a <u>time series</u>. These are useful if something is measured at <u>time intervals</u> — e.g. the sales of a business might be measured quarterly (i.e. four times a year).

1) Like with scatter diagrams, there are <u>two variables</u> to plot. <u>Always</u> plot <u>time</u> on the <u>x-axis</u> and the other variable on the <u>y-axis</u> — but <u>join</u> the points together with straight lines.

2) A <u>trend line</u> (drawn in red) is like a <u>line of best fit</u> through the data points. You can draw it '<u>by eye</u>' — it needs to have more or less <u>equal</u> numbers of points <u>either side</u> of it, but it doesn't have to go through any of the points.

3) The trend line shows <u>general changes</u> with time — the <u>overall trend</u> (e.g. whether the data is going up, down, or staying about constant).

4) You can use it to make a general <u>prediction</u> about <u>future</u> data values — e.g. this trend line suggests sales will continue to increase overall.

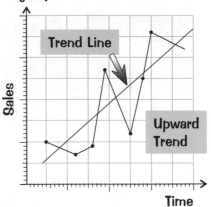

EXAMPLE: The number of people attending band practice at a school is recorded in the table below. Use the table to draw a time series graph.

Week	1	2	3	4	5	6	7	8
Number of people	21	23	26	28	29	24	21	19

1) First <u>label</u> the axes — <u>week</u> goes on the <u>x-axis</u> and <u>number of people</u> goes on the <u>y-axis</u>.

2) Then <u>plot</u> the points and <u>join</u> them with a line.

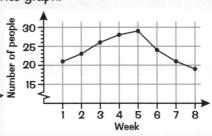

Time Series can have Fluctuations

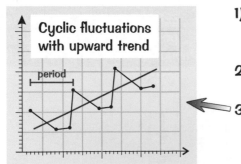

1) Some time series have a <u>regular repeating pattern</u> called <u>cyclic fluctuations</u>. They can also be called <u>seasonal fluctuations</u>, if the data is recorded in each season of a year (i.e. quarterly).

2) The <u>length of time</u> it takes for the pattern to <u>repeat</u> itself is called the <u>period</u> — this is shown on the graph by the <u>blue line</u>.

3) Where you get these cyclic fluctuations, there could be an <u>underlying trend</u> as well.

There's more about time series on pages 77-78.

Sprouts give me seasonal fluctuations...

Time flies when you're revising stats. But make sure you've spent enough time learning this page.

1) In a particular country a swarm of locusts appears once a year for a few weeks. The table below shows an estimate of the number of locusts in the swarm to the nearest 5 billion over 10 years.

Year	2008	2009	2010	2011	2012	2013	2014	2015	2016	2017
Number of locusts (nearest 5 billion)	15	20	45	10	20	40	10	15	35	5

a) Explain why it's suitable to show this data on a time series graph.

b) Draw a time series graph to show the data in the table.   c) Describe the trend of the time series graph.

Choosing How to Represent Data

You've finally covered all the diagrams — now you need to know which one to <u>choose</u> to show your data.

Choose a Diagram That's Suitable for the Data

When <u>choosing a diagram</u> to <u>represent data</u>, you should consider the following points:

1) <u>DATA</u> — think about the type of data you have. Some diagrams are more appropriate for <u>discrete</u> or <u>continuous</u> data. If you have <u>bivariate</u> data, you'll probably want to use a scatter diagram and for <u>grouped</u> data use a frequency polygon or histogram. The <u>amount of data values</u> is also important as you can <u>group</u> the data if you have a lot of it. E.g. histograms work better for lots of data, but are less effective when you've only got a few data values.

2) <u>HYPOTHESIS</u> — choose <u>diagrams</u> and <u>calculations</u> that will be <u>useful</u> for your hypothesis. E.g. stem and leaf diagrams are good for finding the median and bar charts show the mode.

3) <u>TARGET AUDIENCE</u> — if your audience aren't statisticians, or aren't familiar with the data, you should choose diagrams that show the <u>data clearly</u>, are <u>easy to interpret</u> and have a <u>visual impact</u> (e.g. a bar chart or pie chart). For a more <u>technical</u> audience, you can use more <u>complicated</u> diagrams.

EXAMPLE: The test scores (out of 50) of eight boys and eight girls are shown on the right. Explain whether the following diagrams would be suitable to display the data:
a) histogram,   b) scatter diagram,
c) stem and leaf diagram.

Boys	44	31	16	25
	35	24	36	21
Girls	32	33	21	43
	18	38	25	27

a) <u>Not suitable</u> — histograms represent continuous data and the test scores are <u>discrete</u>. There also aren't enough data values for <u>grouping</u> to be effective.

b) <u>Not suitable</u> — scatter diagrams are for <u>bivariate</u> data, but the test scores <u>aren't in pairs</u>.

c) <u>Suitable</u> — stem and leaf diagrams are good for <u>discrete data</u> and there are <u>two data sets</u> (boys and girls), which could be shown <u>back-to-back</u>. There are also only a <u>few data values</u> to plot.

The Same Data can be Shown on Two Diagrams

You might be given <u>multiple diagrams</u> for the <u>same</u> set of data and asked to comment on their suitability.

EXAMPLE: A meteorologist records the midday temperature of a town every day for a year. She uses statistical software to represent the data as a histogram and a cumulative frequency diagram.
a) Give a reason why each diagram may have been chosen to represent the data.
b) Explain which diagram would be more suitable to use in a detailed report.

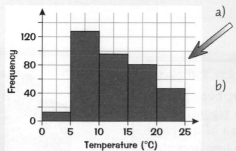

a) <u>Histogram</u> — it shows the frequencies <u>clearly</u>.
<u>Cumulative frequency diagram</u> — it's easy to find the <u>median</u>.

b) The <u>histogram</u> would be more suitable, because it shows the <u>distribution</u> of the data — it has a <u>positive skew</u>.

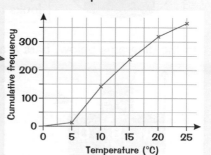

I prefer to represent data by interpretive dance...

You've been given plenty of choice on this page, but now you're out of options — you just have to try this question.

1) A student records the time people spent watching television yesterday (in hours) for 10 males and 10 females. Explain whether the following diagrams would be appropriate for representing the data:
a) time series graph,   b) frequency polygon.

Misleading Diagrams

Now you know lots of different ways to represent data — but sometimes diagrams can be a bit <u>misleading</u>...

Pictograms can Sometimes be Confusing

With <u>pictograms</u> (see page 32) you should use the <u>same symbol</u> for <u>all</u> the categories.

 **EXAMPLE:** Eve sells 52 items one day in her bakery. She records the type of each item sold and draws the pictogram below. Identify four ways that her diagram could be confusing.

(1) There's <u>no key</u> — so you don't actually know how many of each item were sold.

Doughnut	◯ ◯ ◯ ◯ ◯ ◯ ◁
Flapjack	▭ ▭ ▭ ▭
Cake	◯ ◯ ◯

(3) The symbols are <u>different shapes</u> — these could represent <u>different values</u>.

(2) This symbol has been <u>squashed</u> (rather than cut into a fraction) — it could be worth the same as an 'unsquashed' symbol.

(4) The symbols are <u>different sizes</u> and <u>don't line up</u>.

Colour and Volume can Distort Diagrams

Making diagrams look nice with <u>colour</u> and <u>volume</u> can be misleading. You might <u>distort</u> bits of the diagram — which makes it <u>harder</u> to <u>interpret</u>. For example, look at these <u>pie charts</u> with <u>four equal sectors</u>.

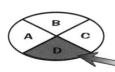

A <u>brighter colour</u> is used for sector D. This can be misleading because it <u>stands out more</u>.

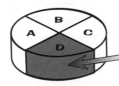

Here the same pie chart looks <u>three-dimensional</u>. Sectors B and D now cover more of the page than A and C. They <u>appear bigger</u> to the eye even though all four sectors are the same. This can be <u>misleading</u>.

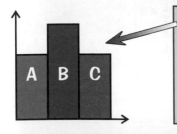

Now it's been given <u>volume</u>. Sector D <u>covers more</u> of the page than any of the other three. The pie chart is still accurate, but sector D looks more <u>important</u> than the others.

Sue's hair was proof that volume should be treated with care.

In the diagrams below, bars <u>A</u> and <u>C</u> are <u>equal</u> in height.

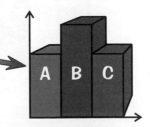

1) The normal 2D bar chart is nice and <u>clear</u>.
2) When the same bar chart has been given <u>volume</u>, bar C appears to be <u>bigger</u>. It covers about the same area of the page as bar B. <u>Bar A</u> might seem <u>less important</u> as it is partly hidden behind bar B.

You need to think when using <u>colour</u> and <u>volume</u>. There's <u>nothing actually WRONG</u> with these diagrams, but you need to <u>read</u> them more <u>carefully</u> because they can be a bit <u>misleading</u>.

Misleading Diagrams

More things can go wrong with graphs than you can shake a stick at...

The Axes and Scales on a Graph can be Misleading

Graph A below shows some crime figures accurately — the others are more confusing or misleading.

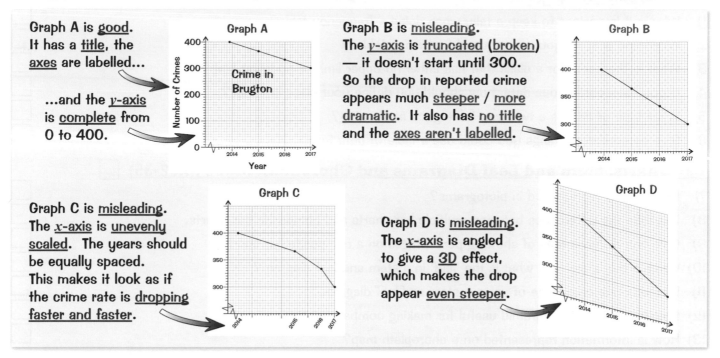

Graph A is good. It has a title, the axes are labelled... ...and the y-axis is complete from 0 to 400.

Graph B is misleading. The y-axis is truncated (broken) — it doesn't start until 300. So the drop in reported crime appears much steeper / more dramatic. It also has no title and the axes aren't labelled.

Graph C is misleading. The x-axis is unevenly scaled. The years should be equally spaced. This makes it look as if the crime rate is dropping faster and faster.

Graph D is misleading. The x-axis is angled to give a 3D effect, which makes the drop appear even steeper.

When drawing a graph you can check that it's not misleading.
1) Make sure your graph has labelled axes, with correct units, and a title explaining what the graph shows.
2) Try not to truncate (break) the y-axis and check the numbers on the axes aren't misleading.
3) Be careful that colour and 3D effects don't make the graph confusing.

Read on for the chance to win a car...

...Sorry — some classic misleading there. Feel free to console yourself by reading the last couple of pages again and trying these questions.

1) Give three ways this pictogram could be misleading.
2) This diagram has several problems. What are they? Explain fully.
3) Explain how each of these three graphs could be misleading.

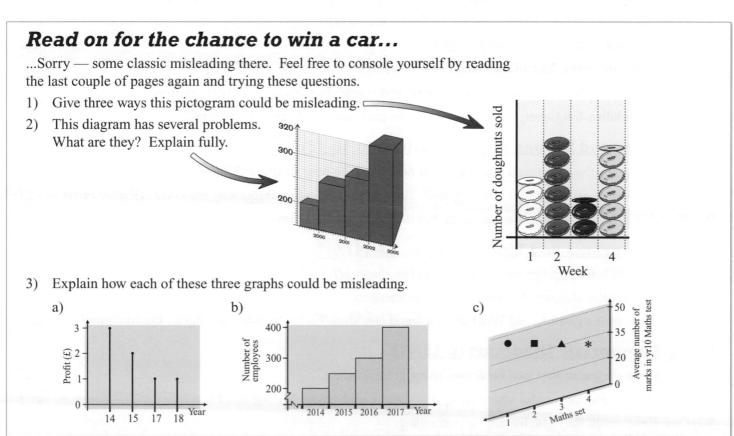

Revision Summary for Section Three

Tuck in that shirt... And do up your tie... You're <u>representing data</u> you know.

• Try these questions and <u>tick off each one</u> when you <u>get it right</u>.

• When you've done <u>all the questions</u> for a topic and are <u>completely happy</u> with it, tick off the topic.

Tables (p.28-31) ☑

1) Why is it important to keep a tally when doing a frequency table?
2) When and why do you use grouped frequency tables?
3) What is the name for a class that has either no upper limit or no lower limit?
4) If you have continuous data, how should you define your class intervals?
5) What type of data is a two-way table good at showing?
6) Give two different things you could use a table of data for.

Bar Charts, Stem and Leaf Diagrams and Choropleth Maps (p.32-35) ☑

7) How is data represented in pictograms?
8) Describe the differences between multiple bar charts and composite bar charts.
9) Give one disadvantage of showing percentages on a composite bar chart.
10) What is the 'stem' and what is the 'leaf' in a stem and leaf diagram?
11) Describe one advantage of using a stem and leaf diagram.
12) How is a population pyramid useful for making comparisons?
13) How is information represented on a choropleth map?

Pie Charts and Line Graphs (p.36-39) ☑

14) Describe the process for drawing a pie chart.
15) Give one advantage of showing data on a pie chart.
16) Explain how to draw comparative pie charts. [Higher only]
17) What type of data can be shown on a vertical line chart?
18) Describe how to plot a frequency polygon.
19) What does the term "cumulative frequency" mean?
20) How are cumulative frequency step polygons and cumulative frequency charts different?
21) On a cumulative frequency chart, where do you plot each cumulative frequency?

Histograms and Shapes of Distributions (p.40-42) ☑

22) Is a histogram the same as a bar chart? If not, describe how they are different.
23) What is frequency density in a histogram? How do you calculate frequency density? [Higher only]
24) Sketch a graph to show a frequency distribution with positive skew.

Scatter Diagrams and Time Series (p.43-44) ☑

25) When would it be appropriate to draw a scatter diagram?
26) Sketch a scatter diagram showing positive correlation.
27) On a time series graph: a) What does a trend line show?   b) What are cyclic fluctuations?

Using Appropriate Diagrams (p.45-47) ☑

28) Name two diagrams that can be drawn using grouped data.
29) Why should you be careful when using 3D, volume and colour in diagrams?
30) Give three ways that graphs can be misleading.

Section Three — Representing Data

Mean, Median and Mode

To make sense of your raw data you need the <u>three 'M's</u>. That's mode, median, mean, not the three musketeers...

The Mode is the One that Appears Most Often

You can find the mode either by just looking at the data or by using a <u>tally chart</u>.
So in the data set: 3, 5, 1, 3, 7, 5, 5, 5, 2, <u>the mode is 5</u> (it appears 4 times).

If you <u>add</u> or <u>remove</u> a value, the mode <u>could change</u> — but only if it changes which value appears the most. In the example above, adding <u>two 3s</u> makes 3 and 5 <u>both</u> modes. Adding <u>three 3s</u> means 5 <u>isn't</u> the mode.

The Median is the Middle Value

In an <u>ordered list</u> of values, the <u>median</u> is the value in the <u>middle position</u>. Here's a handy formula:

n is the number of data values.

Position of Median $= (n + 1)/2$.

EXAMPLE: Find the median of the following data set: 12   5   7   10   8   7   11   6

5   6   7   7   8   10   11   12
position 1   position 8

1) First put the data in <u>ascending order</u>.
2) Then use the <u>formula</u> to find the <u>position</u> of the median. There are 8 values so $(8 + 1)/2 = \underline{4.5}$ — the median is in <u>position 4.5</u>.
3) So the median is halfway between 7 and 8, which is <u>7.5</u>.

If you <u>add</u> a data value that's <u>greater/smaller</u> than the median, the median might <u>increase/decrease</u>.
If you <u>remove</u> a data value that's <u>greater/smaller</u> than the median, the median might <u>decrease/increase</u>.
But if you <u>add/remove</u> one data value that's <u>greater</u> AND one that's <u>smaller</u> than the median, it <u>stays the same</u>.

The Arithmetic Mean is the "Average"

The "arithmetic mean" is usually just called the "mean".

ADD TOGETHER all the data values and DIVIDE by the total number of values in the sample.

1) There's a nifty formula for the <u>mean</u>:

$$\bar{x} = \frac{\Sigma x}{n}$$

$\bar{x}$ is the symbol for the mean
Σ is the Greek letter sigma — it means "the sum of"

x stands for the data values
n is the number of data values

EXAMPLE: Find the mean number of people living in each of nine three-bedroomed houses:
3   5   1   3   7   5   5   5   2

The mean or $\bar{x} = \dfrac{\Sigma x}{n} = \dfrac{(3 + 5 + 1 + 3 + 7 + 5 + 5 + 5 + 2)}{9} = \underline{4}$

2) The <u>mean changes</u> if you <u>add/remove</u> a data value from the sample (unless it's equal to the mean itself).
 • If you <u>add</u> a value <u>greater</u> than the mean or <u>take away</u> a value <u>less than</u> the mean, it <u>increases</u>.
 • If you <u>add</u> a value <u>less</u> than the mean or <u>take away</u> a <u>greater</u> value, it <u>decreases</u>.
3) If you <u>replace</u> a value with another number <u>greater</u> or <u>smaller</u> than the original, the <u>mean</u> will also <u>change</u>.

The three 'M's are so interesting — no, I really mean it...

Make sure you can calculate the averages on this page, then have a go at this question:
1) a) Find the mean, median and mode of these exam scores: 98, 99, 97, 91, 97, 92, 93, 97, 95, 98
   b) Another student sits the exam and scores 85. How will this affect each of the mean, median and mode?
   c) One of the students who scored 98 is caught cheating and their score is removed. What is the median now?

Mean, Median and Mode

This page is about making calculations of the three 'M's <u>easier</u> (sounds pretty good to me), so here we go...

Find the Mean for Large Numbers by Scaling Down

There's a neat little trick you can do to make it easier to find the mean from <u>large numbers</u>.
First <u>take a number away</u> from all the values (so you only have to deal with small numbers)
and find the mean of what's left. Then <u>add</u> the number you took away back onto the result.

 **EXAMPLE:** Find the mean of the following numbers:
191   192   199   198   196   194   195

First take away 190 from each number to give 1, 2, 9, 8, 6, 4 and 5. The mean of these numbers
is $(1 + 2 + 9 + 8 + 6 + 4 + 5) \div 7 = 5$. So the mean of the original numbers is $190 + 5 = \underline{195}$.

For Tricky Data, Use Linear Transformations

When you're calculating an average, sometimes it's tricky to enter <u>large amounts of data</u>
into a calculator — especially if you have <u>really big</u> or <u>really small</u> numbers. But there's a
way to make this easier so you make <u>fewer mistakes</u> — it's called a <u>linear transformation</u>:

1) First, <u>multiply</u> or <u>divide</u> the data values by the same number.
2) Then, you may also have to <u>add</u> or <u>subtract</u> a number from the data values.
3) Now you can calculate the <u>mean</u>.
4) Finally, you must **REVERSE** the transformation.

Remember — you can also do these steps the other way around as well.

 **EXAMPLE:** Calculate the mean of the following set of data:
0.00155   0.00143   0.00152   0.00145   0.00149   0.00141

1) First <u>multiply</u> each value by <u>100 000</u> — this will give whole numbers:
155   143   152   145   149   141

2) Now to make it even easier you can <u>subtract 140</u> from each value:
15   3   12   5   9   1

3) Then calculate the <u>mean</u> of these values:
Mean = $(15 + 3 + 12 + 5 + 9 + 1) \div 6 = \underline{7.5}$

4) Remember you have to <u>reverse</u> the linear transformation
to find the mean for the original values, which is:
$7.5 + 140 = 147.5$, then $147.5 \div 100\ 000 = \underline{0.001475}$

Use Transformations to Find the Mode and Median too

The <u>median</u> and <u>mode</u> can also be worked out more easily by using linear transformations, but remember:

- Whatever you do to the data set, the mean, median and mode are affected in the same way.
- To get the mean, median and mode for the original values you need to reverse the transformation.

I'd say this page was fairly average...

There are some toughies on this page, but once you're happy with them try out these questions for practice:

1) These are the times (in seconds) it takes a dog to fetch a ball: 138, 110, 127, 131, 117, 122, 141, 127, 105, 110
Find the mean time by scaling down.

2) Find the mean, the median and the mode of this data set using linear transformations:
0.00354, 0.00355, 0.00358, 0.00349, 0.00342, 0.00359

Mean, Median and Mode

I bet you're sick of hearing about the three 'M's by now... Well, guess what — they're on this page too.

Choose the Most Appropriate Average

The <u>mean</u>, <u>median</u> and <u>mode</u> all have their <u>advantages</u> and <u>disadvantages</u>:

	Mean	Median	Mode
Advantages	Uses all the data Usually most representative	Easy to find in ordered data Not distorted by extreme values	Easy to find in tallied data Always a data value
Disadvantages	Isn't always a data value Distorted by extreme values	Isn't always a data value Not always a good representation of the data	Doesn't always exist or might be more than one Not always a good representation of the data

<u>MEAN</u>: Takes account of <u>all the data</u>.
May be <u>significantly affected</u> by <u>extreme values</u> or <u>outliers</u> (p.60).
Can be used to calculate the <u>standard deviation</u> (p.57).

<u>MEDIAN</u>: Useful when the data is <u>skewed</u> (p.61) or contains <u>outliers</u>.
Can be used alongside the <u>range</u> and <u>interquartile range</u> (p.54-55).

<u>MODE</u>: Tells you which value is the <u>most popular</u> (useful when considering, e.g. <u>demand</u> for items in a shop).
Can be used with <u>non-numerical</u> data which can't be added up or put in order.
Can give a <u>misleading</u> value that's <u>far away</u> from the mean. May <u>not be unique</u> or <u>may not exist</u>.

The Weighted Mean Gives Values Different Weights

You use the <u>weighted mean</u> to combine different sets of data when one is <u>more important</u> than another. Each number is given a <u>weight</u> depending on its relevance.

GCSE coursework carries a weight of 3, the exam carries a weight of 6 and a controlled assessment carries a weight of 1. Calculate your overall percentage result if you score 70% for coursework, 55% for your exam and 60% for your controlled assessment.

$$\underline{\text{Weighted mean}} = \boxed{\frac{\sum(\text{weight} \times \text{value})}{\sum \text{weights}}} = \frac{(3 \times 70) + (6 \times 55) + (1 \times 60)}{3 + 6 + 1} = \frac{600}{10} = \underline{60\%}$$

No! Mwa ha ha ha...

A weighted meanie

The Geometric Mean Uses Multiplication and Roots

The <u>geometric mean</u> can be used to find the mean of a set of data values that aren't immediately <u>comparable</u> (e.g. a set of scores out of 10 and a set of scores out of 50). It's also used to find the mean of <u>growth</u> or <u>interest rates</u>. It's defined by this <u>formula</u>: $\boxed{\sqrt[n]{x_1 \times x_2 \times ... \times x_n}}$

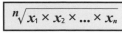
You'll always be told if you should use the geometric mean instead of the arithmetic mean.

Find the geometric mean of the numbers 12, 4, 87, 12, 5.

<u>Multiply</u> the values together: $12 \times 4 \times 87 \times 12 \times 5 = \underline{250\,560}$

Since there are <u>5 values</u>, take the <u>5th root</u>: $\sqrt[5]{250\,560} = 12.016... = \underline{12.0}$ (1 d.p.)

A mean, a median and a mode walk into a bar...

Learn the formulas for the weighted and geometric means (they <u>won't</u> be given to you in the exam), then try these.

1) State which average would be the most suitable for each of these sets of data:
a) 22, 26, 31, 24, 23, 27, 46, 22   b) Red, Blue, Red, Green, Blue, Red, Green, Red   c) 2, 2, 3, 4, 6, 8, 9, 11

2) 15% of passengers arrived at an airport 3 hours before their flight, 68% arrived 2 hours before and 17% arrived 1 hour before. Find the mean number of hours before their flight that these passengers arrived. [Higher only]

3) Calculate the geometric mean of this set of data: 56, 83, 56, 29, 46, 22 [Higher only]

Higher

Higher

Averages from Frequency Tables

Your data might be <u>discrete</u> and recorded in a <u>frequency table</u>, but you'll be pleased to know you can still work out the <u>averages</u>. Time to whip out your calculator and have a go at this...

Find the Mean by Adding a Third Row to the Table

You can find the <u>mean</u> in exactly the same way as you did before (see p.49) — <u>add</u> all the <u>values</u> together (taking the frequencies into account) and <u>divide</u> by the total frequency. Here's a handy formula to help:

$$\overline{x} = \frac{\Sigma fx}{\Sigma f}$$

$\overline{x}$ is the symbol for the mean x stands for the data values

Σ means "the sum of" f stands for the frequencies

The total frequency (Σf) is just like the total number of data values (n)

EXAMPLE: The number of sweets in each of one hundred packets sampled are given in the table below. Find the mean.

Number of sweets per packet	38	39	40	41	42	43
Number of packets (frequency)	5	18	29	33	13	2

There are 2 packets of 43 sweets.

First, to make things easier, add a <u>third row</u> to your table and <u>label</u> the rows as x, f and fx.

Number of sweets per packet, x	38	39	40	41	42	43	Totals
Number of packets (frequency), f	5	18	29	33	13	2	100
Sweets per packet × frequency, fx	190	702	1160	1353	546	86	4037

This gives you the <u>total</u> number of sweets.

Row 1 × Row 2

So $\overline{x} = \dfrac{\Sigma fx}{\Sigma f} = \dfrac{\text{Sum of (frequency} \times \text{sweets per packet)}}{\text{Sum of (frequency)}} = \dfrac{3^{rd} \text{ Row Total}}{2^{nd} \text{ Row Total}} = \dfrac{4037}{100} = \underline{40.37}$

Finding the Median and the Mode is Easy

EXAMPLE: For the data in the example above, find:

     a) the median,   b) the mode.

a) The <u>median</u> is still the middle value but you have to count up through the table to find it.

One <u>advantage</u> of the table is that the data's already in <u>ascending order</u>.

Median position = $(n + 1) \div 2 = (100 + 1) \div 2 = \underline{50.5}$

This means that the median value lies between the <u>50th and the 51st packets</u>.

Looking at the table, there are 5 + 18 = <u>23</u> values in the first two columns, and 23 + 29 = <u>52</u> in the first three.

So the 50th and 51st values must be in the <u>third column</u>, and the median must be <u>40</u>.

b) The <u>mode</u> is easy to find from a frequency table as the frequencies have already been worked out. The mode is <u>41</u> as more packets hold 41 sweets than any other number.

Total revision ÷ number of hours revising gets me mean...

This stuff is really important for the exam, so learn it and then have a go at this question:

1)   a) Calculate the mean number of questions per paper.
    b) Find the median.   c) What is the mode?

Number of questions	15	16	17	18	19	20	21
Number of exam papers	3	6	7	12	9	5	2

Averages from Grouped Data

Sometimes your data will be <u>grouped</u>, which makes estimating <u>averages</u> a bit more <u>tricky</u>...

Grouped Data Has a Modal Class and Estimated Mean

Continuous data is often recorded in a <u>grouped frequency table</u>, using inequalities (p.29). You don't know the <u>actual data values</u>, so you can only <u>estimate</u> the <u>mean</u>. To do this, use the <u>midpoints</u> (or <u>mid-interval values</u>) from each group and multiply by the frequency. The <u>modal class</u> is the <u>group</u> with the <u>highest frequency</u>.

EXAMPLE: The lengths of a sample of 40 slugs were measured and the results are given in the table below. Estimate the mean length of slug and state the modal class.

Length (mm)	$85 < x \le 90$	$90 < x \le 95$	$95 < x \le 100$	$100 < x \le 105$	$105 < x \le 110$	Totals
Frequency, f	3	7	15	10	5	40
Midpoint (mm), x	87.5	92.5	97.5	102.5	107.5	—
Frequency × Midpoint, fx	262.5	647.5	1462.5	1025	537.5	3935

New 3rd row
New 4th row

$$\underline{\text{Mean}} = \boxed{\frac{\Sigma fx}{\Sigma f}} = \frac{\text{4th row total}}{\text{2nd row total}} = \frac{3935}{40} = \underline{98.4 \text{ mm}} \text{ (1 d.p.)}$$

Modal class = $\underline{95 < x \le 100}$ since it's the class with the greatest frequency (15).

In the example above, the <u>class widths</u> were all equal (5 mm). The method is the <u>same</u> when the class widths are <u>unequal</u> — just <u>be careful</u> when you work out the <u>midpoints</u> of each class.

[Higher]

Estimate the Median using Linear Interpolation

EXAMPLE: For the slug data above, state which group the median is in and estimate a value for the median.

1) **FIND WHICH <u>GROUP</u> THE MEDIAN IS IN** — $40 \div 2$

The <u>median</u> is the value in position number 20, in the group $\underline{95 < x \le 100}$.

Use $n/2$ to find the position of the median for grouped data — not $(n + 1)/2$.

2) **FIND THE MEDIAN'S <u>POSITION</u> IN ITS GROUP**

Position in group = overall position − number of positions below median group

The median's overall position is 20 and there are 10 values in the groups below the median group (3 + 7). So position in group = $\underline{20 - 10 = 10}$ — i.e. you want to estimate the 10th value in the group $95 < x \le 100$.

3) **FIND THIS POSITION AS A <u>PROPORTION</u>**

Proportion of the way through group = position in the group ÷ number of values in the group

The median is the 10th value in the group out of a total of 15 values. So it's $\underline{10 \div 15 = 2/3}$ of the way through the group $95 < x \le 100$.

Remember this is just an estimate — it'll only be accurate if the lengths are evenly distributed within the class.

4) **<u>MULTIPLY</u> YOUR ANSWER BY THE <u>CLASS WIDTH</u> OF THE MEDIAN GROUP**

The group starts at 95 mm and goes to 100 mm, so the class width of the group is 5 mm. As the median is $2/3$ of the way through the group you can estimate it'll be at $2/3$ of the way through that 5 mm. So, $2/3 \times 5 = \underline{10/3 \text{ mm}}$ into the group.

5) **<u>ADD</u> THIS NUMBER TO THE MEDIAN GROUP'S <u>LOWER CLASS BOUNDARY</u>**

The median group's lower class boundary is 95 mm, so the median estimate is $\underline{95 + 10/3 = 98.3 \text{ mm}}$ (1 d.p.).

Phew, forget continuous data — this page was continuous stress...

Once you've learnt how to estimate the mean and median for continuous data, try this question:

1 a) Estimate the mean for the data in the table on the right.
 b) Estimate the median. c) What is the modal class?

Weight (g)	$3 < x \le 6$	$6 < x \le 9$	$9 < x \le 12$	$12 < x \le 15$
Frequency	1	9	5	3

Measures of Spread

Next up, the <u>range</u>, along with <u>quartiles</u>, and a bit about <u>percentiles</u> — what a lovely spread...

The Range — How Far the Data Spreads

To find the <u>range</u> of a set of data you work out the <u>difference</u> between the <u>highest</u> and the <u>lowest</u> values.

 **EXAMPLE:** Find the range of these numbers: 7, 12, 5, 4, 3, 7, 5, 11, 6, 4, 9

Highest number − Lowest number = 12 − 3, so the range is <u>9</u>.

Finding the Quartiles is a bit more Tricky

Found one

<u>Quartiles</u> divide the data into <u>four equal groups</u>. The quartiles are the <u>lower quartile</u> Q_1, the <u>median</u> Q_2 and the <u>upper quartile</u> Q_3. If you put the data in ascending order, the quartiles are 25% (¼), 50% (½) and 75% (¾) of the way through the list.

EXAMPLE: Find the value of Q_1, Q_2 and Q_3 for this set of numbers: 7, 12, 6, 4, 3, 9, 7, 11, 7

1) Put the data in <u>ASCENDING ORDER</u> — 3, 4, 6, 7, 7, 7, 9, 11, 12

2) Work out where the <u>QUARTILES</u> come in the list using the following <u>formulas</u>:

$$Q_1 \text{ position number} = (n + 1)/4$$
$$Q_2 \text{ position number} = 2(n + 1)/4$$
$$Q_3 \text{ position number} = 3(n + 1)/4$$

The position is a "half value" so you'll have to find the <u>halfway point</u> of the two numbers <u>either side</u> of this position.

If the position was 2.25, you'd find the value <u>one quarter</u> of the way between the numbers either side of the position (so 4.5 in this case). If it was 2.75, you'd find the value <u>three quarters</u> of the way between the numbers (5.5 here).

Step 1: $n = 9$ so Q_1 position no. $= (9+1)/4 = 2.5$
Q_2 position no. $= 2(9+1)/4 = 5$
Q_3 position no. $= 3(9+1)/4 = 7.5$

Step 2:   3   4   6   7   7   7   9   11   12

position 1 Q_1 Q_2 Q_3 position 9
            $(4 + 6) \div 2 = 5$ $(9 + 11) \div 2 = 10$

3) So, the lower quartile $\underline{Q_1 = 5}$, the median $\underline{Q_2 = 7}$ and the upper quartile $\underline{Q_3 = 10}$.

You Can Find Percentiles too...

You can use other groups to give you a more flexible view of the spread of data. For example, <u>percentiles</u>, P_1 to P_{99}, divide the data into <u>one hundred</u> equal groups.

$Q_2 = P_{50}$, which also represents the median.

The formula to work out the positions of percentiles is really similar to the ones for working out quartiles:
P_1 position no. $= \underline{(n + 1)/100}$, P_2 position no. $= \underline{2(n + 1)/100}$, etc...

Then <u>count along</u> your data to this position. If the position isn't a whole number, you can take the <u>mean</u> of the two data values it <u>falls between</u>. E.g. if the position = 13.3, find the 13th and 14th values (say, x and y) and take $\underline{(x + y) \div 2}$ as the percentile.

Free range data — has plenty of room to spread out...

There are a few different methods for calculating percentiles which give slightly different answers — so it's 100% necessary to show every step of your working to let the examiner see which you've used. Now, have a go at these...

1) For the list of integers from 1 to 999 inclusive:
   a) What is the range?
   b) What is the value of the upper quartile?
   c) Find P_{85}, the 85th percentile.
   d) Find P_{50}. What is the value of the median?

Measures of Spread

Now we're getting to the good stuff. And by good stuff, I mean <u>interquartile</u>/<u>percentile</u>/<u>decile</u> ranges...

Interquartile means "Between Quartiles"

The <u>interquartile range</u> (<u>IQR</u>) is the <u>difference</u> between the <u>upper quartile</u> and the <u>lower quartile</u>: $Q_3 - Q_1$.

> **EXAMPLE:**
> Find the interquartile range of the following set of numbers:
> Put the data in ascending order. → 3 4 ④ 5 5 6 7 7 ⑨ 11 12
> Lower quartile = 4   Upper quartile = 9   <u>Interquartile range = 9 − 4 = 5</u>

There are Other Ranges You Can Find As Well

FINDING AN INTERPERCENTILE RANGE

You can find <u>interpercentile ranges</u> in much the same way.
For any two percentiles, the interpercentile range between them is just their difference.
E.g. the <u>20th to 80th</u> interpercentile range is $P_{80} - P_{20}$.
There are many interpercentile ranges but you find them all in the <u>same way</u>.

FINDING THE INTERDECILE RANGE

<u>Deciles</u>, D_1 to D_9, divide the data into <u>ten</u> equal groups — you work them out in a similar way to quartiles and percentiles. E.g. the position of D_9 is $9(n + 1)/10$.
The <u>interdecile range</u> is just the difference between the first and the ninth deciles: $D_9 - D_1$.
This is the same as the P_{10} to P_{90} percentile range.

The nine deciles are the same as the percentiles $P_{10}, P_{20}, ..., P_{90}$.

You Need to Know What the Ranges Actually Tell You

> A <u>large</u> interquartile/percentile/decile range means the data is
> <u>spread out</u> in this region — it's <u>more varied</u> / <u>less consistent</u>.
> A smaller value means that the data is more consistent / less varied.

1) The <u>interquartile range</u> tells you the range of the <u>middle 50%</u> of the data — where most of the activity's going on — and it's <u>unaffected by outliers</u>, so it's often more useful than the range itself. However, it also <u>omits 50%</u> of the data.

2) <u>Small percentile</u> ranges such as $P_{90} - P_{80}$ let you see what's going on in <u>smaller areas</u> of the data.

3) The <u>interdecile range</u> gives a more <u>realistic</u> idea of the spread of data than the range or interquartile range. It gives the range of the <u>middle 80%</u> of the data, ignoring any <u>outliers</u>.

> **EXAMPLE:**
> Jemima collects a set of data. The $P_{50} - P_{35}$ interpercentile range is 5.25 and the $P_{95} - P_{80}$ interpercentile range is 1.5. Comment on what this tells you about the spread of the data.

The 35th to 50th interpercentile range is <u>higher</u> than the 80th to 95th interpercentile range. This shows that the 15% of the data between the 35th and 50th percentiles is <u>more spread out</u> than the 15% between the 80th and 95th percentiles.

The interquartile ranger — fighting crime between quartiles...

This page is really important, so make sure you understand it, then have a go at this question:

1) Write down the odd numbers between 1 and 13 inclusive. What is the interquartile range?

2) The 85th to 90th and 90th to 95th interpercentile ranges for a set of data are 8.5 and 1.3 respectively. Comment on what this tells you about the distribution of the data. [Higher only]

Measures of Spread — Grouped Data

If you have <u>grouped data</u>, you can only <u>estimate</u> the interquartile/percentile/decile ranges.
One way to do this is by using a similar method to the <u>linear interpolation</u> method for the median on page 53.
An <u>easier way</u>, though, is to use a <u>cumulative frequency curve</u> — see page 39.

Grouped Data — Use a Chart to Estimate...

**EXAMPLE:** The table on the right shows the time taken for 200 birds to each catch a flying fish.

Estimate the interquartile range and the interdecile range for the data.

Time (mins)	Frequency	Cumulative Frequency
$0 \leq t < 5$	8	8
$5 \leq t < 10$	30	38
$10 \leq t < 15$	66	104
$15 \leq t < 20$	58	162
$20 \leq t < 25$	26	188
$25 \leq t < 30$	12	200

If you don't understand this table, check out 'Cumulative Frequency' again (see p.39).

...the Interquartile Range...

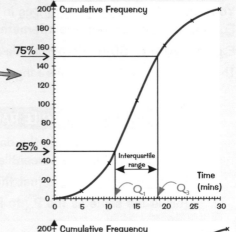

1) First draw a <u>cumulative frequency curve</u> for the data in the table — like the one shown here.

2) <u>Draw lines</u> across from the <u>25%</u> and <u>75%</u> marks on the y-axis — 25% of 200 = 50 and 75% of 200 = 150. These correspond to x-values of (approximately) <u>11</u> and <u>18.6</u> respectively. So $Q_1 = 11$ and $Q_3 = 18.6$.

3) So <u>interquartile range</u>
$= Q_3 - Q_1 = 18.6 - 11 = \underline{7.6 \text{ mins}}$

...or the Interdecile Range

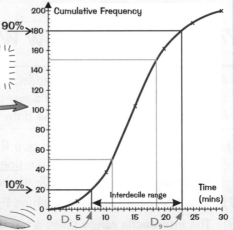

Using the same curve:

1) For the interdecile range, draw your lines from the <u>10%</u> and <u>90%</u> marks (20 and 180 respectively) on the y-axis to the curve. This gives you the x-values: $D_9 = 23$ and $D_1 = 7.5$.

The interdecile range is the same as the $P_{90} - P_{10}$ interpercentile range.

2) So <u>interdecile range</u>
$= D_9 - D_1 = 23 - 7.5 = \underline{15.5 \text{ mins}}$

(margin, left) Higher
(margin, right) Higher

You're opening a flying fish farm? Nah, pal — it'll never take off...

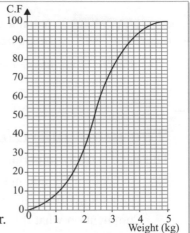

When you're confident with the example above, test yourself with this question:

1) Priscilla collects 100 melons and weighs them. She groups her data and draws a cumulative frequency chart to represent her data, shown on the right.

a) Use the chart to estimate:
    (i) the interquartile range,
    (ii) the 20th to 80th interpercentile range,
    (iii) the interdecile range,
    (iv) the 90th to 95th interpercentile range.

Note: parts (ii)-(iv) and b) are higher only.

b) Priscilla discovers that a few of the melons she collected are unusually heavy. Which of the ranges from a) should she treat with caution? Explain your answer.

Standard Deviation

Ranges are done (sob). Now, for this page there's just one warning — get your <u>calculators</u> ready...

Standard Deviation Measures Spread from the Mean

The <u>standard deviation</u> tells you how <u>spread out</u> the data is. The <u>SMALLER</u> it is, the <u>closer</u> the data is to the <u>mean</u>. Unlike the ranges you met on the last few pages, it uses <u>all</u> the values in a data set to give a measure of spread — this makes it much more useful. It's also good for <u>comparing</u> data sets (see p.62).

For a set of n data values x_1, x_2, ..., x_n whose mean is $\overline{x}$ (p.49), $\sum(x - \overline{x})^2$ is the sum of the "squared deviations from their mean". Then the <u>formulas for standard deviation</u> (σ) are:

> You don't need to learn these formulas — you'll be given them in the exam. You do need to know HOW TO USE THEM though.

$$\sigma = \sqrt{\frac{1}{n}\sum(x - \overline{x})^2}$$ or $$\sigma = \sqrt{\frac{\sum x^2}{n} - \left(\frac{\sum x}{n}\right)^2}$$

This is $\overline{x}^2$ (i.e. the mean^2).

EXAMPLE: Find the standard deviation of the following data:

22   20   25   18   18   18   19   20

First work out the <u>mean</u>: $\overline{x} = (22 + 20 + 25 + 18 + 18 + 18 + 19 + 20) \div 8 = \underline{20}$

Then use a table to work out all the values you need for the formula:

x	x^2	$(x - \overline{x})$	$(x - \overline{x})^2$
22	484	2	4
20	400	0	0
25	625	5	25
18	324	−2	4
18	324	−2	4
18	324	−2	4
19	361	−1	1
20	400	0	0
160	3242	—	42

$\sum x^2$ $\sum(x - \overline{x})^2$

1) List the <u>data values</u> in the first column.

2) What you put in the <u>other columns</u> depends on which set of formulas you're using. I've colour-coded the columns in my table — you only need to use the ones that match the formula you're using.

3) So, using the "blue" formula:

$\sigma = \sqrt{42 \div 8} = 2.29$ (2 d.p.)

Or using the "yellow" formula:

$\sigma = \sqrt{(3242 \div 8) - 20^2} = 2.29$ (2 d.p.)

So the <u>standard deviation = 2.29 (2 d.p.)</u>

EXAMPLE: A set of data contains 16 values. Given that $\sum x = 28$ and $\sum x^2 = 456$, use these summary statistics to find the standard deviation of the data.

The information you're given means you <u>have to use</u> the yellow formula — you can't work out $(x - \overline{x})^2$ from these <u>summary statistics</u> so the blue formula is no use here.

> A <u>summary statistic</u> is just a value used to summarise a data set.

1) First, find the <u>mean</u>: $\overline{x} = (\sum x) \div n = 28 \div 16 = 1.75$

2) Then use the yellow formula: $\sigma = \sqrt{\frac{456}{16} - 1.75^2} = \underline{5.04}$ (2 d.p.)

10g of jam — a measure of spread...

This page was a tough one, but don't be put off by the big formulas. Have a go at these for some practice...

1) Find the standard deviation of the following numbers:

    −1   4   −2   5   3   2   2   1   0   1

2) Calculate the standard deviation of the first six odd numbers.

3) What is the standard deviation of the first six even numbers?

Standard Deviation from Frequency Tables

Here are some more formulas for you, so fasten your seat belts — this page is going to be <u>absolutely wild</u>...

Frequency Distributions — New Formulas for σ

If your data is in a <u>frequency table</u>, you need to use one of these formulas:

$$\sigma = \sqrt{\frac{\sum f(x-\bar{x})^2}{\sum f}}$$ or $$\sigma = \sqrt{\frac{\sum fx^2}{\sum f}-\left(\frac{\sum fx}{\sum f}\right)^2}$$

f is the frequency of an x-value

This is $\bar{x}^2$ for data from a frequency table.

These formulas WON'T BE GIVEN to you in the exam — you'll have to learn them.

EXAMPLE: Find the standard deviation for the following frequency distribution.

values of x →

Number of people in car	1	2	3
Number of cars	3	5	2

frequencies "f" →

To use the "<u>blue</u>" formula — add four columns: fx, $(x-\bar{x})$, $(x-\bar{x})^2$ and $f(x-\bar{x})^2$.

x	f	fx	x^2	fx^2
1	3	3	1	3
2	5	10	4	20
3	2	6	9	18
—	10	19	—	41

$\sum f$ $\sum fx$ $\sum fx^2$

If you're using the "yellow formula" —

1) Make a table and <u>add columns</u> for fx, x^2 and fx^2.
2) Calculate the <u>mean</u> number of people per car: $19 \div 10 = 1.9$.
3) Then work out the answer:

Standard deviation $(\sigma) = \sqrt{\frac{\sum fx^2}{\sum f}-\bar{x}^2} = \sqrt{\frac{41}{10}-1.9^2} = \underline{0.7}$

For Grouped Frequency Distributions, x is the Midpoint

When you've got a <u>grouped frequency distribution</u> you can only <u>estimate</u> the standard deviation. You do this by taking the <u>midpoint of the group</u> as your x-value.

EXAMPLE: Find the standard deviation for the following grouped frequency distribution:

Height (cm)	$50 < x \le 75$	$75 < x \le 100$	$100 < x \le 125$	$125 < x \le 150$	$150 < x \le 175$
Frequency	7	18	42	25	8

x	f	fx	x^2	fx^2
62.5	7	437.5	3906.25	27 343.75
87.5	18	1575	7656.25	137 812.5
112.5	42	4725	12 656.25	531 562.5
137.5	25	3437.5	18 906.25	472 656.25
162.5	8	1300	26 406.25	211 250
—	100	11 475	—	1 380 625

$\sum f$ $\sum fx$ $\sum fx^2$

Again, you make a table with three extra columns — but now the x-column contains the <u>midpoints</u> rather than the actual data values.

Calculate the <u>mean</u>: $11\,475 \div 100 = 114.75$.

Standard deviation $(\sigma) = \sqrt{\frac{\sum fx^2}{\sum f}-\bar{x}^2}$

$= \sqrt{\frac{1380\,625}{100}-114.75^2}$

$= \underline{25.3\ cm}$ (1 d.p.)

The M62 is closed so often, I know all the standard deviations...

Phew... this page is hardcore. And to make matters worse, you need to learn the formulas. But try not to worry, they're not too different from the formulas for σ that you <u>are</u> given — just remember where the fs come in. Practise with this question:

1) Find the standard deviation of the data on the right.

Number of chocolates in box	25	26	27	28	29
Number of boxes	1	5	3	2	1

Box Plots

You'll be glad to hear that this page is a nice little break from those darn formulas. (Hurray)
It's all about <u>drawing</u> and <u>interpreting</u> box plots — time to get your <u>rulers</u> out...

Box Plots are Good for Comparing Data Sets

1) <u>Box plots</u> show the <u>median</u>, <u>quartiles</u> and the <u>highest</u> and <u>lowest</u> values of a set of data. They give a good <u>summary</u> of the spread of data and also show information about the <u>skew</u> (more on this on page 61). Box plots are useful when <u>comparing</u> the <u>distribution</u> of two or more sets of data (page 62).

2) The total length of a box plot represents the range of the data. The <u>middle 50%</u> of the data is the <u>box</u> and the rest is known as the <u>whiskers</u>.

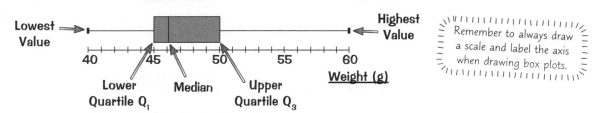

Lowest Value → | Highest Value ← | Weight (g)
Lower Quartile Q_1 | Median | Upper Quartile Q_3

Remember to always draw a scale and label the axis when drawing box plots.

EXAMPLE: Data was collected about how many text messages some students received in a day. The results were as follows: a minimum of 0, a range of 18, a median equal to 13 and upper and lower quartiles equal to 14 and 8 respectively. Draw a box plot to represent this data.

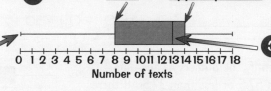

2 Mark the <u>lower</u> and <u>upper quartiles</u> and draw the <u>BOX</u>.

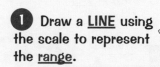

1 Draw a <u>LINE</u> using the scale to represent the <u>range</u>.

Number of texts

3 Finally, draw a <u>LINE DOWN THE BOX</u> at the <u>median</u>.

Interpreting a Box Plot — Read Off the Quartiles

If you know how to draw a box plot, <u>interpreting</u> one should be a doddle.
Just <u>read off</u> the relevant values (the median, quartiles or highest/lowest points).

EXAMPLE: Janine records how many peas are on her plate at dinner each day for a number of weeks. She creates a box plot to illustrate her findings. Use the box plot to find the average and spread of her data.

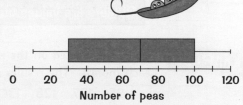

Number of peas

The only <u>average</u> that a box plot tells you is the <u>median</u> — it's the line down the <u>middle</u> of the box. So the average is <u>70 peas</u>.

For the <u>spread</u>, you could find the <u>range</u> or the <u>interquartile range</u>:
The range is the <u>difference</u> between the <u>highest</u> and <u>lowest values</u>: 120 − 10 = <u>110 peas</u>.
The IQR is the <u>difference</u> between the <u>upper</u> and <u>lower quartiles</u>: 100 − 30 = <u>70 peas</u>.

Box and whiskers, like peas in a pod...

Once you're happy drawing and interpreting box plots, have a go at this stupendous question...

1) These are the times in minutes that eleven birthday cake candles stayed alight:

    13   15   12   16   2   14   14   9   13   13   17

    Draw a box plot to represent this data.

Outliers

Outliers — keep them and they could <u>mislead</u> your analysis, exclude them and you could be <u>falsifying</u> the data. And then you'll have your stats qualifications revoked and you'll end up having to write gags for revision guides...

Outliers don't fit the General Pattern

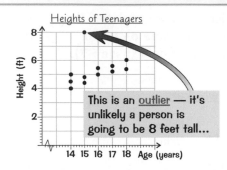

Heights of Teenagers

This is an <u>outlier</u> — it's unlikely a person is going to be 8 feet tall...

1) Outliers are data points that don't fit the <u>general pattern</u> or are a <u>long way</u> from the rest of the data (e.g. the 8-foot tall 15-year-old on this graph).

2) Outliers can show possible <u>errors</u> (e.g. in measuring or data collection).

3) But they aren't <u>necessarily</u> mistakes — they could be valid data values.

4) If you find one on a graph, <u>check</u> the <u>original data</u> to see whether it's been plotted correctly.

Outliers can be found using Box Plots...

<u>Outliers</u> can <u>distort</u> a data set, so you need to be able to <u>identify</u> them. One way to identify outliers is to look for values that are <u>more than 1.5 times</u> the interquartile range away from the upper or lower quartiles.

Outliers are values $> Q_3 + 1.5 \times$ IQR or values $< Q_1 - 1.5 \times$ IQR

A <u>box plot</u> is helpful when finding outliers because it shows the range and the upper and lower quartiles.

EXAMPLE:

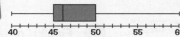

40 45 50 55 60

$Q_3 + 1.5(Q_3 - Q_1) = 50 + 1.5(50 - 45) = \underline{57.5}$
$Q_1 - 1.5(Q_3 - Q_1) = 45 - 1.5(50 - 45) = \underline{37.5}$

In this example you can identify the outliers as any data values that are <u>greater than 57.5</u> or <u>less than 37.5</u>. If there are any outliers, the <u>whiskers should be shortened</u> to extend to the highest and lowest data values that are not outliers.

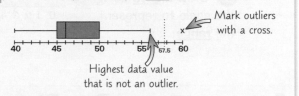

Mark outliers with a cross.

40 45 50 55 57.5 60

Highest data value that is not an outlier.

...or by using the Mean and Standard Deviation

Outliers can also be detected using their <u>distance</u> from the <u>mean</u> — the limit is <u>3 standard deviations</u>.

Outliers are values outside the region $\mu \pm 3\sigma$

μ is the population mean
σ is the standard deviation

EXAMPLE:

Data is collected on the number of minutes workers in an office spend making tea each month. The results are below. The standard deviation is 48.34 mins (2 d.p.).

95 127 128 130 131 138 143 146 147 153 155 303

Use an appropriate calculation to determine whether any of the values are outliers.

The <u>mean</u> is $\sum x \div 12 = \underline{150}$ so outliers are outside 150 ± (3 × 48.34). So, that's values <u>greater than</u> 150 + (3 × 48.34) = <u>295.02</u> and values <u>less than</u> 150 − (3 × 48.34) = <u>4.98</u>. Since <u>303</u> > 295.01, it's an <u>outlier</u>.

The different criteria for detecting outliers won't always give the same results. Have a go at Q2 below to see how the IQR method compares with this one.

My teacher said this would be fun — but he's an outright liar...

You know the drill by now — make sure you know the page then have a go at these:

1) Use inspection only to identify the outlier on the graph. Do you think the outlier is genuine? Explain your answer.

2) a) Draw a box plot for the tea data in the example above.
   b) By finding the IQR, determine if there are any outliers in the data. [Higher only]

Relationship between time spent jogging and distance travelled

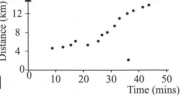

Higher

Section Four — Analysing and Interpreting Data

Skewness of Data

<u>Skewness</u> describes the <u>shape</u> of a distribution. You saw on page 42 how to inspect a histogram for evidence of skew — now it's time to delve into calculating skew by other means (and medians and standard deviations).

Skew Tells You How the Data is Spread

1) If the data is <u>skewed</u>, it means it's packed <u>more tightly</u> to <u>one side</u> of the <u>median</u>.

2) A <u>positive</u> skew means the data values <u>below</u> the median are <u>closer together</u> and the values <u>above</u> the median are more <u>spread out</u>. The <u>majority</u> of the data is <u>relatively low</u>, with a <u>few higher</u> values. The <u>opposite</u> is true for a <u>negative</u> skew.

3) A distribution could be <u>symmetrical</u> — it has <u>no skew</u> and the data is <u>evenly distributed</u> above and below the median.

4) You can get an <u>idea</u> for the skew of a data set using a couple of <u>checks</u>.

These inequalities <u>indicate</u> a <u>positive</u> skew: Mean > Median > Mode   Median – Q_1 < Q_3 – Median

5) If the inequalities are the <u>other way</u> around, it indicates a <u>negative</u> skew.

Today is going to be a good day!

Find the Skew of Data from the Box Plot

It's easy to determine the <u>skew</u> of a distribution just by <u>looking</u> at the box plot.

If the median is near the <u>centre</u> of the box (about halfway between Q_1 and Q_3) and the whiskers are quite <u>even</u> then the distribution is fairly <u>symmetrical</u>.

If the median is towards the <u>left</u> of the box (nearer the lower quartile) then the distribution is <u>positively skewed</u>.

If the median is towards the <u>right</u> of the box (nearer the upper quartile) then the distribution is <u>negatively skewed</u>.

Go back to p.42 to see how a histogram is affected by skew.

Use the Formula to Measure Skewness

You can work out a value to quantify skew, called the <u>coefficient of skew</u>. The coefficient can be between <u>–3 and 3</u>. A <u>negative value</u> means a <u>negative skew</u>, a <u>positive value</u> means a <u>positive skew</u> and <u>zero</u> means the distribution's <u>symmetrical</u>. The <u>closer</u> to ±3, the <u>more skewed</u> the distribution.

This is the <u>formula</u> for the coefficient of skewness: 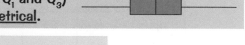 $$\text{skew} = \frac{3\,(\text{mean} - \text{median})}{\text{standard deviation}}$$

The skewness formula will be given in the exam.

EXAMPLE: Data is collected on the weight of 20 hippos. The mean weight was 1650 kg, the median was 1760 kg and the standard deviation was 202 kg. Calculate and interpret the skew.

skew = $\frac{3\,(\text{mean} - \text{median})}{\text{standard deviation}}$

$= \frac{3\,(1650 - 1760)}{202} = \underline{-1.63}$ (2 d.p.)

The value is negative so there is a <u>moderately negative skew</u>. This means the <u>majority of the hippos are heavier</u>, with <u>fewer lighter ones</u>. It also means the weights of the hippos are <u>bunched at the heavier end</u> and there is <u>more spread</u> in the weights of those <u>below</u> the median weight.

I must askew a question, but I'll shave it for — wait, wrong joke...

Once you're sure you understand what the value produced by the skew formula means, have a go at these questions:

1) Look back at the tea example on the previous page.
   a) Predict the skewness of the data using an inequality.
   b) Calculate the skew of the data and interpret it in the context of the data. [Higher only]
2) A data set of 50 values has the following summary statistics: $\sum x = 1382$, $\sum x^2 = 209\,736$. The 25th lowest value is 48 and the 26th is 57. Calculate the skew of the data. [Higher only]

Comparing Data Sets

Entschuldigung, haben Sie einen Apfel, bitte? Oh sorry, wrong book — so, back to STATISTICS then...

You can Compare Two Sets of Data Using...

1) Averages

Compare individual data values by standardising — see page 64.

The results for 20 students' French and English exams were collected and the averages of the two sets of data are shown in the table below.

	French	English
Mean	53.2	52
Median	49.5	51
Mode	43, 47, 65	42, 51, 59, 61

1) The mean and median can be used to give a quick comparison of two or more sets of data. In this example, the mean and median for the English and French scores are pretty similar, so you can't tell which scores were better overall.
2) The MODE, in this case, is not much use at all.

2) Measures of Spread

The table and box plots below show measures of spread for the same two sets of exam results.

	French	English
Range	47	28
Upper Quartile	65	59.5
Lower Quartile	43	44
Interquartile Range	22	15.5
Standard Deviation	13.19	8.60

FRENCH

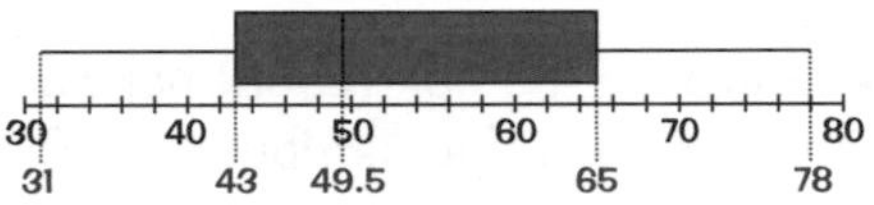
30
40
50
60
70
80
31
43
49.5
65
78
Exam mark

ENGLISH

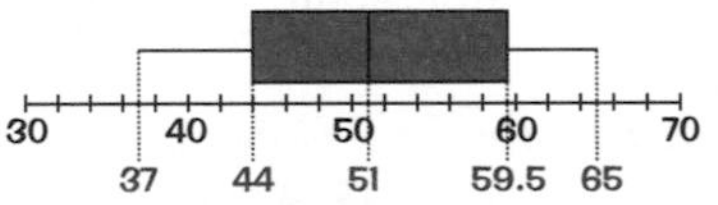
30
40
50
60
70
37
44
51
59.5
65
Exam mark

Look back at page 59 for a reminder on box plots.

1) The table and box plot show that the English results have a smaller range than the French results — this means that the English scores were more consistent. The interquartile range is also smaller for the English results, showing that the middle 50% of English scores were more consistent than the middle 50% of French scores. (Remember, the interquartile range is useful if you have outliers.)
2) The standard deviation is another measure of spread. Here, it's lower for the English scores, which means that they're closer to the mean than the French scores. But that's all the standard deviation shows — unlike box plots, it doesn't give you any idea of the actual values.

Higher

3) Measures of Skew

You can also use the box plots to give you a general idea of the skew (p.61) of a distribution. E.g. the box plots above show that the French scores were more positively skewed than the English scores — this means that the majority of the French scores were relatively low with fewer high scores (and the higher scores were more spread out than the lower ones). The skew of the English scores is still positive but less so, meaning the scores were spread more symmetrically.

	French	English
Skewness	0.84	0.35

You can also calculate the coefficient of skew. The values show the same as the box plots — that the French scores were more positively skewed.

Higher

For comparing data sets — remember, averages, spread & stew...

Erm... oh that's SKEW, not stew. My mistake.
Once you're happy with this page, have a go at this question:

1) The box plots on the right give information about the weights of male and female chipmunks. Compare the two distributions fully.

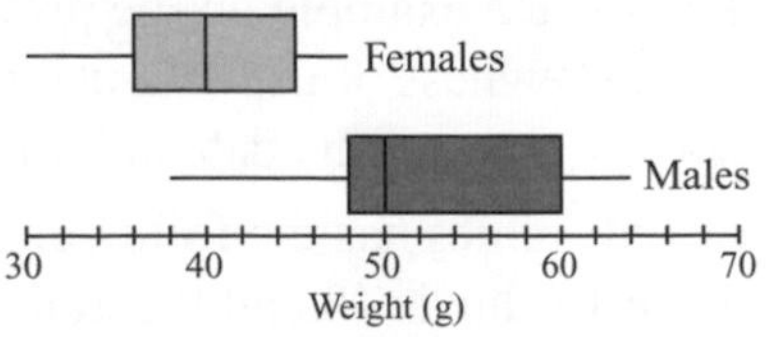
Females
Males
30
40
50
60
70
Weight (g)

Comparing Data Sets

You're not finished comparing data just yet — here are a few more things to bear in mind...

Make Sure to Pair the Appropriate Values

To make valid comparisons, you have to use the right <u>average</u> with the <u>appropriate measure of spread</u>. For example, the standard deviation (p.57) is a measure of deviation from the mean, so you can <u>only</u> use it with the mean. Here are all the <u>pairs</u> you can use together:

> Use the <u>mean</u> with the <u>standard deviation</u> or the <u>range</u>.

> Use the <u>mode</u> with the <u>range</u>.

> Use the <u>median</u> with the <u>interquartile range</u> or the <u>range</u>.

You can also use interpercentile ranges or the interdecile range with the median.

EXAMPLE: Brenda is comparing the ages of people in two cities, Falbrax and Choppleton. She uses statistical software to obtain the values given in the table. Compare the ages of people in the two towns.

	Falbrax	Choppleton
Upper quartile	78	90
Lower quartile	25	21
Median	51	46
Mean	41	48

Use the upper and lower quartiles to calculate the <u>IQR</u>:
$78 - 25 = \underline{53}$ for Falbrax
$90 - 21 = \underline{69}$ for Choppleton

So the IQR is <u>greater for Choppleton</u> than Falbrax, i.e. ages are <u>less consistent</u> / <u>more spread out</u> in Choppleton.

Since you've used the IQR, it makes sense to use the <u>median</u> to compare the average ages. On average, people in Choppleton are <u>younger</u> than in Falbrax since Choppleton has a <u>lower median</u>.

Comparing a Sample with the Population

If you have a <u>subsection</u> (or <u>sample</u>) of the population, it isn't necessarily <u>representative</u> of the population — so you should treat it as a <u>separate data set</u> and <u>make comparisons</u>.

EXAMPLE: The cumulative percentage chart on the right shows the annual incomes of adults in the county of Humbleshire. The boxes below show some statistics about the annual incomes of adults in Humble Town, located within Humbleshire.

Compare the distribution of incomes in the town and the county.

Median	£25 000

IQR	£10 000

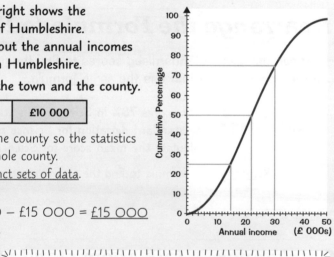

There is <u>no reason</u> to think the town is <u>representative</u> of the county so the statistics for the town are likely to be <u>different</u> from those of the whole county.
So compare the town and the county as if they were <u>distinct sets of data</u>.

Find the median and IQR for the county using the <u>chart</u>:
The <u>median</u> is £22 000 and the <u>IQR</u> = £30 000 − £15 000 = £15 000

So the median in the town is <u>higher</u>, showing people there <u>earn more</u> on average. The IQR for the town is <u>lower</u>, so incomes are <u>more consistent</u> in the town.

A cumulative percentage chart is similar to a cumulative frequency chart, but with percentages on the y-axis instead of frequencies.

Hey everyone, I'll compère — next up, standardised scores...

So that's comparing data sets polished off. Try this question and then you're all set to move on.

1) A school has 750 pupils. All the school's pupils ran around a track and their times, x seconds, were recorded. These statistics are calculated: $\sum x = 43\,500$, $\sum (x - \bar{x})^2 = 75\,321$. For Year 7 pupils only, the mean time was 67 seconds and the standard deviation was 10 seconds. Compare the Year 7 pupils with the school as a whole.

Standardised Scores

Watch out — there's another formula coming right at you. Oh, you're wearing a helmet. Okay, great, nice...

Higher

Compare Individual Data Values by Standardising

1) If you want to compare how far above or below average individual values are, then you can use **STANDARDISED SCORES**.
2) There's another groovy formula for this: $$\text{standardised score} = \frac{\text{value} - \text{mean}}{\text{standard deviation}} = \frac{x - \mu}{\sigma}$$

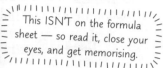

This ISN'T on the formula sheet — so read it, close your eyes, and get memorising.

3) The mean and standard deviation in this formula are for the **WHOLE POPULATION**.
4) Any value equal to the mean has a standardised score of **ZERO** — so zero is an average score.
5) A standardised score **ABOVE ZERO** is higher than average and a **NEGATIVE** one is below average.

EXAMPLE: Nick took Maths and English tests along with the rest of his year. Given the following information, work out his standardised scores and compare his results in Maths and English.

Subject	Score	Mean	Standard Deviation
Maths	60%	70%	10%
English	65%	72%	3%

The scores you compare don't have to be percentages. E.g. you could compare a score out of 50 with one out of, say, 7824.

Standardised score for Maths = $\frac{\text{value} - \text{mean}}{\text{standard deviation}}$ = (60 – 70) ÷ 10 = –1

Standardised score for English = (65 – 72) ÷ 3 = –2.33

Nick did better in Maths — his higher standardised score shows he beat a greater proportion of his fellow students in Maths than in English.

Notice that in this example, Nick actually scored higher in English than Maths. But the mean shows that, on average, everyone did better in English. This is why standardised scores are useful — they take into account the performance of the rest of the population so you can make more reliable comparisons.

Rearrange the Formula to Find Out About the Population

You can use given standardised scores to find the mean and standard deviation of the population — just use the same formula.

EXAMPLE: Nick scores 78% in Science. His standardised score is 0.01. The standard deviation for Science results in his year was 12%. Calculate the mean score for Science.

Since the standardised score is positive, you know the mean will be less than Nick's score.

Rearrange the formula to find the mean: mean = value – (standardised score × standard deviation)
= 78 – (0.01 × 12) = 77.88%

Higher

Chickenpox — talk about standardised sores...

Don't fret if you find this page tough. Make sure you get the examples, learn the formula, then try this question...

1) The table below shows the results for the mock exams for History, Geography and Classics for three students A, B and C, along with the mean, μ, and standard deviation, σ, for the whole year.
   a) Work out the standardised scores in History and Geography for each student.
   b) Which student gave the best performance overall for these two subjects?
   c) (i) Student A has a standardised score in Classics of 0.3. Student B has a standardised score in Classics of 1.2. Find x and y.
   (ii) Find the standardised score in Classics for student C.

	A	B	C	μ	σ
History	78	85	69	74	5
Geography	75	71	83	78	4
Classics	56	59	34	x	y

Summary Statistics — Index Numbers

If your data includes <u>prices</u> it might be helpful to put the values in an <u>index</u>...

Simple Index Numbers — Just Percentages Really

<u>Index numbers</u> are often used to compare <u>price changes</u> over time.
Current values are compared to the values in a particular year — known as the <u>base year</u>.

Here's how you work them out:

$$\text{INDEX NUMBER} = \frac{\text{value}}{\text{value in base year}} \times 100$$

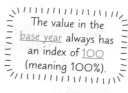

The value in the <u>base year</u> always has an index of <u>100</u> (meaning 100%).

You can tell from the index number whether a value has increased or decreased from the value in the base year.

- If the index number is higher than 100, this means the value has increased. So, if the index number is, say, 120 then the value has risen by **20%**.
- If the index number is lower than 100, this means the value has decreased. So, if the index number is, say, 98 then the value has decreased by **2%**.

EXAMPLE: The table below shows the price of a house over four years as well as the index numbers calculated (to 1 d.p.) using 2015 as the base year.

a) Find the index number for 2017. b) Find the house price in 2018.
c) By what percentage did the house price increase between 2015 & 2016?

Year	2015	2016	2017	2018
House Price	£148,000	£167,000	£174,000	?
Index Number	100	112.8	?	130.2

a) Index number for 2017 = $\frac{174\,000}{148\,000} \times 100 = \underline{117.6}$ (1 d.p.)

b) Index number for 2018 = 130.2 = $\frac{\text{Price in 2018}}{148\,000} \times 100$ So rearrange the equation to find the house price: (130.2 × 148 000) ÷ 100 = £192 696

c) The index number in 2016 is 112.8, which means that the house price increased by <u>12.8%</u> (112.8 − 100).

RPI, CPI and GDP are Commonly Used Index Numbers

1) In your exam, there might be a question that uses a <u>real-life</u> index number. Some of the most common ones used are the <u>retail price index</u> (RPI), <u>consumer price index</u> (CPI) and <u>gross domestic product</u> (GDP).

2) The RPI shows the <u>change in price</u> (e.g. inflation or deflation) of a selection of <u>goods</u> and <u>services</u> in the UK. It is calculated <u>monthly</u> by <u>comparing</u> prices to the <u>same month</u> of the <u>previous year</u>.

3) The CPI is the <u>official</u> measure of inflation used by the UK Government. It's similar to the RPI but some items (e.g. council tax) are <u>excluded</u>. The government updates <u>pensions</u> and <u>benefits</u> in line with the CPI.

4) GDP measures the value of all the goods and services produced in a <u>country</u> in a given amount of time.

EXAMPLE: The table shows the average RPI and the average price of a loaf of bread for two different years. Compare the change in RPI with the change in the price of a loaf of bread for these years.

Year	1987	2017
RPI	100	272.5
Price (pence)	44	103

The RPI increased by 172.5, indicating a percentage increase of <u>172.5%</u>.
But increasing 44 by 172.5% would mean a price of 44 × 2.725 = <u>119.9 pence</u>.
Since <u>103 < 119.9</u>, bread has increased in price at a <u>slower</u> rate than <u>RPI/inflation</u>.

Since the index for the year 1987 is 100, this must be the base year.

Source: Office for National Statistics

Year 7 music lessons — that was my bass year...

Once you've got your head around all these index numbers, cover the page and try out this question:

1) The index numbers in the table show the average monthly rent for a flat, using 2013 as the base year.
   a) In which year did the average monthly rent decrease?
   b) The average monthly rent in 2013 was £530. Calculate the average monthly rent for the years 2014 and 2015.

Year	2013	2014	2015
Index Number	100	85	109

Summary Statistics — Index Numbers

Like you're weighed down with stats revision, <u>index numbers</u> can be <u>weighted</u> too. Poor things.

Weighted Index Numbers Take Proportions into Account

E.g. a dried fruit mixture contains <u>apricots</u> and <u>prunes</u> in the <u>ratio 5:2</u>. If the price of apricots <u>or</u> prunes goes up, then so will the price of the mixture. BUT... a rise in the price of <u>apricots</u> will have <u>more effect</u> on the price of the mixture than an equal rise in the price of <u>prunes</u>.

<u>WEIGHTED INDEX NUMBERS</u> take the <u>difference in importance</u> into account. And there's a lovely formula for it too:

$$\text{WEIGHTED INDEX NUMBER} = \frac{\sum(\text{index number} \times \text{weight})}{\sum \text{weights}}$$

EXAMPLE: The table on the right shows how a publishing company's spending on cheese, biscuits, crisps and wine for the office party has changed over the years. Use the weights in the table to calculate the weighted index number for the items in 2017, using 2014 as the base year.

	2014	2017	Weight
Cost of Cheese	£17.00	£18.50	4
Cost of Wine	£378.00	£351.00	85
Cost of Biscuits	£30.00	£26.40	7
Cost of Crisps	£18.00	£22.50	4

They're weighted according to % of the budget spent on them.

Cheese index number $\times$ weight $= \left(\frac{18.50}{17.00} \times 100\right) \times 4 = 435.2...$

Wine index number $\times$ weight $= \left(\frac{351.00}{378.00} \times 100\right) \times 85 = 7892.8...$

Biscuits index number $\times$ weight $= \left(\frac{26.40}{30.00} \times 100\right) \times 7 = 616$

Crisps index number $\times$ weight $= \left(\frac{22.50}{18.00} \times 100\right) \times 4 = 500$

So, the WEIGHTED INDEX NUMBER $= \dfrac{435.2... + 7892.8... + 616 + 500}{4 + 85 + 7 + 4} = \underline{94.4}$ (3 s.f.)

This means spending has decreased by 5.6% (100 − 94.4).

Chain Base Index Numbers Compare Year to Year

<u>CHAIN BASE NUMBERS</u> are index numbers which show how values change from <u>year to year</u>. They <u>always</u> use the <u>PREVIOUS YEAR</u> as the base year.

EXAMPLE: The prices for pet insurance in three years are given in the table on the right:

Year	2014	2015	2016
Insurance Price	£74	£73	£79

    a) Calculate the index number for 2015 and 2016 using the chain base method.
    b) Describe what the two chain base index numbers show.

a) First, take 2014 as the base year: Index number for 2015 $= \frac{73}{74} \times 100 = \underline{98.6 \ (1 \ d.p.)}$

    Then take 2015 as the base year: Index number for 2016 $= \frac{79}{73} \times 100 = \underline{108.2 \ (1 \ d.p.)}$

b) The 2015 index shows that pet insurance <u>decreased</u> by 100 − 98.6 = <u>1.4%</u> from the <u>previous</u> year (2014). The 2016 index shows that it <u>increased by 8.2%</u> (108.2 − 100) from the <u>previous</u> year (2015).

After that cheese and wine, your weighted index will be ~20 stone...

Another formula here which, guess what, you need to learn off by heart. Once you have, take a stab at these...

1) In 2018, the publishing company above spent £20 on cheese, £325 on wine, £35 on biscuits and £25 on crisps. Use these values and the table in the example to find the weighted index number for 2018 with the base year 2014.

2) CPI is a chain based index number. The table shows the annual percentage change in CPI for a number of years.
    a) Calculate the chain based index numbers missing from the table.
    b) Regina's water bill is linked to this index. Her annual bill for 2015 was £444. Determine what her bill was for 2017.

Year	2014	2015	2016	2017
% change	1.5%	0.0%	0.7%	2.7%
Index				

Source: Office for National Statistics

Higher

Summary Statistics — Rates of Change

Population data can be analysed by calculating certain rates. Sounds like bags of fun...

Crude Rates Tell You How Many In Every 1000

Rates tell you how many instances of a certain factor happen in a population over a period of time — e.g. birth, death, unemployment and marriage rates can be calculated each year. It's often useful to monitor these rates — e.g. if there's a high birth rate in an area, plans could be made to provide more midwives.

> A crude rate is how many times a particular event occurs per thousand of the population in a given time.

So: CRUDE DEATH RATES are the number of deaths per thousand of the population in a given time.

CRUDE BIRTH RATES are the number of births per thousand of the population in a given time.

This is the formula to calculate crude rates:

$$\text{Crude birth/death rate} = \frac{\text{number of births / deaths}}{\text{total population}} \times 1000$$

You'll be given this formula in your exam.

EXAMPLE: At the start of last year, Didston had a population of 142 000. There were 870 deaths there last year. What was the crude death rate in Didston last year?

$$\text{Crude death rate} = \frac{870}{142\,000} \times 1000 = 6.126... = \underline{6.13} \text{ (2 d.p.)}$$

This example shows that last year there were about 6 deaths for every 1000 people in Didston. This is okay as a rough guide to the death rate in Didston alone, but it can be misleading when comparing it with different areas. For example, a town with a lot of retirement homes will have a high proportion of elderly residents, so the town will probably have a higher death rate. Standardised rates on the next page deal with this.

Use Rates of Change to Learn About the Population

You can rearrange the formula to make predictions about the population given a crude rate.
E.g. the number of births one year would be (rate × total population) ÷ 1000.

EXAMPLE: The graph on the right shows the crude birth rates in two towns, Bodbury and Didston, in the years 2010 to 2018.

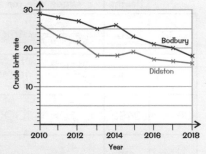

a) Describe the change in birth rates for this period.

b) Can you tell if there were more births in Bodbury or Didston from the graph? Explain your answer.

c) There were 20 671 people in Bodbury at the start of 2018. Estimate how many babies were born there in 2018 (to 3 s.f.).

a) The graph shows that the birth rates are generally declining for both towns. Between 2010 and 2014 the gap between Bodbury and Didston births widened, but this has narrowed since 2014.

b) No, you cannot tell. While the Bodbury birth rate is higher, you would need to know the population of both towns to calculate the actual number of births.

c) Bodbury crude rate in 2018 = 18, so there were (18 × 20 671) ÷ 1000 = 372.0... = 372 births (3 s.f.)

Twenty pence to use the bog — now that's a crude rate...

Nothing too mortifying on this page — a formula which you don't need to memorise and some examples of the different ways you can use it. At this rate, you'll have finished the section in no time...

1) The population of Coldwich at the start of 2016 was 130 000. In 2016, there were 3820 deaths and 5670 births.
   a) Calculate the crude death rate and the crude birth rate for Coldwich for 2016.
   b) The unemployment rate in Coldwich in 2016 was 4.56. Predict how many people were unemployed.

Summary Statistics — Rates of Change

Crude rates can be <u>misleading</u> as they're not always useful for <u>comparing</u> different areas.

Standard Populations Represent the Whole Population

A <u>standard population</u> is a population of <u>1000</u> people that is meant to <u>represent</u> the <u>whole population</u>, taking into account the number of people in each different age/gender/income <u>group</u>. This is the formula:

A standard population can take all sorts of factors into consideration — the groups listed here are just examples.

$$\text{Standard population} = \frac{\text{number of people in group}}{\text{total population}} \times 1000$$

EXAMPLE: The table shows the number of people in each age group in Portlidge. Calculate the standard population of each age group for this town.

<18	5000
18-29	31 000
30-60	20 000
>60	800
	56 800

Use the <u>formula</u> to find the standard population of <u>each group</u>:

<u><18</u>: $\frac{5000}{56\,800} \times 1000 = \underline{88.0}$ (1 d.p.)   <u>30-60</u>: $\frac{20\,000}{56\,800} \times 1000 = \underline{352.1}$ (1 d.p.)

<u>18-29</u>: $\frac{31\,000}{56\,800} \times 1000 = \underline{545.8}$ (1 d.p.)   <u>>60</u>: $\frac{800}{56\,800} \times 1000 = \underline{14.1}$ (1 d.p.)

You might have to work out the total yourself.

The Standardised Rate Uses the Standard Population

A <u>standardised rate</u> allows you to <u>compare</u> populations with different age/gender/income <u>profiles</u> (i.e. where the <u>make-up</u> of the populations is <u>different</u>). The formula for the standardised rate of each group is:

$$\text{Standardised rate} = \frac{\text{crude rate}}{1000} \times \text{standard population}$$

To find the standardised rate for the <u>entire population</u>, <u>add up</u> the rates of each group.

EXAMPLE: The numbers of deaths in Portlidge in each age group over one year are shown below. Calculate the standardised death rate for each age group and for the town of Portlidge.

	Deaths	Crude rate for age group	Standard pop.	Standardised rate (to 1 d.p.)
<18	120	$\frac{120}{56\,800} \times 1000 = 2.11...$	88.02...	$\frac{2.11...}{1000} \times 88.02... = \underline{0.2}$
18-29	2100	$\frac{2100}{56\,800} \times 1000 = 36.97...$	545.77...	$\frac{36.97...}{1000} \times 545.77... = \underline{20.2}$
30-60	3450	$\frac{3450}{56\,800} \times 1000 = 60.73...$	352.11...	$\frac{60.73...}{1000} \times 352.11... = \underline{21.4}$
>60	412	$\frac{412}{56\,800} \times 1000 = 7.25...$	14.08...	$\frac{7.25...}{1000} \times 14.08... = \underline{0.1}$

These add up to give the <u>total crude death rate</u> for the town (107.1 to 1 d.p.).

$0.2 + 20.2 + 21.4 + 0.1 = \underline{41.9}$

1) Calculate the <u>crude rate</u> for <u>each age group</u> using the formula from p.67.

2) Use the formula above with <u>these crude rates</u> and the <u>standard populations</u> for each group.

3) <u>Add up</u> the rates to find the rate for the town.

You can now make useful <u>comparisons</u> with other towns. E.g. a town with a larger proportion of people aged over 60 might have a <u>higher crude death rate</u> than Portlidge — but that doesn't necessarily mean that people in the town are more likely to die. It's better to compare <u>standardised rates</u> rather than crude rates.

The standard rate of revision — 5 in every 1000 minutes...

Try out this question to see what you know.

Age	Standard pop.	Crude death rate
<18	110	0.02
18-29	280	8
30-60	260	12
>60	350	56

1) a) Calculate the standardised death rate for the town shown on the right.
    b) Add up the crude death rates to give the total rate, then compare the crude and standardised rates of this town with those of Portlidge.

Estimating Population Characteristics

Don't worry — you're only a couple of pages away from the end of Section Four* and a well-deserved break.
First up, you need to know how to make <u>estimates</u> about a <u>whole population</u> from your <u>sample</u> data...

Use your Data to Estimate the Whole Population

1) Often you'll have collected data from a <u>sample</u> that represents the <u>whole population</u> (see page 10).

2) You can then use this data to make <u>estimates</u> about the size, mean weight etc. of the whole population.

 A gardener has a field of 500 potato plants. He randomly selects 30 plants from different areas and finds the mean weight of a potato to be 120 grams and the median weight to be 140 grams. He also counts the number of potatoes in his sample and finds that each plant produces an average of 9 potatoes.

> *See Section One for more on sampling.*

a) Estimate the mean weight of each potato in the whole crop.

b) Estimate the total number of potatoes in the whole crop.

c) Estimate how many potatoes in the whole crop will weigh more than 140 grams.

d) 9 of the plants in his sample have been found to have a disease. Estimate how many plants in the field have the disease.

> *You can also use the range and quartiles of your sample as an estimate for the range and quartiles of the population.*

a) You can use the <u>sample mean</u> as the <u>estimate</u> for the <u>population mean</u>. So, an estimate for the mean weight of each potato in the whole crop is <u>120 g</u>.

b) Estimated total number of potatoes = 9 × 500 = <u>4500 potatoes</u>.

c) The median is 140 g so <u>half</u> of the potatoes in the <u>sample</u> weigh more than this value. You can use the <u>sample median</u> as an <u>estimate</u> for the <u>population median</u>, so you can estimate that half of the potatoes in the population will weigh more than this — i.e. 4500 ÷ 2 = <u>2250 potatoes</u>.

d) First work out the number of plants with the disease in his <u>sample</u> as a <u>proportion</u> of the sample: 9 ÷ 30 = <u>0.3</u>. Then find this proportion of the whole population: 0.3 × 500 = <u>150 plants</u>.

This method's fine, but you need to know how many <u>units</u> (e.g. plants) there are in the whole population — and sometimes you don't have this much <u>information</u>. Another way of estimating a population size is by <u>capture and recapture</u> (p.70).

The Size of Your Sample is Really Important

1) Any conclusions or estimates you make will only be <u>reliable</u> if your <u>sample size</u> is <u>large</u> enough.

2) The size of the sample should be <u>appropriate</u> for the size of the <u>population</u>.

3) For example, a sample of 50 people should be fine to estimate the music tastes of a small <u>town</u>, but probably not the music tastes of the whole <u>country</u>. The results probably won't be <u>accurate</u>, because the sample is <u>too small</u>.

> *Page 11 goes into more detail about the issues to consider when sampling.*

4) You'd have to be very careful if you planned to use the music tastes of the town to predict the music tastes of the country, because the town might <u>not be representative</u> of the whole country.

Free samples? Well, I'd better try 100 to make a reliable decision...

Don't forget that unless you were unbelievably lucky, your sample wouldn't perfectly reflect the population. So everything you calculate about the population is only ever an estimate. Now, have a go at this question...

1) 1 000 000 tourists visit the city of New Londoblin annually. A survey of 200 tourists is conducted.

a) The poll revealed that 30 tourists from the sample had visited the Empire Temple Palace. What is the approximate total number of tourists visiting the Palace in a year?

b) The mean amount of spending money brought by a tourist in the sample of 200 was £750. Estimate the mean amount of spending money brought by the 1 000 000 tourists in New Londoblin.

c) 50 of the tourists in the sample have travelled more than 250 miles and 50 of the tourists in the sample have travelled less than 50 miles. Estimate the interquartile range of the distance travelled by the 1 000 000 tourists.

Estimating Population Sizes

If you ever wanted to know the population of fish in a lake or snakes on a plane then it's your lucky day...
I have just the thing — Petersen's capture recapture method.

Capture Recapture Uses Two Random Samples

It's often impractical to count the exact size of a population — luckily, sampling can help.
Petersen's capture recapture method is used to estimate the size of large populations.
Call the unknown size of the population N and use this method to find it:

- Take a representative sample of size n and tag or mark each subject in the sample.
  Then release them back into the population.

- Once they've mixed back in, take a second representative sample of size M.

- Count the number in the second sample that are tagged. Suppose there are m
  of them. Assuming the proportion of tagged things in the new sample ($^m/_M$) is
  the same as in the first sample ($^n/_N$), you can rearrange $\frac{m}{M} = \frac{n}{N}$ to find N.

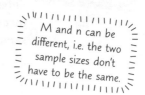
M and n can be different, i.e. the two sample sizes don't have to be the same.

EXAMPLE: A fisherman nets 50 fish from a lake. He marks all of them with a small tag and returns them alive to the lake. A few days later another fisherman nets 60 fish. 15 of them are found to have been tagged by the first fisherman. Find an estimate of the number of fish in the lake.

Assuming that the sample of 60 fish is representative of the whole population,
you can work out roughly how many fish there are in total.

1) The fraction of tagged fish in the second net will be the same as the fraction tagged in the whole lake.

2) Call the total population N. So... $\frac{15}{60} = \frac{50}{N} \Rightarrow 15N = 50 \times 60 \Rightarrow 15N = 3000 \Rightarrow N = \underline{200}$

Capture/recapture only works in constant populations — the population has to be made up of
exactly the same members when the two samples are taken (i.e. there's no birth, death or migration).

You Need to Make a Lot of Assumptions

You make a lot of ASSUMPTIONS when you use this method — so it's only an ESTIMATE.

1) You assume that the second sample is perfectly representative of the whole population.
E.g. the tagged fish in the example above will need to have had time (and opportunity) to fully
mix back in with the rest of the population before the second net is cast. On the other hand, the
time between the capture and recapture can't be so long that the population has changed.

2) You have to assume that the capture and recapture are completely random. If the person
doing the catching can see the tags, you could end up with a biased second sample.

3) You also assume that fish from the first sample are unaffected by the capture or the tagging/marking.
For example, the fish above are returned alive and well, but some types of tag might make them easier
to catch in the second sample (so it wouldn't be representative). Or it might affect their
survival rates (e.g. by making them more attractive to predators),
which would mean the population would then not be constant.

4) The sample size needs to be large enough. While it's impractical to
capture the whole population, you still need to capture enough of it
for it to be representative.

I can see you...
Fish

Capture/recapture — it's a hard life being a juggling ball...

Lots of assumptions on this page. But don't make the assumption that you don't need to know all this.
Instead, read back over it all and then have a go at answering this...

1) Evelyn captures 30 frogs from her garden pond and carefully marks each before returning them to the water.
The next day she captures 20 frogs and finds that 10 are marked. Estimate the number of frogs in her pond.

Revision Summary for Section Four

Section Four — at last, it's over. I bet you thought you'd never get here. Give yourself a medal, you earned it.
- Try these questions and tick off each one when you get it right.
- When you've done all the questions for a topic and are completely happy with it, tick off the topic.

Averages (p.49-53) ☑

1) What is the modal number of days in a month?
2) What is the median?
3) What is another term for 'mean'?
4) How do you work out the mean?
5) Suggest a way to make finding the mean of some very large numbers easier.
6) What type of average can most easily be used with qualitative data?
7) Give one advantage of finding the mean instead of the median or mode.
8) What is a weighted mean? What's the formula for it? [Higher only]
9) How do you find the geometric mean? [Higher only]
10) What is the formula for the mean if the data is in a frequency table?
11) Why can you only estimate the mean for grouped data?

Measures of Spread (p.54-58) ☑

12) What is the range of a set of data?
13) How would you work out the position of the lower quartile of a set of data?
14) Which interpercentile range is the interdecile range the same as? [Higher only]
15) How would you estimate the interquartile range of grouped data?
16) What does a small standard deviation tell you about the data? [Higher only]
17) What are the formulas for standard deviation for data in a frequency table? [Higher only]

Box Plots, Outliers and Skew (p.59-61) ☑

18) What information is shown on a box plot?
19) What is an outlier?
20) What are two different criteria for detecting outliers? [Higher only]
21) The mean of your data is less than the median. What type of skew does this indicate?

Comparing Data, Summary Statistics and Populations (p.62-70) ☑

22) You know the mean of your data. Which measure of spread should you use for comparisons?
23) How do you find a standardised score? [Higher only]
24) What value does an index number have in the base year? What's the formula for an index number?
25) What do weighted index numbers take into account? [Higher only]
26) What is the difference between simple and chain based index numbers? [Higher only]
27) What is a crude rate?
28) What is a standard population and how is it used to calculate standardised rates? [Higher only]
29) A lightbulb manufacturer wants to test the lifetime of its bulbs, so it finds the mean lifetime of a sample of 200 bulbs. Why is this sample mean only an estimate of the population mean?
30) Explain the process of capture/recapture for estimating populations. [Higher only]
31) State one assumption you make about the population when using capture/recapture. [Higher only]

Scatter Diagrams — Correlation

Are GCSE Statistics exam marks related to the amount of revision a person does? Hmmmmm...

Scatter Diagrams Show If Two Variables are Related

An <u>association</u> is just a fancy term for a <u>relationship</u> between two things. You can plot a <u>scatter diagram</u> to see if there's an association between <u>two variables</u>. Correlation is a <u>linear</u> association — for correlated variables, the points on the scatter diagram will lie close to a <u>straight line</u>.

You can also <u>interpret</u> the <u>direction</u> and <u>strength</u> of the correlation from the diagram:

Take a look back at p.43 for how to plot scatter diagrams.

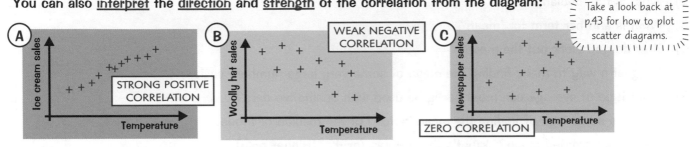

- A shows <u>positive correlation</u> — as the temperature increases, ice cream sales also increase.
- B shows <u>negative correlation</u> — as the temperature increases, woolly hat sales decrease.
- C shows <u>zero correlation</u> — the points are randomly scattered, so temperature and newspaper sales aren't linearly related.

<u>Strong</u> and <u>weak</u> are words used to describe the <u>strength</u> of correlation. <u>Strong correlation</u> is when the points make a fairly <u>straight line</u> (graph A). <u>Weak correlation</u> is when they <u>don't line up</u> as nicely (graph B).

**EXAMPLE:**

A study asks a number of workers to give their age and a score out of 10 to describe their job satisfaction, where 10 is extremely satisfied and 0 is not at all satisfied. The results are shown in the scatter diagram. Describe and interpret the correlation shown.

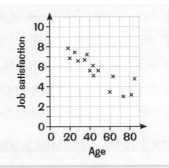

Age and job satisfaction show a <u>strong negative</u> correlation.
So as a worker's age <u>increases</u>, their job satisfaction <u>decreases</u>.

Causation is when a Variable Causes Change in Another

If a change in one variable <u>causes</u> a change in another variable, they're said to have a <u>causal link</u>, e.g. a rise in the temperature outside could cause an increase in ice cream sales. However, an increase in ice cream sales <u>wouldn't</u> cause the weather to improve — unfortunately.

The <u>dependent</u> variable (ice cream sales here — they <u>depend</u> on the temperature) is always plotted on the <u>y-axis</u> in a scatter diagram.

You have to be <u>**VERY CAREFUL**</u> with causality, though. Just because there's a correlation between two things, it <u>doesn't</u> necessarily mean there's a causal link — CORRELATION DOESN'T IMPLY CAUSATION.

There could be <u>multiple factors</u> interacting. For example, the number of pairs of sunglasses sold per week in a particular town is positively correlated with the amount of algae in a local pond. Neither one <u>causes</u> the other, though. Both of these increases are due to a <u>third</u> factor: an increase in the amount of sunshine.

I broke up with my boyfriend — we just had no correlation...

When you think you understand correlation, test yourself with this question.

1) Describe the correlation you would expect for each of the following pairs of variables:
   a) Adult shoe size and waist size
   b) Hours of sunshine in a day, and hours of rain in a day
   c) No. of power cuts and no. of candles sold
   d) Age and height of primary school children

Scatter Diagrams — Using Lines of Best Fit

Yep, there's more about scatter diagrams... painful but true. So grab a biscuit and have a read...

Line of Best Fit — A Straight Line Through the Data

If a scatter diagram shows <u>correlation</u>, you can draw a '<u>line of best fit</u>' through the data points.

1) The line of best fit should be a <u>straight</u> line passing <u>close</u> to as <u>many points</u> as possible.

2) You should end up with roughly the <u>same number</u> of plotted points on <u>either side</u> of the line.

3) To make your line of best fit more <u>accurate</u>, plot it through the <u>double mean point</u> $(\bar{x}, \bar{y})$, where $\bar{x}$ is the mean of the x-values and $\bar{y}$ is the mean of the y-values — see page 49 for how to find the mean.

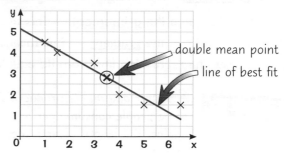

The <u>closer</u> the points are to the line, the <u>stronger</u> the correlation. A <u>positive gradient</u> (slope) means <u>positive correlation</u> and a <u>negative gradient</u> means <u>negative correlation</u>. The <u>y-intercept</u> of the line (where it <u>meets the y-axis</u>) tells you the value of y if the value of x is <u>zero</u>.

Interpolation & Extrapolation — Making Predictions

You can use lines of best fit to predict <u>unknown values</u> by either <u>interpolation</u> or <u>extrapolation</u> — scary words, but they're not too bad really...

1) <u>Interpolation</u> is when you make predictions <u>inside</u> the <u>range</u> of the <u>known data</u>. It tends to give <u>fairly reliable</u> results — so long as you get the line of best fit right.

2) <u>Extrapolation</u> is when you make predictions <u>outside</u> the <u>range</u> of the <u>known data</u>. <u>BE VERY CAREFUL WITH EXTRAPOLATION</u> — you're going into unknown territory. You have <u>no idea</u> what happens to the relationship between your variables once you go outside your data set — the <u>pattern</u> might <u>not continue</u>. So it's best not to extrapolate <u>too</u> far from what you <u>do</u> know.

EXAMPLE: The scatter diagram on the right shows the chest and waist sizes of a sample of men.
a) Estimate the waist size of a man with a 115 cm chest.
b) Predict the waist size of a man with a 140 cm chest.
c) Comment on the reliability of your estimates.

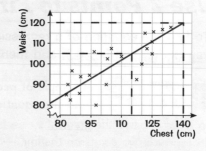

a) 115 cm is <u>inside</u> the range of the plotted data, so this is <u>interpolation</u>:
1) First draw a <u>vertical line</u> from 115 on the x-axis to the line of best fit.
2) Then draw a <u>horizontal line</u> from this point to the y-axis.
3) Finally <u>read off</u> the value — <u>105 cm</u> is the estimate for waist size... it's as easy as that.

b) 140 cm is <u>outside</u> the plotted data, so this is <u>extrapolation</u>: Using the method above you can predict that a man with a 140 cm chest would have about a <u>120 cm waist</u>.

c) The estimate in part a) should be <u>reliable</u> since it's <u>interpolating</u> well within the range of the known data. However, the estimate in b) might be <u>unreliable</u> as it's <u>extrapolating</u>.

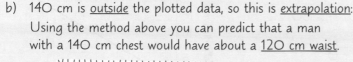
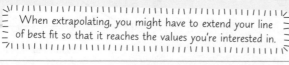

When extrapolating, you might have to extend your line of best fit so that it reaches the values you're interested in.

If you're going to extrapolate, take some spare pants and a torch...

You don't know what lies beyond... ooh sounds like the stuff of nightmares. Try this question, if you dare...

1) The table shows the weekly sales of toads and bats over a nine-week period at Witchworths.
a) Plot the data on a scatter diagram and draw a line of best fit through the double mean point.
b) How many bats are they likely to sell in a week if they sell 48 toads?
c) Why shouldn't they use the line of best fit to predict how many bats they will sell in a week if they sell 180 toads?

| toads | 80 | 49 | 38 | 58 | 68 | 72 | 46 | 70 | 59 |
| bats | 20 | 18 | 6 | 12 | 18 | 14 | 14 | 15 | 18 |

Scatter Diagrams — Regression Lines

A <u>regression line</u> is basically a line of best fit — but now it has an <u>equation</u> to represent it. Wowzers.

The Regression Line is Written in the Form y = a + bx

The <u>regression line</u> is a straight line so you can write its equation as: $y = a + bx$

1) The value 'a' is the <u>y-intercept</u> — this means that if <u>$x = 0$</u> then <u>$y = a$</u>.
2) The value 'b' is the <u>gradient</u> — this means that every time x changes by <u>1 unit</u>, y changes by <u>b units</u>.
3) To <u>draw</u> the regression line from its equation, use the equation to plot <u>two points</u>, then <u>join</u> them up.

EXAMPLE: A scatter diagram is produced showing the amount of caffeine some people consume per day (x hundreds of milligrams), against the length of time they sleep for (y hours). The regression line is given by the equation $y = 9 - 0.5x$.

a) Draw the regression line using its equation.

b) Interpret the values of the y-intercept and the gradient of this line.

c) The mean amount of caffeine consumed is 800 mg. Use this information to find the mean length of time spent sleeping.

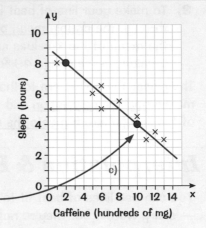

a) Pick <u>two x-values</u> between 1 and 13 and substitute into the equation to <u>find y</u>. If $x = \underline{2}$, then $y = 9 - 0.5 \times 2 = \underline{8}$. If $x = \underline{10}$, then $y = 9 - 0.5 \times 10 = \underline{4}$. <u>Plot</u> these points on the scatter diagram and <u>draw</u> the line <u>between</u> them.

b) The y-intercept is <u>$a = 9$</u> — this means that someone who consumes <u>no caffeine</u> is expected to sleep for <u>9 hours</u>. The gradient is <u>$b = -0.5$</u>, so for every <u>100 mg</u> of caffeine consumed, a person is expected to sleep <u>half an hour less</u>.

c) There are <u>two methods</u> you could use here:
- <u>Read</u> up from 8 on the x-axis to the line, and then read across to the y-axis to get <u>5 hours of sleep</u>.
- Use the <u>equation</u> of the line: $y = 9 - 0.5 \times 8 = 5$, so <u>5 hours of sleep</u>.

> Don't try to work out the mean using the method on page 49 — the question specifically tells you to use the information you're given.

Use 2 Points to Find the Equation of the Regression Line

To <u>find</u> the equation of a regression line, you need to <u>choose two points</u> on the line, say (x_1, y_1) and (x_2, y_2), and then use them to <u>calculate</u> a and b.

EXAMPLE: A sample of people each threw a cricket ball and a welly and the distances were recorded. Find the equation of the regression line shown on the scatter diagram.

First, find the <u>gradient</u>.
Pick <u>two points</u> on the line — (0 ,0) and (30, 20) look good.

Then use the <u>formula</u> $b = \dfrac{y_2 - y_1}{x_2 - x_1}$ with (0 ,0) and (30, 20):

> You could use (x_2, y_2) instead here.

$\underline{b} = \dfrac{20 - 0}{30 - 0} = \dfrac{2}{3}$.

Next, find the <u>y-intercept</u> using $a = y_1 - bx_1$: $\underline{a} = 0 - \dfrac{2}{3} \times 0 = 0$.

So the <u>equation</u> of the line is $y = 0 + \dfrac{2}{3}x$, i.e. $y = \dfrac{2}{3}x$.

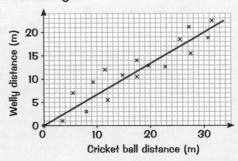

What's harder than learning y = a + bx...

...erm, writing a gag about it. Try this out to check you know what's occurring...

1) The height of water in a water tank is measured every 30 minutes, as shown.
   a) Find the equation of the regression line given on the scatter diagram.
   b) Interpret the value of the gradient of the line.
   c) Estimate the height of the water after 100 minutes.

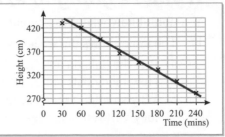

Section Five — Analysing and Interpreting Diagrams

Spearman's Rank Correlation Coefficient

This page is all about rank data... oh sorry, I meant rank<u>ed</u> data...

r_s is Always Between –1 and 1

Spearman's rank correlation coefficient (SRCC), often shortened to r_s (bit less of a mouthful), is used with data that can be <u>ranked</u> into <u>place order</u> — highest to lowest or first to last. It measures the <u>rank correlation</u> — i.e. whether there is <u>agreement</u> between two sets of <u>ranks</u>.

Values of r_s are always between <u>–1 and +1</u>:

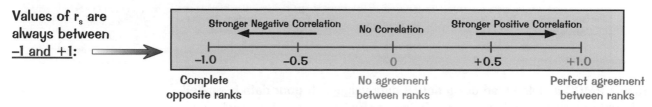

Stronger Negative Correlation	No Correlation	Stronger Positive Correlation
–1.0 –0.5	0	+0.5 +1.0
Complete opposite ranks	**No agreement between ranks**	**Perfect agreement between ranks**

EXAMPLE: Two races take place with the same five competitors. The competitors are ranked in places 1 to 5 for each race. The Spearman's rank correlation coefficient for these ranks is calculated to be 0.85. What type of correlation does this show? Interpret the value in the context of the races.

0.85 is <u>fairly close</u> to 1 so there is <u>strong positive</u> correlation. This means there is <u>agreement</u> between the ranks in the two races — i.e. the <u>placings were similar</u> for each race.

There's a Nasty Formula for Working Out r_s

To <u>calculate</u> r_s, you need to use a pretty nasty-looking <u>formula</u>. But quell your fear — it'll be on the <u>formula sheet</u> in your exam. And you might even have a function on your <u>calculator</u> that does all the hard work for you — just plug the <u>ranks</u> in (<u>NOT the raw data</u>) and it'll give you r_s.

EXAMPLE: The table on the right shows the marks two judges awarded to high-board divers from six different countries.

By using appropriate calculations, comment on how much agreement there is between the two judges.

	Aus	Bul	Ch	Den	Est	Fra
Judge Judy	5.7	4.9	6.0	6.3	5.9	5.5
Judge Dredd	5.0	5.2	5.8	6.0	6.1	5.6

1) First <u>rank</u> both sets of data. For each set, give the highest value a rank of 1, the next highest a rank of 2, and so on.

2) Find the <u>difference</u> in rank (d) between the two values in each data pair.

3) Then find d^2.

	Aus	Bul	Ch	Den	Est	Fra
Judge Judy	4	6	2	1	3	5
Judge Dredd	6	5	3	2	1	4
d	–2	1	–1	–1	2	1
d^2	4	1	1	1	4	1

4) Count the <u>number</u> of data pairs, n. There are 6 data pairs, so $n = 6$.

5) Use the <u>formula</u> to find r_s:

$$r_s = 1 - \frac{6\sum d^2}{n(n^2 - 1)}$$

The data in your exam might be ranked already.

$\sum d^2 = 4 + 1 + 1 + 1 + 4 + 1 = 12$

So $r_s = 1 - \dfrac{6 \times 12}{6(6^2 - 1)}$

$= 1 - \dfrac{72}{210} = \underline{0.657}$ (3 d.p.)

6) <u>Interpret</u> r_s: 0.657 is <u>positive</u> and between <u>0.5 and 1</u>, so there is <u>fairly strong agreement</u> between the judges.

(margin:) Higher

Get off the sofa and back to revision — go on, move your r_s...

Now would be a good time to check if your calculator has a function for calculating r_s — if it does, you can use it.

1) Lewis and Dee tried eight flavours of ice cream (A-H) and gave each flavour a mark from 1 to 20, where 20 is the best mark. Their results are shown in the table.

   a) Work out Spearman's rank correlation coefficient for the data. [Higher only]

   b) How do their tastes compare? [Higher only]

	A	B	C	D	E	F	G	H
Lewis	13	19	1	10	14	18	15	6
Dee	20	6	15	13	2	8	16	10

Interpreting Correlation Coefficients

If you thought Spearman had the monopoly on correlation coefficients, think again. Step up Mr Pearson...

Pearson's PMCC Measures Linear Association

Pearson's product moment correlation coefficient (PMCC) measures the correlation (linear relationship) between two variables. It can take a value between –1 and 1 — the value indicates the strength and direction of the correlation, as shown here:

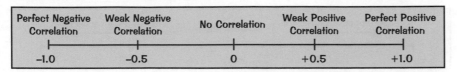

Perfect Negative Correlation	Weak Negative Correlation	No Correlation	Weak Positive Correlation	Perfect Positive Correlation
–1.0	–0.5	0	+0.5	+1.0

You won't have to calculate the PMCC — how delightful.

Pearson's PMCC is calculated using actual data values. If your data is ranked, you should use Spearman's rank correlation coefficient — see the previous page.

 **EXAMPLE:** A study is conducted on the relationship between the amount of green space and the number of cases of lung disease in various cities. Pearson's PMCC for these two variables is –0.6. Comment on what this shows about the association between the two variables.

Since Pearson's PMCC is negative, there is (moderate) negative correlation between green space and cases of lung disease.
So cities with more green space generally have fewer cases of lung disease.

Remember that this doesn't provide evidence that green spaces actually reduce cases of lung disease — correlation doesn't imply causation.

The PMCC and SRCC Tell You Different Things

You need to be clear on the difference between what Pearson's product moment correlation coefficient and Spearman's rank correlation coefficient tell you.

- Pearson's PMCC measures how close the data points on a scatter diagram lie to a straight line — it only detects a linear association between variables.

- The SRCC measures correlation between ranks — this can be strong even if the data values themselves have a non-linear relationship. So the SRCC can detect linear and non-linear association.

If there's a non-linear positive (or negative) association between two variables, both the PMCC and SRCC will be positive (or negative) — but the SRCC will be closer to 1 (or –1).

 **EXAMPLE:** The scatter diagram below shows the relationship between the amount of precipitation and the number of fish falling from the sky in a town.

Spearman's rank correlation coefficient is r_s = 0.9.
What can you say about the value of Pearson's product moment correlation coefficient for this data?

There is a positive association between the two variables so you'd expect the PMCC to be positive.

But the relationship is non-linear (the points don't sit close to a straight line) — therefore the value of the PMCC is going to be lower than r_s.

So the PMCC will be somewhere between 0 and 0.9.

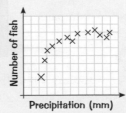

You use Pearson's PMCC? Me, I'm much more of a Spear-man...

Correlation coefficients sound nastier than they really are. Have a bash at this question to see how much you know.

1) Sacha calculates Pearson's product moment correlation coefficient for two variables x and y to be –0.2.

   a) Describe what this tells you about how x and y are correlated.

   b) Sacha also calculates the Spearman's rank correlation coefficient. He says that he thinks x and y have a strong negative association. Could he be correct? Explain your answer.

Time Series

You can use <u>data</u> to make <u>predictions</u> for the future — no crystal balls necessary...

Use a Time Series Graph to Spot Trends

1) A <u>time series</u> is a set of data collected over a <u>period of time</u> at <u>equal intervals</u>, which can then be plotted on a <u>line graph</u> (page 44).

2) From the graph, you can identify the <u>trend</u> — whether the data is generally <u>going up</u> or <u>going down</u>.

3) You can draw a <u>trend line</u> by ignoring <u>fluctuations</u> in the graph and just following the <u>general pattern</u>.

4) If the <u>gradient</u> of the line is <u>positive</u>, it shows an <u>upwards (rising) trend</u>. If it's <u>negative</u>, there is a <u>downwards (falling) trend</u>.

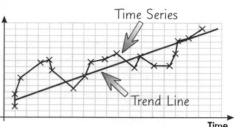

Plot Moving Averages for a More Accurate Trend Line

1) A <u>moving average</u> "<u>smooths out</u>" fluctuations in the data and makes the trend line more <u>accurate</u>.

2) Data often fluctuates in <u>cycles</u> that <u>repeat</u> over time. The <u>number</u> of individual data points you use to calculate a moving average depends on the <u>length of time</u> it takes the cycle to repeat. So, for example, if you had <u>quarterly</u> data you would use a <u>4-point</u> moving average.

EXAMPLE: The number of sun hats sold by a department store is recorded every quarter in 2016 and 2017. The results are given in the table.

a) Work out the moving averages for the data.

b) Plot the moving averages on the graph and draw a trend line through the points.

	2016				2017		
Q1	Q2	Q3	Q4	Q1	Q2	Q3	Q4
780	970	840	760	1030	1140	920	990

1st average = (780 + 970 + 840 + 760)/4   2nd average = (970 + 840 + 760 + 1030)/4

a) As the data is <u>quarterly</u> you can use a <u>4-point</u> moving average. That means taking the <u>average</u> of each group of four <u>consecutive</u> data values. So you'd start by taking the average of <u>780, 970, 840 and 760</u>, then <u>move along one</u> and average the <u>next group</u> of values, <u>970, 840, 760 and 1030</u> — and so on through the data.

The <u>moving averages</u> are 837.5, 900, 942.5, 962.5 and 1020.

b) You plot the moving averages at the <u>centre point</u> of the time interval. So the first point will be <u>halfway</u> between Q2 and Q3 for 2016, and so on.

You can then draw a trend line by eye — a <u>line of best fit</u> through the moving average points.

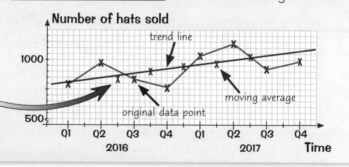

You can use your time series graph to <u>predict future values</u> — but since this is <u>extrapolating</u> (see p.73), you have to be <u>careful</u>, especially if it looks like the trend might <u>not continue</u>.

> You'd use a <u>different number</u> of points for your moving average if the cycle isn't of length 4. E.g. if the data seems to cycle weekly, a 7-point moving average might be more <u>appropriate</u>.

Higher   Higher

Vogue — always predicting trendy lines...

Make sure you understand how to calculate moving averages, then have a go at this question:

2015				2016			
Q1	Q2	Q3	Q4	Q1	Q2	Q3	Q4
13	12	14	18	15	17	14	19

1) a) Work out the moving averages for the data in the table.

    b) Plot the moving averages on a graph and draw a trend line through the moving average points.

Time Series

If a time series has <u>fluctuations</u> which <u>cycle</u> at <u>regular intervals</u>, then this is evidence of <u>seasonality</u>.

Seasonal Trends are Repeated Fluctuations

You need to be able to <u>spot</u> and <u>interpret</u> seasonal variation.

EXAMPLE: The graph on the right shows the quarterly profits (in £) for a perfume department over three years. A trend line has been plotted using moving averages. Interpret the seasonal variation for the data.

Perfume profits <u>increased</u> from their <u>lowest</u> point in <u>Q1</u> to their <u>highest</u> point in <u>Q4</u> every year.

⟍ You need to <u>interpret</u> the seasonality in the <u>context</u> of the question. ⟋

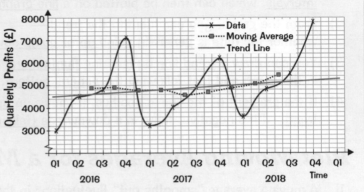

Seasonal Effect Measures the Seasonality

1) The <u>difference</u> between a <u>real value</u> and the value taken from the <u>trend line</u> (plotted through the moving averages) is known as the <u>seasonal effect</u>.

> **SEASONAL EFFECT = REAL VALUE — VALUE FROM TREND LINE**

2) The <u>average seasonal effect</u> is the <u>mean</u> of all the seasonal effects for the <u>same point in each cycle</u>. In the example above, the average seasonal effect could be calculated for each quarter.

3) You can use this average to make more <u>accurate predictions</u> for future values.

EXAMPLE: Using the data in the graph above:
  a) calculate the seasonal effect for the 4th quarter in 2016,
  b) work out the average seasonal effect for the first quarter,
  c) predict the profit for the first quarter in 2019.

a) The <u>seasonal effect</u> for the 4th quarter in 2016 is:

  £7100 – £4700 = <u>£2400</u>

  REAL value   TREND LINE value

  ⟍ Read up from 2016 Q4 to the trend line and then across to the y-axis to read off the profit. ⟋

b) The <u>average seasonal effect</u> for the 1st quarter is:

  [(3000 – 4500) + (3200 – 4800) + (3600 – 5000)] ÷ 3 = <u>–£1500</u>

c) The <u>predicted profit</u> is the value taken from the <u>trend line</u> <u>PLUS</u> the <u>average seasonal effect</u>. So the predicted profit for the 1st quarter in 2019 is £5300 – £1500 = <u>£3800</u>

However, this is a form of <u>extrapolation</u> (page 73) — so there are <u>limitations</u> to making predictions in this way. For example, <u>random events</u> could mean that the predicted value <u>varies greatly</u> from the actual value.

Adding salt and pepper — the seasoning effect...

This stuff is <u>pretty tough</u>. So have another read and then try out this question for practice.

1) The table shows the quarterly electricity bills (in £) for the Green family over the last three years.

  a) Plot these points on a time series graph.
  b) Calculate and plot the moving averages on the same graph.
  c) Draw the trend line for the moving averages.
  d) What is the average seasonal effect for the fourth quarter? [Higher only]
  e) Predict their bill for the fourth quarter of 2018. [Higher only]

	Q1	Q2	Q3	Q4
2015	280	180	140	210
2016	260	150	150	230
2017	250	160	140	220

Higher (left margin)

Higher (right margin)

Revision Summary for Section Five

Section Five is all done and dusted. That wasn't too bad... and now you only have two more sections to go.
- Try these questions and tick off each one when you get it right.
- When you've done all the questions for a topic and are completely happy with it, tick off the topic.

Scatter Diagrams (p.72-74) ☑

1) What does it mean if two variables are correlated? ☑
2) If the points on a scatter diagram lie very close to a line of best fit with negative gradient, how would you describe the association between the variables? ☑
3) What is causation? ☑
4) Two variables are positively correlated. What does this tell you about the causation between them? ☐
5) What point would you draw a line of best fit through to make it more accurate? ☑
6) What is the difference between interpolation and extrapolation? ☐
7) Which is more reliable — interpolation or extrapolation? Why? ☑
8) What does the 'b' represent in $y = a + bx$? What about the 'a'? [Higher only] ☑
9) How do you draw a regression line if you know its equation? [Higher only] ☑
10) How many points do you need to know to work out the equation of the regression line? [Higher only] ☐
11) What's the formula for the gradient of a regression line? [Higher only] ☑

Correlation Coefficients (p.75-76) ☑

12) What range of values can the Spearman's rank correlation coefficient take? ☑
13) What does a rank correlation of zero mean? ☑
14) What is the formula for the SRCC? [Higher only] ☑
15) A set of data has a product moment correlation coefficient of –0.99. What does this tell you about the correlation? [Higher only] ☑
16) Your data is ranked. Should you use the SRCC or Pearson's PMCC? [Higher only] ☑
17) You find that Pearson's PMCC for two variables is 0.3 but the SRCC is 0.8. Explain why the SRCC might be higher than Pearson's PMCC. [Higher only] ☑

Time Series (p.77-78) ☑

18) A set of data is plotted on a time series graph. The gradient of the trend line is positive. What can you say about the trend in the data? ☑
19) How many data points would you use to calculate a moving average [Higher only]:
    a) if you'd collected data every quarter?
    b) if you'd collected data every month? ☑
20) Give an example of data that features seasonal variation. ☑
21) How do you find a seasonal effect? [Higher only] ☑
22) You want to make predictions about the future which are as accurate as possible. Would you use the seasonal effect or the average seasonal effect? [Higher only] ☑
23) Why should you be careful when making predictions from a trend line? [Higher only] ☑

Probability

Next up is probability. There's a 50/50 chance you'll like it...

Probability is a Measure of How Likely an Event is

Some things are <u>more likely</u> to happen than others.
The <u>probability</u> of any event happening is somewhere between <u>impossible</u> and <u>certain</u>.

"Even chance" means that something is equally likely to happen or not happen.

Certain	The Sun will set tomorrow
	On your next birthday you will be older than you are now
Highly likely	
	Hollyoaks will be on TV tonight
Likely	
Even chance	The next baby born will be a boy
	If you toss a coin it will land on heads
Unlikely	You will correctly predict the results of every match in the next football World Cup
Highly unlikely	
	You can find a snowman on the Sun
Impossible	Your Aunt Mabel will become King of England in July

You can use Numbers instead of Words

1) You can put the probability of something happening on a scale from <u>0 to 1</u> — 0 means <u>impossible</u> and 1 means <u>certain</u>.

2) You can write probabilities as <u>fractions</u> or <u>percentages</u> too — so you can say the probability of picking a red card is 0.5, $\frac{1}{2}$ or 50%.

Impossible = 0   Even chance = 0.5   Certain = 1

A whale will walk across England this week

A card picked at random from a pack of 52 cards will be red.

If you throw a ball in the air, it will fall down again

An Outcome is What Might Happen

1) An <u>OUTCOME</u> is something that can happen <u>as a result of a TRIAL</u>.
(A trial can be anything from spinning a spinner to a horse race.)

2) For example, when you <u>toss a coin</u>, the only possible <u>outcomes</u> are <u>heads</u> and <u>tails</u>.

ALWAYS THINK ABOUT <u>ALL</u> THE POSSIBLE OUTCOMES.

3) An <u>EVENT</u> is a specific thing that has a probability of happening, e.g. picking a king from a pack of cards. More than one <u>outcome</u> can lead to the same <u>event</u>, e.g. 4 outcomes match this event: K♣, K♦, K♥, K♠.

EXAMPLE: If you roll a fair 6-sided dice, how many outcomes match each of these events?
Event A: Rolling a 1   Event B: Rolling an even number
Event C: Rolling a number less than or equal to 5

1) The <u>outcomes</u> of rolling a normal dice are the numbers <u>1</u>, <u>2</u>, <u>3</u>, <u>4</u>, <u>5</u> and <u>6</u>.
2) There is only <u>one outcome</u> that matches <u>Event A</u> — the number <u>1</u>.
3) There are <u>three outcomes</u> that match <u>Event B</u> — the numbers <u>2</u>, <u>4</u> and <u>6</u>.
4) There are <u>five outcomes</u> that match <u>Event C</u> — any of the numbers <u>1</u>, <u>2</u>, <u>3</u>, <u>4</u> and <u>5</u>.

Steve's chance of winning is 50% — they call him Evens Steven...

Nothing too scary here — except maybe the idea of a walking whale. To take your mind off that, try these questions:

1) Put the probability of the following events on a scale of 0 to 1:
   a) If you roll an unbiased 6-sided dice it will land on an even number.
   b) Pigs will fly in the sky tonight.   c) The tide will go out today.

2) List the possible outcomes of tossing a coin three times.

Probability

Another page on probability, featuring an important formula that you'll wonder how you ever lived without...

You can find Probabilities of Events using a Formula

If outcomes of a trial have <u>the same chance</u> of happening, they are called <u>equally likely outcomes</u>.

If <u>all</u> the possible outcomes are <u>equally likely</u>, you can use the following <u>formula</u> to find <u>probabilities</u>:

$$P(\text{event}) = \frac{\text{number of outcomes matching event}}{\text{total number of outcomes}}$$

 P(event) is just a short way of writing 'Probability of an event happening'.

Don't worry if this is a bit confusing — it'll become clear when you <u>work through an example</u>:

EXAMPLE: Calculate the probability of landing on green and the probability of landing on red when spinning this fair spinner:

If you spin this spinner, there are <u>six possible outcomes</u> because there are six sections it might land on — 3 red, 1 yellow, 1 green and 1 blue. Each section on the spinner is <u>equally sized</u>, so there is the <u>same chance</u> of landing on each section. So there are six <u>equally likely outcomes</u> — one giving the event "green" and three giving the event "red". Using the formula:

The probability of landing on <u>green</u> is: $P(\text{green}) = \dfrac{\text{The number of GREEN sections}}{\text{The TOTAL number of sections}} = \dfrac{1}{6}$

The probability of landing on <u>red</u> is: $P(\text{red}) = \dfrac{\text{The number of RED sections}}{\text{The TOTAL number of sections}} = \dfrac{3}{6} = \dfrac{1}{2}$

The event "landing on red" is much more likely to occur than the event "landing on green" because there are more outcomes that match this event.

The Probabilities of All Outcomes Add Up to 1

For a set of events that cover <u>every possible outcome</u> exactly once, their probabilities <u>always</u> add up to <u>1</u>.

1) For one spin of this fair spinner that has 8 sections, the probabilities are:

$P(\text{green}) = \dfrac{3}{8}$
$P(\text{blue}) = \dfrac{3}{8}$ $\Longrightarrow$ $\dfrac{3}{8} + \dfrac{3}{8} + \dfrac{2}{8} = \dfrac{8}{8} = 1$
$P(\text{red}) = \dfrac{2}{8}$

 It's all about me.

2) When the probabilities are written as percentages, they add up to 100%:

$P(\text{green}) = 37.5\%$
$P(\text{blue}) = 37.5\%$ $\Longrightarrow$ $37.5\% + 37.5\% + 25\% = 100\%$
$P(\text{red}) = 25\%$

To find the percentage, divide the numerator by the denominator and multiply by 100.

P(Green) = a beautiful colour for a boat...

That formula at the top of the page is crucial — but don't forget that it only applies if the outcomes are equally likely. When you've learnt the stuff on this page, try this question:

1) In a race between 5 pink poodles and 3 green poodles, all equally matched, what is the probability of a pink poodle winning?

Relative Frequency and Risk

Sometimes outcomes <u>aren't equally likely</u>, so you can't use the formula on p.81 to work out probabilities. Instead, you have to base the probabilities on <u>what's happened before</u>. So take a look at this...

Relative Frequency is an Estimated Probability

1) If you repeat a <u>trial</u> (or experiment) a whole load of times, you can use the results to <u>estimate</u> the <u>probability</u> of a certain <u>event</u> happening if you do the trial again. A trial could be as simple as rolling a dice to see what number comes up. This type of <u>estimated probability</u> is called <u>relative frequency</u>.

> Relative frequency is the frequency relative to the total number of trials.

2) <u>Relative frequencies</u> can be used to <u>predict</u> things like sports results. If a certain team or player has won a high percentage of their recent matches, there's a <u>higher probability</u> they'll win the next one.

There's a Formula for Relative Frequency

OK, you need to do the experiment over and over ...over.

1) To <u>calculate relative frequency</u>, you need to do lots of <u>trials</u> (i.e. repeat the experiment over and over again), <u>record</u> the results and then do a quick <u>calculation</u>.

2) Once you have the results of the trials, you can put them into this handy <u>formula</u>:

$$\text{Probability of something happening} = \frac{\text{Number of times it happened}}{\text{Number of trials}}$$

3) The important thing to remember is:

> The <u>more trials</u> there are, the <u>more accurate</u> the probability should be.

4) This means that relative frequencies will <u>get closer and closer</u> to the theoretical probabilities as the number of trials <u>increases</u>.

You can work out the relative frequencies as fractions, but they're usually easier to compare if you convert them to decimals.

EXAMPLE: A dice was rolled 100 times and the results were recorded in the table below.

a) What is the relative frequency of rolling a 5?
b) What is the relative frequency of rolling a 3?
c) What can be done to increase the accuracy of this experiment?

Number on the dice	1	2	3	4	5	6
Number of times rolled	17	20	30	7	14	12

a) A 5 was rolled <u>14</u> times. Use the above formula to work out the <u>relative frequency</u>:

$$\frac{\text{Number of times a 5 was rolled}}{\text{Number of trials}} = \frac{14}{100} = 0.14$$ So the relative frequency of rolling a 5 is <u>0.14</u>.

b) A 3 was rolled <u>30</u> times. Using the formula again:

$$\frac{\text{Number of times a 3 was rolled}}{\text{Number of trials}} = \frac{30}{100} = 0.3$$ So the relative frequency of rolling a 3 is <u>0.3</u>.

c) The more trials you do, the more <u>accurate</u> the probability is likely to be. So to increase the accuracy of the experiment you could <u>roll the dice many more times</u> (e.g. another 100 rolls).

Relative frequency — how often your gran comes to visit...

Make sure you learn that lovely formula for working out relative frequency and remember that doing more trials should increase the accuracy of the probabilities. Then try this question:

1) A spinner was spun a number of times. It landed on magenta 69 times, silver 98 times and turquoise 83 times.

   a) Estimate the probability of spinning each colour on this spinner.

   b) How could you improve your estimate? Explain your answer.

Relative Frequency and Risk

Relative frequency can also be used to <u>predict bias</u> and <u>assess risk</u>.

Relative Frequency Can Help You Spot Bias

1) You can use <u>relative frequency</u> to find out if, e.g. a coin, spinner or dice is <u>fair</u>.

2) For example, if a dice is <u>fair</u>, you should get each number coming up about $\frac{1}{6}$ of the time. If the dice is a bit wonky (or "<u>biased</u>") then each number <u>won't</u> have an <u>equal chance</u> of being rolled, and the relative frequencies of some numbers will be <u>more or less</u> than $\frac{1}{6}$.

 The dice from the previous page is suspected of being biased towards the number 3. What is the evidence for this?

The number 3 is rolled <u>way more often</u> than $\frac{1}{6}$ (= 0.166...) — nearly <u>twice</u> as much in fact. This is a lot <u>more</u> than you would expect from an <u>unbiased</u> dice. This suggests that there's <u>evidence</u> that the dice is <u>biased</u>.

Probabilities are Used to Assess Risk

1) Relative frequencies can be used to <u>assess</u> how likely something is to happen.

2) Insurance companies use <u>probabilities</u> to decide <u>how likely</u> you are to make a claim. This is <u>risk assessment</u>. They'll use this information to decide how much to charge you.

3) For example, if you want insurance against your yacht sinking, the insurance company will look at the <u>absolute risk</u> of <u>how many</u> yachts like yours sink each year and <u>compare</u> it to the <u>total</u> number of yachts like yours.

$$\text{Estimated probability of your yacht sinking} = \frac{\text{number of yachts that sink}}{\text{total number of yachts}}$$

They'll also consider how much money they'll need to pay out if your yacht does sink.

4) There are <u>two</u> types of risk:
   - <u>Absolute risk</u> — <u>how likely</u> an event is to happen. This is just the relative frequency.
   - <u>Relative risk</u> — how much <u>more likely</u> an event is to happen to one group <u>compared</u> to another group. To find this, <u>divide</u> the absolute risk for the <u>first group</u> by the absolute risk for the <u>second group</u>.

$$\text{Relative risk} = \frac{\text{risk for group A}}{\text{risk for group B}}$$

 Two groups of hikers are walking in the countryside on an unexpectedly sunny day. One group decides to walk up a large hill in the sun while the second group strolls through a wood. Neither group brought any sun cream. The probability that the first group will get sunburnt is 0.6. The probability that the second group will get sunburnt is 0.2.

What's the relative risk of getting sunburnt for the first group compared to the second group?

<u>Divide</u> the risk of the <u>first group</u> by the risk of the <u>second group</u>:

$$\text{Relative risk} = \frac{\text{risk for group A}}{\text{risk for group B}} = \frac{0.6}{0.2} = 3$$

The relative risk is <u>3</u>, so the <u>first group</u> of hikers is <u>3 times more likely</u> to get sunburnt than the second group.

Better not risk missing this page out of your revision...

Make sure you understand that <u>absolute risk</u> is the estimated probability of an event happening while <u>relative risk</u> is comparing the estimated probabilities of two events happening to different groups. Then have a go at these:

1) Tennis player A hits the ball on 32 out of 40 shots. Tennis player B has a 60% probability of hitting the ball.

   a) What is the relative frequency of tennis player A hitting the ball?

   b) Using this, what is the absolute risk that tennis player A will miss the ball?

   c) Work out the relative risk that tennis player A will miss the ball compared to tennis player B.

Expected and Actual Frequencies

The last page was about using the results of trials (or experiments) to estimate probabilities. But just 'cause we like to mix things up a bit, this one's about the opposite — using probabilities to predict results...

The Expected Frequency is What's Likely to Happen

Once you know the probability of something happening, you can predict how many times it will happen in a certain number of trials, e.g. the number of sixes you could expect if you rolled a fair dice 20 times. This prediction is called the EXPECTED FREQUENCY.

> EXPECTED FREQUENCY = NUMBER OF TIMES you are going to do something (the number of trials) × The PROBABILITY of the outcome happening

EXAMPLE: What is the expected frequency of heads when you toss a fair coin 200 times?

1) First work out the probability of the outcome happening.
There are two possible outcomes when you toss the coin — it's either going to land heads up or tails up, and both are equally likely. So the probability of getting heads is 0.5.

2) Now use the formula for expected frequency.

Expected Frequency = 200 × 0.5 = 100
  tosses   probability of heads

So the EXPECTED FREQUENCY would be 100 heads (out of 200 tosses).

Results Might be Different from Expected Frequencies

The expected frequency tells you the most likely number of times something will happen — but if you test it you'll probably get slightly different results. Often the easiest way to compare your actual results with the predicted results (i.e. the expected frequencies) is to draw a graph.

EXAMPLE: Anna was investigating how the expected frequency of each number on a standard dice compared with the actual frequencies she got when she rolled the dice 60 times.

First, she rolled the dice and recorded the actual number of times each number was rolled out of 60. She plotted these actual frequencies on the graph below.

a) Work out the expected frequency for each number on the dice and plot them on the graph.
b) Compare the expected frequencies with the actual frequencies.

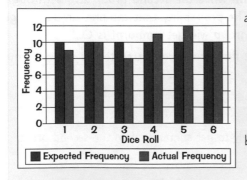

a) 1) There are six sides on the dice and each is equally likely to come up, so the probability of getting each number is $\frac{1}{6}$.
2) If you roll the dice 60 times, the expected frequency of each number is $\frac{1}{6}$ × 60 = 10 (i.e. in your test you expect to roll each number 10 times).
3) Draw bars on the graph to show these expected frequencies.

b) The actual frequencies are quite close to the expected frequencies, but not exactly the same.

Come in, Mr Frequency — I've been expecting you...

Don't panic if your actual frequencies don't match the expected frequencies exactly — you'd only start thinking about bias if they were way off. Ooh look, some more questions...

1) If you roll a standard dice 24 times, how many 4s would you expect to get?
2) This fair spinner is spun 200 times. How many times would you expect it to land on blue?

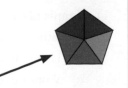

Section Six — Probability

Sample Space Diagrams

Just when you thought the section was going okay, we go and give you problems with <u>two or more</u> things happening at once. Oh well, bring on the spinner and dice, that's what I say. Yeehaw.

A Sample Space is a List of ALL Possible Outcomes

If you roll a normal dice, there are <u>6</u> possible outcomes — all of these possible outcomes make up the <u>sample space</u>.

If you spin a spinner with 3 sections, there are <u>3 possible outcomes</u> — these make up the <u>sample space</u>.

Rolling the dice <u>AND</u> spinning the spinner give <u>6 × 3 = 18 different combinations altogether</u> (since any number on the dice could come up with any colour on the spinner). Here, the sample space is a <u>list</u> of these <u>18 outcomes</u>. Luckily, there are some easy ways to work out what these outcomes can be.

Use a Sample Space Diagram to List all the Outcomes

Sample Space Diagram

A <u>sample space diagram</u> is basically a posh name for a <u>table</u>. If you use one, you're less likely to miss out any <u>outcomes</u>.

This table uses columns for the spinner outcomes and rows for the dice. It doesn't matter which way round you do it though.

	Red	Blue	Green
1	1R	1B	1G
2	2R	2B	2G
3	3R	3B	3G
4	4R	4B	4G
5	5R	5B	5G
6	6R	6B	6G

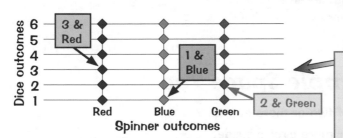

Cartesian Grids

<u>Cartesian grids</u> are <u>graphs</u> of sample space diagrams. To draw one of these, use a grid with each <u>line</u> showing an outcome for the spinner or the dice. Then each <u>point</u> where <u>two lines cross</u> shows an outcome for <u>the spinner AND the dice</u>.

EXAMPLE: Two dice are rolled and the total of their results are found. The sample space diagram shows all the outcomes of the total of the dice.

a) What is the probability of getting a total of 9?

b) What is the probability that the total is an even number?

	1	2	3	4	5	6
1	2	3	4	5	6	7
2	3	4	5	6	7	8
3	4	5	6	7	8	9
4	5	6	7	8	9	10
5	6	7	8	9	10	11
6	7	8	9	10	11	12

a) 1) <u>Count up</u> all the outcomes in the table where the total is <u>9</u>.

2) Then <u>divide</u> this by the <u>total number of possible outcomes</u> (it's the formula from p.81). There are <u>four 9s</u> in the table and <u>36 possible outcomes</u>:

$$P(\text{total of } 9) = \frac{4}{36} = \frac{1}{9}$$

b) <u>Count up</u> all the outcomes that are <u>even</u> and <u>divide</u> it by the total number of possible outcomes. There are <u>18 even outcomes</u> and <u>36 possible outcomes</u>:

$$P(\text{total is an even number}) = \frac{18}{36} = \frac{1}{2}$$

I had a go at being an astronaut — I wanted to sample space...

Believe me, if you've got a systematic way to make sure you've counted all the possible outcomes it makes this probability stuff a whole lot easier. This question should test if you've got the gist of Cartesian grids:

1) Set up a Cartesian grid to list the possible outcomes of tossing a coin and randomly choosing one day next week to go shopping.

Venn Diagrams and Two-Way Tables

Thought you'd finished with sample spaces for now? Think again...
You can also find more two-way tables on p.30.

Two-Way Tables can be used to Find Probabilities

A <u>two-way table</u> is a sample space diagram that can be used to show <u>bivariate data</u> (see p.5)
— e.g. the results of a survey, or other real data where <u>two pieces of information</u> have been collected.
You can use a two-way table to find probabilities, including <u>conditional probabilities</u> (see p.91).

EXAMPLE: A company employs 200 people. The table on the right
shows information about these employees.

a)   Complete the table.

b)   Calculate the probability that a randomly
chosen employee works part-time.

	Full-time	Part-time	Total
Females		62	106
Males	45		94
Total			200

a)   1)   The <u>right-hand column</u> tells you the totals for each <u>row</u>. You can use it to complete the first two rows:
       Number of females who work full-time = 106 − 62 = <u>44</u>.
       Number of males who work part-time = 94 − 45 = <u>49</u>.

	Full-time	Part-time	Total
Females	44	62	106
Males	45	49	94
Total	89	111	200

   2)   Then you can add up the <u>totals</u> in the <u>first two columns</u>:
       44 + 45 = <u>89</u> employees work full-time.
       62 + 49 = <u>111</u> employees work part-time.

b)   P(randomly chosen
employee works part-time) = $\dfrac{\text{Total number working part-time}}{\text{Total number of employees}} = \dfrac{111}{200}$

> Check your numbers — the bottom row should add up to the same as the right-hand column. 89 + 111 = 200. Phew.

A Venn Diagram Shows a Sample Space Too

Venn diagrams can be used to show the outcomes of two or more events.

1)   A <u>Venn diagram</u> looks like a rectangle with two or more circles inside.

2)   Each circle represents a set of <u>data</u> matching an event —
the data can be <u>theoretical outcomes</u> or <u>real data</u>, like survey results.

3)   Venn diagrams are often <u>labelled</u> with the number of data values that match each section of the diagram.

4)   The whole rectangle represents all the <u>possible outcomes</u> or <u>results</u> — the <u>sample space</u>.

5)   So, back to the dice and spinner from the previous page... The Venn diagram below represents
the sample space and two events, where <u>Event A</u> is 'rolling an even number on the dice' and
<u>Event B</u> is 'the spinner landing on blue'.

The <u>left circle</u> represents all the outcomes matching <u>Event A</u>. There are <u>nine</u> in total — 2R, 4R, 6R, 2B, 4B, 6B, 2G, 4G, 6G.

The bit where the two circles <u>overlap</u> represents the outcomes that match <u>both events</u> — even and blue. There are <u>three</u> — 2B, 4B and 6B.

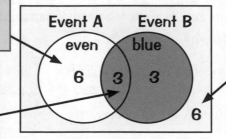

The bit <u>outside</u> the circles represents the outcomes that <u>don't match either of the events</u>. There are <u>six</u> — 1R, 3R, 5R, 1G, 3G, 5G.

Best page of the section so far? There's no two-ways about it...

Both Venn diagrams and two-way tables can be used to show data made up of <u>two pieces of information</u>.
Have a go at this question to make sure you understand how they work.

1)   By drawing a circle for 'female' and another for 'full-time', draw a Venn diagram
to show the information in the two-way table in the example above.

Venn Diagrams and Two-Way Tables

Venn diagrams can do more than just show you the outcomes of multiple events... Read on to discover more.

You Can Use Venn Diagrams to Work Out Probabilities

EXAMPLE:

MENU
Soup
Beef
Jelly

A class was surveyed to find out how many students had bought each of three items from the school canteen on a particular day. The Venn diagram below shows the results of the survey.

a) How many students are there in the class?

b) What is the probability that a randomly chosen student had jelly?

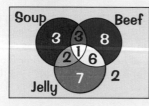

a) The Venn diagram shows all the results of the survey, so you just need to <u>add up</u> all the numbers from each section to get the total number of students:

3 + 3 + 8 + 2 + 1 + 6 + 7 + 2 = <u>32 students</u>

b) Work out the number of students who had jelly by <u>adding up</u> all the numbers in the circle representing jelly — the <u>green circle</u>:

7 (jelly only) + 2 (soup and jelly) + 6 (beef and jelly) + 1 (soup, beef and jelly) = <u>16</u>.

So P(randomly chosen student having had jelly)

$= \dfrac{\text{Total number having had jelly}}{\text{Total number of students}} = \dfrac{16}{32} = \dfrac{1}{2}$

The student was randomly chosen, so there's an equally likely chance of picking ANY student. This means you can use the formula for working out probability from p.81.

Remember, 'P' is just short for probability.

Venn Diagrams Can Also Show Probabilities of Events

You've just seen how Venn diagrams can be used to show the <u>outcomes</u> of multiple events. They can also show the <u>probabilities</u> of events. Each section of the diagram is <u>labelled</u> with the <u>probability</u> of that event happening and the total sum of all the bits of the Venn diagram is 1. To work out the probabilities of an event or combination of events happening, <u>add up</u> all the <u>relevant outcomes</u>.

EXAMPLE:

The Venn diagram shows the probability that it will be sunny, raining, both or neither on any given day.

a) Find the probability that it will be sunny.

b) Find the probability that it won't rain.

c) Find the probability that it will rain and won't be sunny.

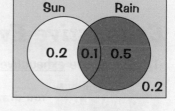

a) 1) Find all the outcomes where it will be sunny. There are <u>two</u> outcomes — if it's <u>just sunny</u> (0.2) and if it's <u>both sunny and raining</u> (0.1).

2) <u>Add</u> these together to get the probability that it'll be sunny: 0.2 + 0.1 = <u>0.3</u>

b) To find the probability that it <u>won't rain</u>, add up all the probabilities of the outcomes where it won't rain. This is the probability that it'll be <u>sunny</u> (0.2) and the probability that it'll be <u>neither</u> (0.2): 0.2 + 0.2 = <u>0.4</u>.

c) To find the probability that it'll rain <u>without</u> the sun shining, find the probability that it'll rain (the blue circle) but <u>ignore</u> the probability that it'll rain AND be sunny (the green overlap): <u>0.5</u>.

Venn in doubt, draw a diagram...

These types of question come up a lot in exams. So get this stuff learnt, then have a go at this question:

1) A school has a choir and a football team. The probability that a random student is a member of each is shown in the Venn diagram on the right. What is the probability that a randomly chosen student:

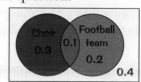

a) is in the choir and the football team
b) isn't in the football team

The Addition Law

On the next few pages you can find some lovely <u>probability laws</u> to learn for the exam — they're in <u>blue boxes</u>.

Mutually Exclusive Events Can't Happen Together

1) When <u>two</u> events <u>can't happen at the same time</u>, they are called <u>MUTUALLY EXCLUSIVE EVENTS</u>. You can use the <u>ADDITION LAW</u> to find the probability of <u>either</u> one <u>OR</u> the other of these events happening.

$$P(A \text{ or } B) = P(A) + P(B)$$ ← The probability of A or B is equal to the probability of A plus the probability of B

EXAMPLE: You roll a fair dice once. What's the probability of rolling a 2 OR a multiple of 3?

The probability of rolling a 2 is $\frac{1}{6}$.

The probability of rolling a multiple of 3 is $\frac{2}{6}$ (as you can roll a 3 or 6).

You can't roll a 2 and a multiple of 3 at the same time,
so the events are <u>mutually exclusive</u>.

So P(getting a 2 or a multiple of 3) = $\frac{1}{6} + \frac{2}{6} = \frac{3}{6} = \frac{1}{2}$

> The addition law works for more than two events — as long as they're mutually exclusive. E.g. P(A or B or C or D) = P(A) + P(B) + P(C) + P(D).

The General Addition Law is for Non-Mutually Exclusive Events

You need to use this when <u>two events</u>, A and B, <u>can</u> happen together. You don't want to count the overlap twice, so you have to <u>take it away</u> — simple as that.

$$P(A \text{ or } B) = P(A) + P(B) - P(A \text{ and } B)$$

EXAMPLE: You roll a fair dice once. What's the probability of rolling a multiple of 2 OR a multiple of 3?

The probability of rolling a multiple of 2 is $\frac{3}{6}$ because you could get a 2, 4 or 6,

and the probability of rolling a multiple of 3 is $\frac{2}{6}$ because you could get a 3 or 6.

Rolling a 6 has been counted twice (since it's a multiple of 2 <u>and</u> a multiple of 3), so you

need to take away the probability of rolling a 6 ($\frac{1}{6}$). So the answer is: $\frac{3}{6} + \frac{2}{6} - \frac{1}{6} = \frac{4}{6} = \frac{2}{3}$

(Higher) *(Higher)*

Exhaustive Events — at least One of them Must Happen

1) Events are <u>exhaustive</u> if together they include <u>all possible outcomes</u>, so at least one of them <u>must</u> happen.

EXAMPLE: You draw a card randomly from a standard pack of 52 playing cards. What's the probability of picking a spade, a heart, a diamond or a club?

Here, the four events are "<u>picking a spade</u>", "<u>picking a heart</u>", "<u>picking a diamond</u>" and "<u>picking a club</u>".
There are <u>no other possibilities</u>, so the probability of one of the 4 events happening must be <u>1</u>.

2) If you <u>add together</u> the probabilities of <u>exhaustive</u> mutually exclusive events, you <u>ALWAYS</u> get <u>1</u>. So the probability of any event is <u>1</u> minus the probability of <u>all the other possible events</u>. (In other words the probability of an event happening is 1 minus the probability of it <u>not happening</u>.) For example, the probability of picking a spade, heart or club from a pack of cards is 1 minus the probability of picking a diamond.

> There's more about this on the next page.

Phew... that page was what I call an exhaustive event...

It's absolutely essential you know the formula(s) for the tier you're doing — and always take the time to check whether or not you're dealing with mutually exclusive events before you use one of them. Now for some questions:

1) What is the probability of rolling an odd number or a six on a fair six-sided dice?

2) Find the probability of picking a diamond or a king at random from a standard pack of 52 cards. [Higher only]

Independent Events

Right, now's the time to make a bit more space in your brain for some more brilliant formulas...

Independent Events are Unconnected

Two events are INDEPENDENT if one has no effect on the other.

EXAMPLE: You toss a coin and then pick a card at random from a standard pack.
What's the probability of the coin showing heads and the card being a heart?

It doesn't matter which way the coin lands — it won't affect the card you pick out of the pack, so the two events are independent. The possible results are shown in this sample space diagram:

	Clubs	Diamonds	Hearts	Spades
Heads	H, C	H, D	H, H	H, S
Tails	T, C	T, D	T, H	T, S

There are 8 equally likely possible outcomes, so the probability of getting any one of them is $\frac{1}{8}$. So P(hearts and heads) = $\frac{1}{8}$.

The Law of Independent Events Saves a Lot of Counting

You don't have to draw a sample space diagram and count outcomes each time. There's a quicker way of calculating the probability of two independent events happening — the probability of A AND B. All you need to do is to multiply the probabilities of each event together. It's called the Multiplication Law for Independent Events:

CAREFUL — it only works when you've got an 'and'.

$$P(A \text{ and } B) = P(A) \times P(B)$$

Prithee, Abraham, what are we doing here?

I have no idea, William. We're totally unconnected to this page.

So you could answer the example above using the multiplication law instead:

The probability of the coin showing heads is $\frac{1}{2}$ and the probability of picking a heart is $\frac{1}{4}$. So P(heads and hearts) = $\frac{1}{2} \times \frac{1}{4} = \frac{1}{8}$

It doesn't matter how many events there are as long as they're independent — just keep multiplying to find the probability of them all happening. So for 4 events, P(A and B and C and D) = P(A) × P(B) × P(C) × P(D).

You can Find Out the Probability of At Least 1

From the previous page you know that the probability of an event is 1 minus the probability of all the other possible events (i.e. the probability of it not happening). Here's a special version of that law and how to use it:

$$P(\text{at least 1}) = 1 - P(\text{none})$$

EXAMPLE: A woman has four children. Find the probability that at least one of them is a girl, assuming that boys and girls are equally likely.

"At least one girl" means "1 girl", "2 girls", "3 girls" or "4 girls", which could take a while to work out. It's easier to work out P(no girls) and subtract the answer from 1.

P(no girls) = P(boy) × P(boy) × P(boy) × P(boy) = $\frac{1}{2} \times \frac{1}{2} \times \frac{1}{2} \times \frac{1}{2} = \frac{1}{16}$ — This is the Multiplication Law for Independent Events.

So P(at least one girl) = $1 - \frac{1}{16} = \frac{15}{16}$

You made it to the end of the page — give yourself a big 'and'...

Now when you read 'at least one' or 'and' in a question, you'll know what to do. Test yourself with these:

1) What is the probability of rolling a 6 on a fair, 6-sided dice and then rolling an even number?

2) The probability of a daily train service arriving late on any given day is $\frac{1}{3}$.
If all the days are independent, what's the probability of it being late at least once in a five-day period?

Tree Diagrams

When you're working out probabilities for several events there'll be a whole lorra multiplying going on. So to make sure you don't make a mistake, you can use <u>tree diagrams</u>. They might crop up in the <u>exam</u> too.

You Can Use Tree Diagrams for Probability Questions

Follow these <u>four simple steps</u> and you'll know how to use any tree diagram:

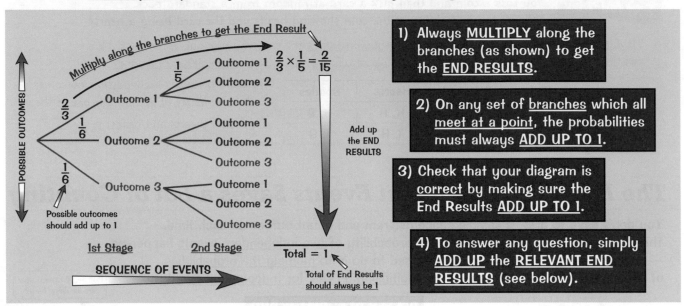

1) Always <u>**MULTIPLY**</u> along the branches (as shown) to get the <u>END RESULTS</u>.

2) On any set of <u>branches</u> which all <u>meet at a point</u>, the probabilities must always <u>ADD UP TO 1</u>.

3) Check that your diagram is <u>correct</u> by making sure the End Results <u>ADD UP TO 1</u>.

4) To answer any question, simply <u>ADD UP</u> the <u>RELEVANT END RESULTS</u> (see below).

A Likely Tree Diagram Question

This example shows you how the information in a question can be <u>magically transformed</u> into a tree diagram.

EXAMPLE: There are five coloured balls in a bag. Three balls are blue and two are green. One ball is drawn out of the bag at random and its colour recorded. It is put back into the bag and another ball is drawn out.

What is the probability that both balls will be the same colour?

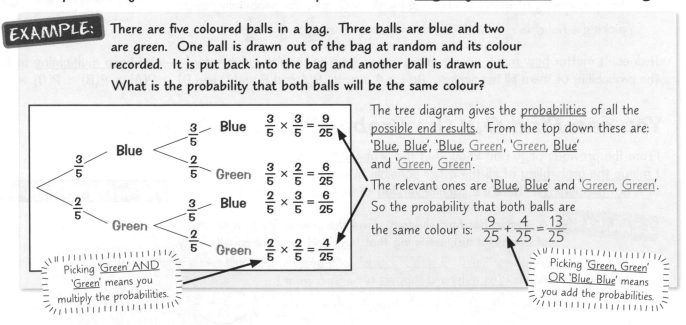

The tree diagram gives the <u>probabilities</u> of all the <u>possible end results</u>. From the top down these are: '<u>Blue, Blue</u>', '<u>Blue, Green</u>', '<u>Green, Blue</u>' and '<u>Green, Green</u>'.

The relevant ones are '<u>Blue, Blue</u>' and '<u>Green, Green</u>'.

So the probability that both balls are the same colour is: $\frac{9}{25} + \frac{4}{25} = \frac{13}{25}$

Picking '<u>Green</u>' AND '<u>Green</u>' means you multiply the probabilities.

Picking '<u>Green, Green</u>' OR '<u>Blue, Blue</u>' means you add the probabilities.

So the answers really do grow on trees...

The best way to get good at tree diagrams is to practise. A lot. Learn this page, then try these questions:

1) J Foods is a company that makes ready meals. 65% of the ready meals it makes contain chicken and the rest contain beef. Each day a ready meal is selected at random for quality control tests.
   a) Use a tree diagram to work out the probability that a chicken meal is chosen on two consecutive days.
   b) Use the tree diagram to find the probability of choosing one beef meal and one chicken meal.

2) Use a tree diagram to find the probability of rolling a 1 then an even number in two rolls of a normal dice.

Conditional Probability

When the <u>outcome</u> of one trial <u>affects</u> the outcome of the <u>next</u>, things start to get more complicated. However, one way you can solve these sorts of problems is by treating them like <u>logic puzzles</u>...

Conditional Probability — When an Event Affects Another

1) Sometimes the <u>probability</u> of the <u>second event depends on the first</u>. This is called <u>Conditional Probability</u> — the probability that event B will happen, given that event A happens.

2) P(B given that A happens) can be written as: $\boxed{P(B|A)}$

 **EXAMPLE:**

A bag contains 3 red balls and 1 white ball.
Two balls are chosen at random from the bag and not replaced.

What is the probability that the second ball chosen is red given that the first ball is:
a) red   b) white?

If the first ball chosen is <u>red</u>, that leaves <u>2 red</u> and <u>1 white</u>, so P(2nd ball is red|1st ball is red) = $\frac{2}{3}$

If the first ball chosen is <u>white</u>, that leaves <u>3 red</u>, so P(2nd ball is red|1st ball is white) = $\frac{3}{3} = \underline{1}$

You Don't Always Need the Whole Sample Space

If you've got information in a <u>sample space diagram</u> (like a Venn diagram or two-way table), you usually need to concentrate on <u>one bit</u> of the diagram to find a <u>conditional probability</u>.

 **EXAMPLE**

A survey was carried out to find out how many households in a street of 30 houses owned cats and dogs. The Venn diagram below shows the results of the survey. One household is chosen at random. Given that the household has a dog, what is the probability that it also has a cat?

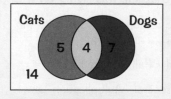

1) You know the household in question has a dog, so you're only interested in what's going on in the circle representing households with dogs.

2) Inside the '<u>dogs</u>' circle, there are 4 + 7 = <u>11 outcomes in total</u>, and <u>4</u> outcomes matching the event '<u>owning a cat</u>'.

3) So P(household has a cat|household has a dog) = $\frac{4}{11}$

Sneakily, questions about <u>conditional probability</u> don't always include the words '<u>given that</u>'.

EXAMPLE

The two-way table on the right shows the results of a survey of 140 people to find out which of three types of hat they prefer. What is the probability that:

a) a randomly chosen person from this group is male, if that person prefers top hats?

b) a randomly chosen female member of this group prefers berets?

	Beret	Top hat	Fez	Total
Male	20	35	20	75
Female	33	20	12	65
Total	53	55	32	140

a) You know the person prefers top hats, so you're only interested in the '<u>top hat</u>' column. So there are <u>55</u> possible outcomes, and <u>35</u> of them match the event '<u>choosing a male person</u>'. So P(male|top hat) = $\frac{35}{55} = \frac{7}{11}$

b) This time you know the person is <u>female</u>, so you're only interested in that row. There are <u>65</u> possible outcomes, and <u>33</u> of them match the event '<u>choosing someone who prefers berets</u>'. So P(beret|female) = $\frac{33}{65}$

P(passing exam | not revising) = 0...

Conditional probability isn't too bad, really. Make sure you understand the examples on this page, then try these:

1) Using the Venn diagram above, find the probability that a randomly chosen household does not own a dog, given that the household owns a cat.

2) Using the two-way table above, find the probability that a randomly chosen person:
a) is male, if that person prefers fezzes,   b) prefer fezzes, given that they are male.

Conditional Probability

Now you have a good idea how to work out <u>conditional probability</u>, here's a lovely formula...

There's a General Law for Combining Events

If you can work out conditional probability, you can use it to work out the probability of <u>any</u> two events <u>both happening</u>, when one <u>depends</u> on the other — this is called the <u>General Multiplication Law</u>.

It looks like this: $\boxed{P(A \text{ and } B) = P(A) \times P(B|A)}$ This is the conditional probability bit from p.91 — the probability of event B, given that event A occurs.

EXAMPLE A basket of fruit contains 2 apples and 4 pears. If two pieces of fruit are picked out at random, without being replaced, what's the probability that they're both pears?

The chance of picking out a <u>pear first</u> is $\frac{4}{6}$. You then have <u>only 5 pieces of fruit left</u> in the basket.

The probability of picking a <u>second pear</u>, given that you have already picked a pear, is $\frac{3}{5}$.

So the probability of picking out <u>two pears</u> is: $\frac{4}{6} \times \frac{3}{5} = \frac{12}{30} = \frac{2}{5}$

For <u>independent</u> events, $P(A|B) = P(A)$ and $P(B|A) = P(B)$ because neither outcome <u>depends</u> on the other. So the General Multiplication Law gives $P(A \text{ and } B) = P(A) \times P(B)$ — the Multiplication Law for Independent Events from page 89.

Use the Formula to Find Conditional Probabilities

Sometimes you'll get a question where working out the conditional probability is really tricky. To make it easier you can rearrange the <u>General Multiplication Law</u>: $\boxed{P(B \mid A) = \dfrac{P(A \text{ and } B)}{P(A)}}$

EXAMPLE A skier is twice as likely to fall on old snow as fresh snow. On fresh snow, she falls on one tenth of her runs down the slope. There's an even chance of fresh snow on any particular day. Given that she fell on her first run today, find the probability that she was skiing on fresh snow.

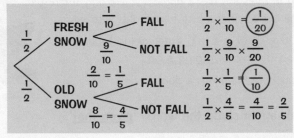

You should always start a question like this by drawing a <u>tree diagram</u>. The diagram tells you that:

$P(\text{fall and fresh}) = \frac{1}{20}$ and $P(\text{fall}) = \frac{1}{20} + \frac{1}{10} = \frac{3}{20}$

So, using the rearranged General Multiplication Law,

$P(\text{fresh}|\text{fall}) = P(\text{fall and fresh}) \div P(\text{fall}) = \frac{1}{20} \div \frac{3}{20} = \frac{1}{3}$

A Likely Tree Diagram Question

You can use <u>tree diagrams</u> to answer questions involving <u>conditional probabilities</u>.

EXAMPLE A card is picked at random from a standard pack. Without replacing the first card, a second card is picked. What is the probability that both cards are aces?

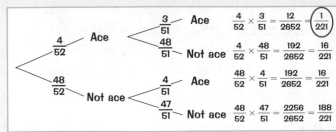

The probabilities in the second stage of the tree diagram are <u>conditional</u> — they depend on whether or not an ace is picked at the first stage.

There is only <u>one</u> relevant end result, so:

$P(\text{both aces}) = \frac{1}{221}$

Combination — that's what you need...

This stuff's just a little more tricky, but learn how to use the formulas properly, and you won't go far wrong.

1) Two cards are picked from a standard pack at random, without replacement. What is the probability that:
   a) both cards are hearts?   b) the first card was a heart, given that the second card was a heart?

Revision Summary for Section Six

Phew... That was a lot of probability to do — but you got through it all, hurrah!
Now here are some revision questions just to make sure it's all really gone in...

*   Try these questions and <u>tick off each one</u> when you <u>get it right</u>.
*   When you've done <u>all the questions</u> for a topic and are <u>completely happy</u> with it, tick off the topic.

Probability (p.80-84) ☑

1) What is the numerical probability of an event which:
    a) is certain?
    b) is impossible?
    c) has an even chance? ☑

2) How do you calculate the probability of an event using the number of equally likely outcomes? ☑

3) If two events include between them every possible outcome of a trial,
    what does that tell you about their probabilities? ☑

4) What is bias and how can it affect the probability of a particular outcome of an event? ☑

5) How are probabilities used by insurance companies? ☑

6) Describe what a relative frequency is, and suggest two things it might be used for. ☑

7) What is the difference between absolute risk and relative risk? ☑

8) How do you work out an expected frequency? ☑

9) Will your actual results always match the expected frequency? ☑

10) What's a good way of comparing actual results with the expected frequencies? ☑

Sample Spaces (p.85-87) ☑

11) What is a sample space? ☑

12) Other than a Venn diagram, name two ways of showing a sample space. ☑

13) Sketch a Venn diagram with two circles, and label what each section represents. ☑

Probability Laws (p.88-90) ☑

14) What are mutually exclusive events? ☑

15) Write out the formula that can be used to work out the probability
    that either one of two mutually exclusive events will happen. ☑

16) What similar formula can be used for events that aren't mutually exclusive? [Higher only] ☑

17) What is meant by exhaustive events? ☑

18) What can you say about the total probability of exhaustive, mutually exclusive events? ☑

19) Suggest a way of tackling "at least one" questions. ☑

20) Give an example of two events that are independent. ☑

21) Write out the formula used to find the probability of two independent events happening. ☑

22) On a tree diagram, how do you calculate the results at the end of the branches? ☑

Conditional Probability (p.91-92) ☑

23) Give a brief description of what is meant by conditional probability. ☑

24) Write out the formula that can be used to find the probability of two events happening,
    when the second event is conditional on the first. ☑

The Binomial Distribution

All of Section Seven is Higher Level only. A <u>probability distribution</u> is a model used to find <u>expected</u> <u>probabilities</u> of events. The first distribution you need to know about is called the <u>binomial distribution</u>.

Binomial Distribution — Two Possible Outcomes

Some events have only <u>two possible outcomes</u> — e.g. toss a coin and it will land on either heads or tails. Throw in a few more <u>conditions</u>, and if they hold then you can use a <u>binomial distribution</u>:

1) There is a <u>fixed number</u> of trials (n). This probability distribution is <u>discrete</u> — it can only take values 0, 1, 2, ..., n.	**2) Each trial results in either '<u>success</u>' or '<u>failure</u>'.** There are <u>two mutually exclusive outcomes</u> — e.g. the score on a dice can be a 'six' or 'not a six'.
3) All the trials are <u>independent</u>. This means that each trial has <u>no effect</u> on any of the others.	**4) The <u>probability</u> of 'success' (p) is <u>constant</u>.** The probability of 'failure' (q) also stays the <u>same</u> — you can calculate it using $q = 1 - p$.

If the conditions are met then the <u>total number of 'successes'</u> can be modelled by the <u>binomial distribution</u>. This can be written <u>B(n, p)</u>, where n is the <u>number of trials</u> and p is the <u>probability of success</u>. You might need to explain whether a binomial distribution is a <u>suitable</u> model, using the conditions.

EXAMPLE: 8 cards are randomly picked from a standard deck of playing cards with replacement.
a)   Give a reason why you can use the binomial distribution to model the number of hearts picked.
b)   Explain why you need to replace the cards for this to be a suitable model.

a)   A deck of cards has 4 suits, but there are only <u>two outcomes</u> (i.e. 'success' = a heart, 'failure' = not a heart).

Here, n = 8 and p = 0.25 — so the distribution is B(8, 0.25).

b)   Cards are replaced so the <u>probability</u> of picking a heart is <u>constant</u>. If there was <u>no replacement</u>, p would <u>change</u> — e.g. from $\frac{13}{52}$ to $\frac{12}{51}$ if the first card was a heart.

Use $(p + q)^n$ to Find Probabilities

1)   Identify the <u>two outcomes</u> (success and failure) and find their <u>probabilities</u> — i.e. p and $q = 1 - p$.
2)   Find the <u>expansion of $(p + q)^n$</u>, where n is the number of trials — e.g. for two trials, $n = 2$, so $(p + q)^2 = p^2 + 2pq + q^2$. However, this gets tough for <u>higher values</u> of n (see the next page).
3)   To find the probability of <u>x successes</u>, find the <u>term</u> of the expansion that has <u>p raised to the power of x</u> (i.e. p^x). So to find P(2 heads), you'd look for the term with p^2 in it.
4)   Stick the numbers for <u>p</u> and <u>q</u> into the <u>term</u> to get the answer.

EXAMPLE: Use the binomial distribution to find the probability of getting one head if you toss a fair coin twice.

Let <u>P(heads) = 0.5 = p</u> and <u>P(tails) = 1 − 0.5 = q</u>. There are two trials, so <u>n = 2</u> and you use the expansion of <u>$(p + q)^2$</u> = $(p + q)(p + q) = \underline{p^2 + 2pq + q^2}$. You want to know the probability that heads occurs once in the two trials — so find the term that includes $p^1 = p$. The term you need is <u>2pq</u>.
So P(1 head) = 2pq = 2 × 0.5 × 0.5 = <u>0.5</u>

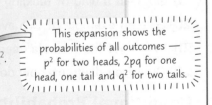

This expansion shows the probabilities of all outcomes — p^2 for two heads, 2pq for one head, one tail and q^2 for two tails.

This page really puts the 'Noooooooooooo!' in Binomial...

Toss a coin. If it lands on heads, do the question below. If it lands on tails, toss the coin again.

1)   At a doctor's surgery, 20% of patients have a cold. There are two patients in the waiting room.
   a)   State one assumption needed for this situation to be modelled by a binomial distribution.
   b)   Use the binomial distribution to find the probability that there are no patients in the waiting room with a cold.

The Binomial Distribution

Now that you've seen the basics of binomial distributions, let's look at some other ways of finding probabilities.

Find Probabilities with Your Calculator

Expanding $(p + q)^n$ by hand is <u>hard</u> for <u>big values of n</u> — so use these other ways to find the terms needed:

1) PASCAL'S TRIANGLE

Pascal's triangle starts with 1 in row 0 and has 1s down both sides. All the other numbers are found by <u>adding the two numbers directly above</u>. E.g. in row 2, the <u>2</u> comes from <u>1 + 1</u>. The triangle gives you the <u>numbers</u> that go <u>in front</u> of p and q — e.g. to expand $(p + q)^4$, use <u>row 4</u> to get $(p + q)^4 = 1p^4 + 4p^3q + 6p^2q^2 + 4pq^3 + 1q^4$.

row 0					1				
row 1				1	+	1			
row 2			1		=2		1		
row 3		1		3		3		1	
row 4	1		4		6		4		1

2) YOUR CALCULATOR'S nCr BUTTON

The <u>nCr button</u> on your calculator gives the numbers in Pascal's triangle. The probability of <u>r successes</u> from <u>n trials</u> is $nCrp^rq^{n-r}$. E.g. for 4 trials with 3 successes, type '4', 'nCr', '3', '=' and you'll get 4 — and the probability is $4p^3q^1$. (The powers of p and q always <u>add up to n</u>.)

You might see nCr written ^nC_r or $\binom{n}{r}$.

3) CALCULATOR FUNCTIONS

Some calculators can find the <u>probability</u> you want <u>directly</u>. All you have to do is find the <u>binomial probability function</u> and enter the number of <u>successes</u> (x), number of <u>trials</u> (n) and probability of <u>success</u> (p) — make sure you know how to find probabilities on <u>your</u> calculator.

To find a <u>range of probabilities</u>, e.g. P(more than 4 successes), simply <u>add up</u> the individual parts (or just use your <u>calculator</u> if it's fancy enough to have <u>binomial probability functions</u>).

EXAMPLE: The probability of an unfair coin landing on heads is 0.75. Use the binomial distribution to find the probability of getting fewer than two heads if you toss the coin five times.

You need to find <u>P(less than 2 heads) = P(1 head) + P(0 heads)</u>.
Let <u>p = P(head) = 0.75</u> and <u>q = P(tail) = 1 − 0.75 = 0.25</u>. The number of trials n = 5, so calculate the 5th row of <u>Pascal's triangle</u>: 1, 5, 10, 10, 5, 1.
So $(p + q)^5 = p^5 + 5p^4q + 10p^3q^2 + 10p^2q^3 + 5pq^4 + q^5$.
The two green terms above are the probabilities for 1 head and 0 heads.
<u>P(1 head)</u> $= 5pq^4 = 5 \times 0.75 \times 0.25^4 = $ <u>0.014648...</u> and <u>P(0 heads)</u> $= q^5 = 0.25^5 = $ <u>0.000976...</u>
So <u>P(less than two heads)</u> = 0.014648... + 0.000976... = <u>0.015625</u>

You could use the nCr button to find the numbers in front of the terms you need — e.g. typing '5', 'nCr', '1' gives 5.

Sometimes, it's easier to do <u>1 minus a probability</u> instead of adding up all the possibilities (see p.88). E.g. if you wanted the probability of <u>at least one</u> head in the example above, it'd be quicker to find <u>1 − P(0 heads)</u> than P(1 head) + P(2 heads) + P(3 heads) + P(4 heads) + P(5 heads).

The Mean of B(n, p) is np

The <u>mean</u> (or <u>expected value</u>) of a binomial distribution is <u>np</u> — e.g. if B(8, 0.7), then the mean is $8 \times 0.7 = 5.6$. This means that if you repeated the 8 trials over and over again, you'd <u>expect</u> an <u>average</u> of 5.6 successes (see p.84 for more on expected and actual frequencies).

All this coin tossing is driving me flipping mad...

Well that was a bit of a tricky topic. And there's plenty more where that came from. For starters, this question:

1) Each day, 9 people take their driving test at a particular test centre. The probability that they pass is 0.4.
   a) Find the probability that three or fewer learners pass their driving test on any day.
   b) How many people would you expect to pass their test each day?

The Normal Distribution

The second (and last) probability distribution you need to know about is the normal distribution.
The name is pretty boring, but it's 'normal' because it's a common model for lots of real-life situations.

A Normal Distribution is Drawn as a Smooth Curve

There are many situations where there are lots of data values near the middle and fewer data values further away. E.g. the weights of apples in an orchard — there'd be lots with similar weights and fewer heavier or lighter ones. Data like this can be modelled by a normal distribution, if the following conditions are met:

1) The data is continuous — e.g. heights, lengths, times, etc.
2) The distribution is symmetrical (p.42) with a peak at the mean (μ) — this means that mean = median = mode (approximately).
3) There are fewer data values as you get further from the mean. This is affected by the standard deviation (σ) — see below.

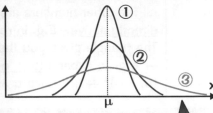

The normal distribution can be written $N(\mu, \sigma^2)$, where μ is the mean and σ is the standard deviation. A graph showing a normal distribution is 'bell' shaped — as shown by the three curves above. Curves 1, 2 and 3 have the same mean but 1 has the smallest standard deviation and 3 has the largest.

Most Data is in the Middle of a Normal Distribution

You need to learn these facts about data values that are modelled by a normal distribution:

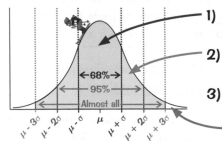

1) Approximately 68% (just over two thirds) of values are within one standard deviation of the mean ($\mu \pm \sigma$).

2) Approximately 95% of values are within two standard deviations of the mean ($\mu \pm 2\sigma$).

3) Values more than three standard deviations from the mean ($\mu \pm 3\sigma$) are very uncommon — these are considered outliers (see page 60).

Approximately 99.7% of the data values lie within 3 standard deviations of the mean.

EXAMPLE: The histogram shows the lengths (in mm) of 57 worms. Find an estimate for the standard deviation of the lengths of the worms using the summary statistics $\sum fx^2 = 129\,243.75$ and $\overline{x} = 46.62$. Then use this to decide whether you think the data can be modelled by a normal distribution.

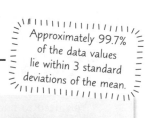

Find the standard deviation using the formula from page 58.

$$\sigma = \sqrt{\frac{\sum fx^2}{\sum f} - \overline{x}^2} = \sqrt{\frac{129\,243.75}{57} - 46.62^2} = 9.6958... = \underline{9.70}\text{ (2 d.p.)}$$

The data is continuous and the distribution is roughly symmetrical, so a normal distribution seems like it might be a good model. If the data is normally distributed then you'd expect about 68% of the data to be within one standard deviation of the mean — so in the range $(46.62 - 9.6958..., 46.62 + 9.6958...) = (\underline{36.92...}, \underline{56.31...})$.

Using frequency = frequency density × class width (page 41), the number of worms in this interval is:
$[0.9 \times (40 - 36.92...)] + [3 \times 5] + [3.2 \times 5] + [0.8 \times (56.31... - 50)] = \underline{38.82...}$

So that's $(38.82... \div 57) \times 100 \approx \underline{68\%}$ of the worms
— suggesting the data is normally distributed.

Alternatively, you could show that 95% of the data is within 2 standard deviations of the mean.

Move along... Nothing to see here... Just a normal distribution...

The normal distribution can be used to model loads of situations in the real world. This one, for instance...

1) The lifetime (in hours) of some batteries can be modelled by $N(100, \sigma^2)$. On average 2.5%, of the batteries last for less than 75 hours. Find an estimate for the standard deviation of the life of the batteries, σ.

Quality Assurance

I assure you this page is going to be absolute quality...

Quality Assurance is Making Sure Products are OK

1) On a <u>production line</u>, people can make mistakes and machinery can stop working. <u>Quality assurance</u> is about making sure that certain <u>measured values</u> stay as close as possible to <u>target values</u>, so that the products are all of the <u>same quality</u>.

2) For quality assurance, you take <u>regular samples</u> and calculate the <u>sample mean</u>, <u>median</u> or <u>range</u>. These sample averages or ranges can then be <u>plotted</u> to see how far they are from the value you'd <u>expect</u> if everything was <u>running properly</u>.

3) You use <u>sample</u> averages or ranges because they'll be <u>more closely distributed</u> than actual data values from the population — so there'll be <u>less variation</u> between them.

The graphs below show some possible results from a quality-assurance procedure:

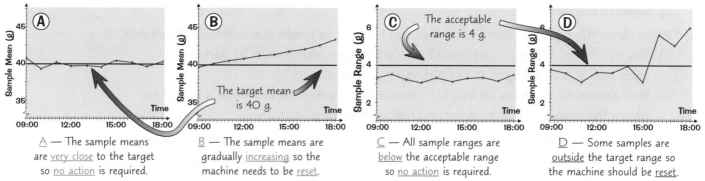

<u>A</u> — The sample means are <u>very close</u> to the target so <u>no action</u> is required.

<u>B</u> — The sample means are gradually <u>increasing</u> so the machine needs to be <u>reset</u>.

<u>C</u> — All sample ranges are <u>below</u> the acceptable range so <u>no action</u> is required.

<u>D</u> — Some samples are <u>outside</u> the target range so the machine should be <u>reset</u>.

Quality Assurance Graphs — Warning and Action Limits

1) Sometimes the quality assurance graphs shown above are more detailed and include:

   WARNING LIMITS — these are set at <u>2 standard deviations</u> above and below the target value. Only <u>1 in 20</u> of the sample averages or ranges should fall outside them.

   ACTION LIMITS — these are set at <u>3 standard deviations</u> above and below the target value. Almost <u>ALL</u> of the sample averages or ranges should fall within them.

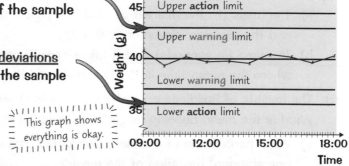

2) If a sample average or range lies <u>between the warning limits</u> the process is working <u>okay</u> and the quality of the product is acceptable.

3) If a sample average or range lies <u>between the warning and action limits</u>, <u>another sample</u> is taken at once to see if there is a problem. If that is <u>also</u> outside the warning limits then production should be <u>stopped</u>.

4) If a sample average or range is <u>outside the action limits</u> the production line is <u>stopped</u> straight away.

This page is quality assured — it's been checked by at most 3 chimps...

When you think you've cracked the page, have a go at this lovely question.

1) A factory makes trousers with an 80 cm inside leg. As a quality control check, samples were taken each hour and the mean lengths recorded. The mean lengths should be normally distributed with $\mu = 80$ and $\sigma = 0.4$.

   a) Plot the sample means against time.

   b) Draw lower and upper warning lines on the graph.

   c) Describe what action should be taken, if any.

   d) What can you say about the standard deviation of the lengths of the inside leg of the trousers?

	10:00	11:00	12:00	13:00	14:00	15:00	16:00	17:00
Sample mean	79.5	79.3	80.6	80.2	80.4	80.0	80.1	81.1

Revision Summary for Section Seven

Section Seven done, and that means you're at the end of the book. Once you've got through this page, that is.
- Try these questions and tick off each one when you get it right.
- When you've done all the questions for a topic and are completely happy with it, tick off the topic.

The Binomial Distribution (p.94-95) ☑

1) List four conditions that must be met to use a binomial distribution to model a sequence of trials. ☑
2) If the probability of success is p, write down an expression for the probability of failure in terms of p. ☑
3) For each of the situations below, give a reason why you couldn't use a binomial distribution.
   a) The number of 'sixes' obtained by rolling a six-sided dice an indefinite number of times.
   b) The number of clubs drawn from a deck of cards after withdrawing 8 cards, without replacement. ☑
4) A sequence of coin tosses is modelled by B(50, p).
   a) How many times was the coin tossed?
   b) What is the value of p? ☑
5) Write down the binomial distribution that can be used to model the following situations:
   a) The number of bullseyes achieved by a darts player who throws 10 darts,
      each with a probability of 0.1 of hitting the bullseye.
   b) The number of windows broken by a vandal who throws 50 stones at a building,
      where the probability of each stone breaking a window is 0.35. ☑
6) a) Write down an expression you can use to find probabilities from a binomial distribution. ☑
   b) Give three ways that you can expand your expression from part a) if you have a lot of trials. ☑
7) What is the mean of the binomial distribution B(n, p)?

The Normal Distribution (p.96) ☑

8) Give three conditions for modelling data with a normal distribution. ☑
9) Make a rough sketch of a normal distribution graph. Mark the mean μ on the x-axis. ☑
10) Write down the normal distribution that can be used to model the following situations:
    a) The mass (to the nearest g) of all the piglets on a farm, where the mean mass is 2.4 kg
       and the standard deviation is 0.2 kg.
    b) The time (in seconds) that it takes Year 10 pupils to run 100 metres,
       where the mean time is 12.8 seconds and the standard deviation is 0.5 seconds. ☑
11) The heights of buildings on a street (in metres) are normally distributed with N(5.7, 0.8).
    What is the mean building height? What is the standard deviation of the heights? ☑
12) a) What percentage of normally distributed data would you expect to find within
       one standard deviation of the mean?
    b) Within how many standard deviations of the mean would you expect to find
       95% of normally distributed data? ☑
13) A data value lies more than 3 standard deviations from the mean. What can you say about this value? ☑

Quality Assurance (p.97) ☑

14) What is the purpose of quality assurance? ☑
15) Describe how to plot a graph for quality assurance. ☑
16) Which would be more consistent — sample means or actual data values? ☑
17) How many standard deviations should a) warning limits and b) action limits be from the mean? ☑
18) What would you do if there was a sample average outside the action limits? ☑
19) What would you do if there was a sample average in between the warning limits and the action limits? ☑

Do Well in Your Exams

Deep breaths everyone. This page is all about how you'll be examined. Oooo errr...

You'll Sit Two Exams

- You'll sit <u>two exams</u> — each one can test <u>any</u> of the topics that you've been taught.
- Each exam will last for <u>1 hour and 30 minutes</u> and will be out of <u>80 marks</u>.
  This works out as roughly <u>1 minute per mark</u> (with about <u>10 minutes</u> left over
  to <u>check</u> your answers) so use this to judge <u>how long</u> to spend on each question.
- There'll be a mix of <u>short</u> questions, <u>medium</u> questions and <u>extended</u> response questions.
- You can use your <u>calculator</u> in <u>both</u> exams.

> Extended response questions require you to explain, discuss or justify something, so you'll have to write more for them.

Top Tips for the Exams

1) General Hints

1) <u>Read</u> each <u>question carefully</u> and make sure you <u>actually answer the question</u>.
   E.g. You don't want to draw a cumulative frequency step polygon instead of a cumulative frequency curve.

2) Make sure you know which <u>formulas</u> you'll be <u>given</u> in the exam and which you need to <u>learn</u>.
   If you're doing the Higher tier exam, you'll be given a formula sheet (see the back cover of this book).

3) Make sure your <u>answers</u> are <u>clear</u> and in the <u>correct form</u> — e.g. if you get your
   answer from a table labelled <u>per thousand</u>, you'll probably need to <u>multiply by 1000</u>.

4) If you're asked to "<u>interpret</u>" some data, it means you need to <u>relate</u> it to the
   <u>context of the question</u>. E.g. if a question about height and hand span asks you to describe
   the correlation and it's positive, you need to say that as height increases, hand span increases.

5) <u>Don't panic</u> if you <u>don't recognise</u> a question or context. You'll be given <u>enough information</u>
   to answer the question, so work out what you <u>know</u> and what it is you're being <u>asked for</u>.

6) Do <u>all the steps</u> in a method or calculation — e.g. when using <u>transformations</u> to help
   you find an average, you need to remember to <u>reverse the transformation</u> (see p.50).

7) <u>Don't rush</u> a question that you think is <u>easy</u> — you could make a
   <u>silly mistake</u> (like using numbers from the wrong part of a Venn diagram).

8) For <u>longer questions</u>, write in <u>full sentences</u> with correct <u>spelling</u> and <u>grammar</u>.

9) Don't forget to use <u>statistical language</u> in your answers — e.g. positive or negative skew.

EXAM SKILLS

Steve brushed up on his exam skills.

2) Diagram Questions

1) <u>Label</u> all <u>diagrams</u> clearly — e.g. the axes of a graph or the sectors of a pie chart.

2) Use a <u>suitable scale</u> that covers the <u>full range</u> of data and is
   <u>large enough</u> so that you can clearly see what's going on.

3) <u>Plot</u> points on a graph <u>accurately</u> and <u>double-check</u> them.

4) Make sure you <u>include all the data</u> — check that you haven't <u>missed out</u> any values.

3) Calculation Questions

1) <u>Draw a sketch</u> if it'll help — e.g. a tree diagram or a sketch of the normal distribution.

2) <u>Show your working clearly</u>. You might get marks for your method even if the answer's wrong.

3) If you get a question that uses the <u>answer</u> of a <u>previous bit</u>, but you're not sure if it's right,
   <u>try the question anyway</u> — you might still get some of the <u>method marks</u>.

4) <u>Check</u> your <u>answer</u> to see if it's <u>sensible</u> — e.g. probabilities can only be between 0 and 1.

Answers

Section One — Planning Data Collection

Page 2 — Planning an Investigation

1) **a)** E.g. 'Children solve the logic puzzle faster than adults.'

b) Think about the different stages of the statistical enquiry cycle.
<u>Collecting data:</u>
E.g. collect primary data by doing an experiment. This data should be reliable as the researcher can measure and record the times fairly and accurately.
<u>Processing and presenting data:</u>
E.g. put the data into grouped frequency tables, with one for children and one for adults. Then averages, such as the mean, can be found and diagrams, such as histograms, can be drawn.
<u>Interpreting results:</u>
E.g. Compare the mean times for children and adults. This shows whether the children were generally faster or slower at solving the puzzle than the adults.
There are loads of things that could be included in an investigation plan — they depend on the hypothesis you've chosen.

Page 3 — Planning an Investigation

1) **a)** It's unethical — showing a scary film to children could cause them distress.

b) Confidentiality — mental health is a sensitive issue, which people may not want to answer questions about.

c) Time — the report has to be finished by the end of the week, so Misha is unlikely to be able to collect her own data.

d) Convenience — it would be extremely difficult for Polly to get access to the royal family.

Page 4 — Types of Data

1) **a) (i)** Processed   **(ii)** Discrete

b) (i) Raw   **(ii)** Qualitative

c) (i) Raw   **(ii)** Continuous

Page 5 — Types of Data

1) **a)** Race position

b) Bivariate

Page 6 — Simplifying Data

1) **a)**

Film Rating	V. bad	Bad	Good	V. good
Total No. of People	17	19	31	33

b) E.g. Advantage — it's easier to see that generally there were more positive film reviews than negative ones.
E.g. Disadvantage — you've lost information about the ticket types (e.g. children and concessions gave quite different film ratings).

Page 7 — Grouping Data

1) **a)** E.g. 1-20, 21-40, 41-60, 61-80, 81-100, 101-120 (amount spent to the nearest pound)

b) E.g. Finding the mean amount of money spent from the grouped data will only give an estimate.

Page 8 — Grouping Data

1) **a)** Rounding gives: 15.3, 15.0, 15.7, 16.4, 16.9, 15.9, 17.0, 15.0, 15.9, 16.5, 16.7, 15.9.
Putting these in a grouped table gives:

Time (t seconds)	$14 < t \leq 14.5$	$14.5 < t \leq 15$	$15 < t \leq 15.5$	$15.5 < t \leq 16$	$16 < t \leq 16.5$	$16.5 < t \leq 17$
Frequency	0	2	1	4	2	3

b) E.g. Rounding the data to the nearest 0.1 seconds affects which class some of the times are in — no snails had a time of 15 seconds or less, but the table suggests that two did.

c) The classes would be wider, so there would be a loss of information — e.g. you lose the fact that there were no times in the $14 < t \leq 14.5$ group.

Page 9 — Data Sources

1) **a)** E.g. People might lie about how much pocket money they get, so her data could be unreliable. / It might be difficult or time-consuming to get answers from the students.

b) E.g. It would be difficult to find secondary data about pocket money or it might not match her hypothesis exactly.

Page 10 — Populations and Sampling

1) **a)** The population is all the people that live on the street, which is a fairly small number, so a census is suitable.

b) The population is all 16-year-olds in the UK (thousands of people), so it probably isn't suitable for the student to do a census.

c) The population is every grain of sand on the beach — it would be impossible to measure them all, so a census isn't suitable.

d) The population is everyone in the UK. The population is large but the government can ask people's names on the national census, so it is suitable.

Page 11 — Populations and Sampling

1) A list of all the registered patients.

2) E.g. Pablo's sample is not likely to be representative. Year 7 pupils might have different tastes in music compared to other year groups.

Page 12 — Random Sampling

1) Get a list of all the 748 students (a sample frame) and number them 1 to 748. Generate 40 random numbers (e.g. using a random number table or computer) between 1 and 748. Match the 40 random numbers to the students to create the sample.

2) E.g. To generate random numbers use the last two digits of each number in the random number table. Start in the top left of the table and read across to generate your random numbers, ignoring any numbers that are outside the range 01 to 28, or repeated. This gives: 12, 10, 9, 25, 2, 23, 18, 21, 14. Match the random numbers to the children.

Answers

Page 13 — Stratified Sampling

1) a) Stratified sampling is suitable because how much people earn might affect who they vote for, and the groups are well defined.

   b) Less than £20 000: (600 / 1500) × 100 = 40 adults
   £20 000 to £40 000: (750 / 1500) × 100 = 50 adults
   More than £40 000: (150 / 1500) × 100 = 10 adults

Page 14 — Systematic and Cluster Sampling

1) Number the biscuits from 1 to 150.
   Divide the batch size by the sample size: 150 ÷ 30 = 5.
   Choose a random start number between 1 and 5 —
   e.g. 2 (from a calculator). Start with the 2nd biscuit and then sample every 5th biscuit after that — so the sample would be the 2nd, 7th, 12th, etc.

2) E.g. Advantage — the restaurants could be spread over a wide area, so it's more convenient to focus on one.
   E.g. Disadvantage — the sample could be biased because this particular restaurant might be better or worse than / different to the other restaurants in the chain.

   You need to recognise from the description that the restaurant chain is using cluster sampling.

Page 15 — Quota, Opportunity and Judgement Sampling

1) a) Opportunity sampling — the sample is done at a place and time that is convenient to the researcher (the high street of a town at 10 am on a Monday morning).

   b) Quota sampling — Paul surveys a certain number of people, based on their eye colour.

   c) Judgement sampling — the teacher uses their knowledge of the students to choose a sample.

Section Two — Collecting Data

Page 17 — Questionnaires

1) a) It's a leading question (because of "Do you agree"). An improved question would be, e.g. "What is the most important subject taught in schools?".

   b) It's ambiguous and there's no time frame — people could interpret 'a lot' differently.
   An improved question would be, e.g. "How many hours do you spend watching television in a week?".

   c) There aren't enough options — they don't allow for all possible answers. An improved question would be, e.g. "What is your favourite drink?
   Answer A, B, C, D, E or F.

   A) Tea   B) Milk   C) Coffee
   D) Soft drink   E) Water   F) Other"

Page 18 — Questionnaires

1) a) E.g. Advantage — it should be quick and cheap to carry out.
   E.g. Disadvantage — the results might be biased depending on who takes a questionnaire and who responds.

   b) E.g. He could enter people who respond into a prize draw.

Page 19 — Questionnaires

1) a) E.g. To spot any questions that are unclear or ambiguous.

   b) You'd expect roughly 328 ÷ 2 = 164 people to toss heads and tick the 'yes' box. Since there are actually 203 'yes' responses, approximately 203 − 164 = 39 people have tossed tails and answered the question with 'yes'. So the estimated proportion in the sample who have used a mobile phone when driving in the last three months is: 39 ÷ 164 = 0.24 or 24% (2 s.f.)

Page 20 — Interviews

1) E.g. Questions about technology might be complicated and Anna could explain these in an interview.
   E.g. The interviews should have a higher response rate.

Page 21 — Observation and Reference Sources

1) E.g.

Day	Mon	Tues	Wed	Thur	Fri	Sat	Sun
Tally							
Freq.							

2) E.g. The number of endangered orangutans probably changes a lot, so there's a good chance the data could be out of date.
   E.g. Hans may not know the reliability of the data.

Page 22 — Experiments

1) a) Explanatory variable — age
   Response variable — amount of sleep

   b) E.g. Physical activity — if you've had an active day you might be more tired and therefore sleep more.
   Food and drink consumed — if you've drunk a lot of caffeine you might get less sleep.
   Amount of stress — stress can make it difficult to sleep, which may reduce the amount of sleep.

Page 23 — Experiments — Lab, Field and Natural

1) a) Lab

   b) Natural

   c) Field

Page 24 — More on Experiments

1) All the extraneous variables like temperature, humidity, etc. haven't been kept constant and will affect the results — e.g. the temperature in the cellar will be very different to that in the greenhouse. There also aren't enough plants (only one in each location) to get reliable results.

Page 25 — Simulation

1) E.g. Find the probabilities of getting each type of chocolate. For every 6 chocolates 1 is white, 1 is dark and 4 are milk. So white has probability $\frac{1}{6}$, dark has probability $\frac{1}{6}$, and milk has probability $\frac{4}{6} = \frac{2}{3}$.
   Roll a dice to generate random numbers between 1 and 6, and assign 1 to white, 2 to dark and 3, 4, 5 and 6 to milk. Roll the dice three times and match the numbers rolled to the type of chocolate.

   You could get random numbers in other ways —
   e.g. on a calculator use RanInt(1, 6), or use a computer.

Answers

Page 26 — Problems with Collected Data

1) E.g. The data is written in different formats — the genders are written in different ways and the times are given in different units (minutes and seconds).
E.g. The last person is an outlier — their time of 0 is probably inaccurate.

You could also mention that the first data entry is in the wrong order, the fourth data entry has missing data (for gender) or that units should be removed.

Section Three — Representing Data

Page 28 — Frequency Tables

1)

No. of coins	0	1	2	3	4	5
Tally	I	II	JHT II	JHT III	JHT IIII	III
Frequency	1	2	7	8	9	3

Page 29 — Grouped Frequency Tables

1)

Height	$0 < h \leq 4$	$4 < h \leq 8$	$8 < h \leq 12$	$12 < h \leq 16$	$16 < h \leq 20$
Tally	II	JHT	II	II	I
Frequency	2	5	2	2	1

Page 30 — Two-Way Tables

1)

	Boy	Girl	Total
Pass	13	24 − 13 = 11	24
Fail	16 − 13 = 3	4	3 + 4 = 7
Total	16	11 + 4 = 15	24 + 7 = 31

You might have used different calculations here.

2) a) Add up the $70 \leq l < 90$ row: 3 + 8 + 4 = 15 newts

b) Add up the $70 \leq w < 100$ column:
0 + 4 + 10 = 14 newts

c) Add up all the values:
7 + 4 + 0 + 3 + 8 + 4 + 0 + 2 + 10 = 38 newts

Page 31 — Interpreting Tables

1) a) Divide the profit for Maltby by the total profit and multiply by 100: 50.2 ÷ 103.3 × 100 = 48.6% (1 d.p.)

b) Profit has decreased from £105 200 in 2014 to £94 900 in 2018, so there is a downwards trend.

The general trend is still downwards, even though there is a slight increase in total profit from 2016 to 2017.

c) E.g. The values for the three branches might have been rounded, whereas the total might have been calculated using unrounded data.

Page 32 — Bar Charts

1) a) Tuesday

b) Mon = 3 × 40 = 120 books, Tues = 40 ÷ 4 = 10 books,
Wed = 40 × 2.5 = 100 books,
Thur = 40 × 3 = 120 books, Fri = 40 books
Total = 120 + 10 + 100 + 120 + 40 = 390 books

Page 33 — Bar Charts

1)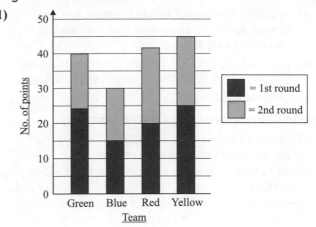

Page 34 — Stem and Leaf Diagrams

1) a)

CITY 1   CITY 2

```
8 8 4 3 2 | 1 | 6 8
  8 7 6 3 | 2 | 6 7 8
      9 6 | 3 | 2 2 2 3 7
          1 | 4 | 2 4
```

key: City 1
2|1 = 12 miles

key: City 2
1|6 = 16 miles

b) City 1: modal distance = 18 miles
City 2: modal distance = 32 miles

c) City 1: commuting range = 41 − 12 = 29 miles
City 2: commuting range = 44 − 16 = 28 miles

d) City 2

Page 35 — Population Pyramids and Choropleth Maps

1) Any two from, e.g.: population A is smaller than population B (the total size of all the bars is smaller) / population A has a higher proportion of younger people / population B has a higher proportion of older people / population B has a higher life expectancy than population A etc.

Page 36 — Pie Charts

1) a) Sparrow angle = (16 ÷ 30) × 360° = 192°
Pigeon angle = (11 ÷ 30) × 360° = 132°
Robin angle = (3 ÷ 30) × 360° = 36°
Draw a circle with a radius of 2.5 cm, accurately draw the angles and add a key (or labels):

b) Measure the angle for pigeons in the afternoon: 144°
So number of pigeons = (144° ÷ 360°) × 20 = 8 pigeons

Page 37 — Comparative Pie Charts

1) Plumson: total = 11 + 13 + 21 = 45 cups
Large = (11 ÷ 45) × 360° = 88°
Medium = (13 ÷ 45) × 360° = 104°
Small = (21 ÷ 45) × 360° = 168°
Area for 45 cups = $\pi r^2 = \pi \times 2^2 = 4\pi$ cm²
Area for 1 cup = $(4\pi) ÷ 45 = 0.279...$ cm²

Coffee Group Place: total = 82 + 62 + 62 = 206 cups
So area for Coffee Group Place pie chart
= 0.279... × 206 = 57.5... cm²
57.5... = πr^2, therefore r^2 = 18.3... $\Rightarrow$ r = 4.3 cm (1 d.p.)
Large = (82 ÷ 206) × 360° = 143.3° (1 d.p.)
Medium/Small = (62 ÷ 206) × 360° = 108.3° (1 d.p.)

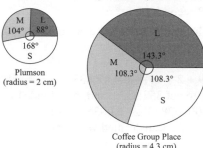

Page 38 — Vertical Line Charts and Frequency Polygons

1)

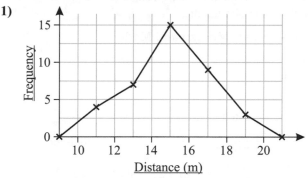

Page 39 — Cumulative Frequency Diagrams

1) Work out the cumulative frequencies:

Age (yrs)	$0 \le y < 20$	$20 \le y < 40$	$40 \le y < 60$	$60 \le y < 80$	$80 \le y < 100$
Frequency	40	50	50	30	20
Cumulative frequency	40	90	140	170	190

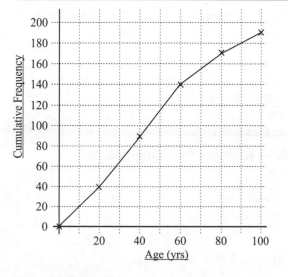

Page 40 — Histograms

1) a) The first bar represents 4 people, so each division on the vertical axis represents 2 people. Use this to work out the number of people for the other bars — e.g. the second bar is 3.5 lines tall and 3.5 × 2 = 7 people.

Time (minutes)	$0 \le t < 2$	$2 \le t < 4$	$4 \le t < 6$	$6 \le t < 8$	$8 \le t < 10$	$10 \le t < 12$
Frequency	4	7	2	3	1	8

You could have labelled the classes differently — i.e. $0 < t \le 2$, $2 < t \le 4$, etc.

b) Find the area to the right of 5 minutes on the histogram — this includes half of the $4 \le t < 6$ bar and all of the $6 \le t < 8$, $8 \le t < 10$ and $10 \le t < 12$ bars. Using the frequency table from part a):
(2 ÷ 2) + 3 + 1 + 8 = 13 people.

Page 41 — Histograms

1) Find the area between 155 and 162 cm on the histogram.
$155 \le h < 160$ area = 5 × 5 = 25
$160 \le h < 162$ area = 3.5 × 2 = 7
25 + 7 = 32 sunflowers.

Page 42 — The Shape of a Distribution

1) a) The distribution for species A is fairly symmetrical, whereas the distribution for species B is negatively skewed (most of the data is to the right).

b) Species B is generally longer — its modal class ($30 \le l < 40$) is larger than the modal class of species A ($20 \le l < 30$) and there are more higher values in general (because of the negative skew).

Page 43 — Scatter Diagrams

1) a), b)

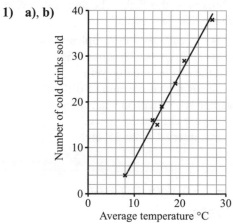

c) The data shows positive correlation.

Page 44 — Time Series Graphs

1) a) The data is measured at time intervals (each year) and is bivariate.

b)

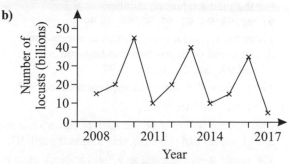

c) There is a cyclic fluctuation with a period of 3 years and a downward trend.

Answers

Page 45 — Choosing How to Represent Data

1) a) Not suitable — e.g. the data isn't bivariate or recorded at time intervals.

b) E.g. suitable — you could group the data and use two different lines to represent males and females.
/ E.g. not suitable — there aren't enough values to group the data.

Page 47 — Misleading Diagrams

1) Any three from — e.g. there's no key / some symbols have been squashed / the symbols are different colours or some are more brightly coloured than others / there's a missing label (for week 3).

2) E.g. Neither of the axes are labelled, there's no title, the scales are not evenly spaced on either axis, one of the bars is far more brightly coloured than the other three (making it stand out more), it is unclear which part of the bar you ought to read the y-value from, the 3D effects are misleading (making the orange bar look far bigger than the others).

3) a) The y-axis is unlikely to be labelled correctly — there should be a key showing that the figures are in thousands or millions of £s, etc.
The x-axis years are not placed correctly — 15 to 17 is a two-year gap, so there should be a space 2 divisions wide between them.

b) The y-axis is broken — this makes the increases look a lot more dramatic than they actually are.

c) The 3D effect is misleading — the graph appears horizontal across ability sets. This gives the impression that the sets do equally well.
The symbols are so big that it would be difficult to read off average scores with any accuracy.
The y-axis values are not equally spaced — 0-20 has the same interval as 20-35, etc.

Section Four — Analysing and Interpreting Data

Page 49 — Mean, Median and Mode

1) a) Mean = (98 + 99 + 97 + 91 + 97 + 92 + 93 + 97 + 95 + 98) ÷ 10
= 957 ÷ 10 = 95.7
For the median, put the numbers in order:
91, 92, 93, 95, <u>97, 97</u>, 97, 98, 98 99
There are ten values so the median is between the fifth and sixth positions, so between 97 and 97. So, the median is 97.
The mode is the value that appears the most: 97.

b) The mean will decrease.
The median will now be the sixth position since there are 11 values. In this case, this means it's still 97.
The mode stays the same as 97 still appears most often.

c) The median is now between the fifth and sixth positions again, but now this is between 95 and 97. So the median is 96.

Page 50 — Mean, Median and Mode

1) Subtract 100 from each of the values:
38, 10, 27, 31, 17, 22, 41, 27, 5, 10
The mean of these values is (38 + 10 + 27 + 31 + 17 + 22 + 41 + 27 + 5 + 10) ÷ 10 = 22.8
Then add 100 back on so the mean of the times is 122.8 seconds.

2) Multiply each value by 100 000 and then subtract 340:
14, 15, 18, 9, 2, 19
The mean of these values is
(14 + 15 + 18 + 9 + 2 + 19) ÷ 6 = 12.833...
Add 340 back on to get 352.833... and then divide by 100 000 to get 0.00352833... = 0.00353 (3 s.f.)
In ascending order, the transformed values are:
2, 9, 14, 15, 18, 19. The median of the transformed values is between 14 and 15 so it's 14.5. Reversing the transformation, this gives a median of 0.003545.
There is no mode for this data since all the values are unique.

Page 51 — Mean, Median and Mode

1) a) Median

b) Mode

c) Mean

2) Use the weighted mean:
$$\frac{(15\times 3)+(68\times 2)+(17\times 1)}{15+68+17}=\frac{198}{100}=1.98 \text{ hours}$$

3) $\sqrt[6]{56\times 83\times 56\times 29\times 46\times 22}=\sqrt[6]{7\,638\,932\,224}$
= 44.378... = 44.4 (1 d.p.)

Page 52 — Averages from Frequency Tables

1) a)

Number of questions (x)	15	16	17	18	19	20	21	
Number of exam papers (f)	3	6	7	12	9	5	2	44
fx	45	96	119	216	171	100	42	789

$$\text{mean}=\frac{\Sigma fx}{\Sigma f}=\frac{789}{44}=17.9318...=17.9 \text{ (1 d.p.)}$$

b) Median position = (44 + 1) ÷ 2 = 22.5 so the median lies between the 22nd and 23rd values.
There are 3 + 6 + 7 = 16 values in the first three columns and 16 + 12 = 28 values in the first four columns, so the median is in the fourth column. Hence, the median is 18.

c) The column with the highest frequency is the fourth, so the mode is 18.

Page 53 — Averages from Grouped Data

1) a)

Weight (g)	$3<x\le 6$	$6<x\le 9$	$9<x\le 12$	$12<x\le 15$	
Frequency (f)	1	9	5	3	18
Midpoint (x)	4.5	7.5	10.5	13.5	
fx	4.5	67.5	52.5	40.5	165

$$\text{Mean}=\frac{\Sigma fx}{\Sigma f}=\frac{165}{18}=9.166...=9.17 \text{ (2 d.p.)}$$

b) 18 ÷ 2 = 9 so the median is in the 9th position. This is in the group $6<x\le 9$. There is only one value in the group below this, so the median is the 8th value in the group $6<x\le 9$.

Answers

There are 9 values in this group so, as a proportion, the median is $8 \div 9 = 0.88...$ of the way through the group. The class width is 3 g so the median is $0.88... \times 3 = 2.66...$ g into the group. Therefore, the median is $6 + 2.66... = 8.66... = 8.67$ g (2 d.p.).

c) The modal group is $6 < x \le 9$ as it has the greatest frequency.

Page 54 — Measures of Spread

1) a) Range $= 999 - 1 = 998$

b) Upper quartile: $3(999 + 1) \div 4 = 750^{th}$ value $= 750$

c) P_{85}: $85(999 + 1) \div 100 = 850^{th}$ value $= 850$

d) P_{50}: $50(999 + 1) \div 100 = 500^{th}$ value $= 500$
So the median is also 500.

Page 55 — Measures of Spread

1) $1, \underline{3}, 5, 7, 9, \underline{11}, 13$
$Q_1 = 3$, $Q_3 = 11$ so IQR $= 11 - 3 = 8$

2) The $P_{95} - P_{90}$ interpercentile range is much smaller than the $P_{90} - P_{85}$ interpercentile range so the 5% of the data between the 90th and 95th percentiles is packed much more tightly than the 5% of the data between the 85th and 90th percentiles.

Page 56 — Measures of Spread — Grouped Data

1) a) Find the quartiles, deciles and percentiles by drawing lines across the chart.

(i) $Q_1 \approx 1.8$ kg, $Q_3 \approx 3$ kg so IQR $\approx 3 - 1.8 = 1.2$ kg

(ii) $P_{20} \approx 1.6$ kg, $P_{80} \approx 3.2$ kg
so 20th to 80th interpercentile range
$\approx 3.2 - 1.6 = 1.6$ kg

(iii) $D_1 \approx 1.1$ kg, $D_9 \approx 3.7$ kg
so interdecile range $\approx 3.7 - 1.1 = 2.6$ kg

(iv) $P_{90} \approx 3.7$ kg, $P_{95} \approx 4.1$ kg so
90th to 95th interpercentile range
$\approx 4.1 - 3.7 = 0.4$ kg

b) The interdecile range and the 90th to 95th interpercentile range both use high values in their calculations and so may be affected by the unusually heavy melons.

Page 57 — Standard Deviation

The "yellow" formula has been used here but using the "blue" formula would give you the same answers.

1) $\overline{x} = (-1 + 4 - 2 + 5 + 3 + 2 + 2 + 1 + 0 + 1) \div 10 = 1.5$
$\sum x^2 = (-1)^2 + 4^2 + (-2)^2 + 5^2 + 3^2 + 2^2 + 2^2 + 1^2 + 0^2 + 1^2$
$= 65$
$\sigma = \sqrt{\dfrac{\sum x^2}{n} - \overline{x}^2} = \sqrt{\dfrac{65}{10} - 1.5^2} = 2.061... = 2.06$ (2 d.p.)

2) The first six odd numbers are: 1, 3, 5, 7, 9, 11
$\overline{x} = (1 + 3 + 5 + 7 + 9 + 11) \div 6 = 6$
$\sum x^2 = 1^2 + 3^2 + 5^2 + 7^2 + 9^2 + 11^2 = 286$
$\sigma = \sqrt{\dfrac{\sum x^2}{n} - \overline{x}^2} = \sqrt{\dfrac{286}{6} - 6^2} = 3.415... = 3.42$ (2 d.p.)

3) The first six even numbers are: 2, 4, 6, 8, 10, 12
$\overline{x} = (2 + 4 + 6 + 8 + 10 + 12) \div 6 = 7$
$\sum x^2 = 2^2 + 4^2 + 6^2 + 8^2 + 10^2 + 12^2 = 364$
$\sigma = \sqrt{\dfrac{\sum x^2}{n} - \overline{x}^2} = \sqrt{\dfrac{364}{6} - 7^2} = 3.415... = 3.42$ (2 d.p.)

The values in Q2 and Q3 may be different but they're spread out in the same way (the values are every second integer), so their standard deviations are equal.

Page 58 — Standard Deviation from Frequency Tables

1)

x	f	fx	x^2	fx^2
25	1	25	625	625
26	5	130	676	3380
27	3	81	729	2187
28	2	56	784	1568
29	1	29	841	841
	12	321		8601

The mean is $321 \div 12 = 26.75$. Then, using the "yellow formula", the standard deviation is:
$\sigma = \sqrt{\dfrac{\sum fx^2}{\sum f} - \overline{x}^2} = \sqrt{\dfrac{8601}{12} - 26.75^2}$
$= 1.089... = 1.09$ (2 d.p.)

Page 59 — Box Plots

1) Put the numbers in ascending order:
$2, 9, \underline{12}, 13, 13, \underline{13}, 14, 14, \underline{15}, 16, 17$
The median is the sixth value (13), the lower quartile is the third value (12) and the upper quartile is the ninth value (15). On the box plot, the ends of the box are at the quartiles and the line down the box is at the median. The ends of the lines (the whiskers) are at the smallest and greatest values (2 and 17).

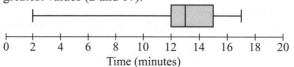

Page 60 — Outliers

1) The outlier is the point that doesn't fit the general pattern (circled below).

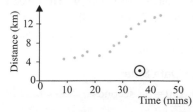

The outlier is probably not genuine. Whilst people run at very different speeds, it seems unlikely that someone would take nearly 40 minutes to travel about 2 km.

2) a) The median is $(138 + 143) \div 2 = 140.5$.
The lower quartile is $(128 + 130) \div 2 = 129$.
The upper quartile is $(147 + 153) \div 2 = 150$.

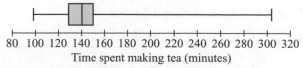

b) IQR $= 150 - 129 = 21$
$Q_3 + (1.5 \times IQR) = 150 + (1.5 \times 21) = 181.5$
Since $303 > 181.5$, this value is an outlier.

Answers

$Q_1 - (1.5 \times IQR) = 129 - (1.5 \times 21) = 97.5$
Since $95 < 97.5$, this value is an outlier.
The method using the mean and the standard deviation in the example on page 60 didn't return 95 as an outlier.

Page 61 — Skewness of Data

1) a) E.g. mean $= 150$, median $= 140.5$
So mean $>$ median, indicating a positive skew.
Or median $- Q_1 = 11.5$, $Q_3 -$ median $= 9.5$
So median $- Q_1 > Q_3 -$ median,
indicating a negative skew.
Since the two inequalities give contradicting indications, this question shows why you shouldn't solely rely on inequalities to find the skewness of a data set.

 b) $skew = \dfrac{3(mean - median)}{standard\ deviation} = \dfrac{3(150 - 140.5)}{48.34}$
$= 0.589... = 0.59$ (2 d.p.)
So the data is (slightly) positively skewed. This means most of the times are lower, with fewer higher times (or the times are more spread out above the median).

2) Mean $= 1382 \div 50 = 27.64$
Median $= (48 + 57) \div 2 = 52.5$
$\sigma = \sqrt{\dfrac{209\,736}{50} - 27.64^2} = 58.572...$
$skew = \dfrac{3(27.64 - 52.5)}{58.572...} = -1.273... = -1.27$ (2 d.p.)

Page 62 — Comparing Data Sets

1) The median for females (40 g) is lower than the median for males (50 g) so female chipmunks weigh less on average. (You can also see that the females generally weigh less since the entire box is to the left of the box for the males.)
$IQR_{female} = 45 - 36 = 9$ g, $IQR_{male} = 60 - 48 = 12$ g
The IQR for males is higher than the IQR for females so the middle 50% of the weights of the male chipmunks was more varied than that of the females.
Looking at the position of the median lines in the boxes, both males and females have positive skew. However, the skew in the male chipmunks is stronger than the females. So the weights of the female chipmunks were spread more symmetrically than the weights of the males.

Page 63 — Comparing Data Sets

1) $mean_{school} = 43\,500 \div 750 = 58$ seconds
$\sigma_{school} = \sqrt{\dfrac{1}{750} \times 75\,321} = 10.021...$
The mean time for Year 7 pupils was higher than the mean time for the school so Year 7 pupils were slower on average. The standard deviations were almost equal so the spread of the times for Year 7 was consistent with that of the school.

Page 64 — Standardised Scores

1) a) **History** Student A: $\dfrac{78 - 74}{5} = 0.8$,
Student B: $\dfrac{85 - 74}{5} = 2.2$, Student C: $\dfrac{69 - 74}{5} = -1$

 Geography Student A: $\dfrac{75 - 78}{4} = -0.75$,
Student B: $\dfrac{71 - 78}{4} = -1.75$, Student C: $\dfrac{83 - 78}{4} = 1.25$

 b) Student B has the greatest total standardised score so they performed best overall.

 c) (i) Student A: $0.3 = (56 - x) \div y$
Student B: $1.2 = (59 - x) \div y$
Solving these equations simultaneously:
$1.2y + x = 59$
$- 0.3y + x = 56$
$\overline{\quad 0.9y = 3\quad}$
$y = 3.333... = 3.33$ (2 d.p.)
$\Rightarrow x = 59 - (1.2 \times 3.333...) = 55$

 (ii) Student C: $\dfrac{34 - 55}{3.333...} = -6.3$

Page 65 — Summary Statistics — Index Numbers

1) a) Average monthly rate decreased in 2014 ($85 < 100$).

 b) $85 = \dfrac{price\ in\ 2014}{£530} \times 100 \Rightarrow price\ in\ 2014 = £450.50$
$109 = \dfrac{price\ in\ 2015}{£530} \times 100 \Rightarrow price\ in\ 2015 = £577.70$

Page 66 — Summary Statistics — Index Numbers

1) Cheese index number $\times$ weight $= \left(\dfrac{20}{17} \times 100\right) \times 4$
$= 470.58...$
Wine index number $\times$ weight $= \left(\dfrac{325}{378} \times 100\right) \times 85$
$= 7308.20...$
Biscuits index number $\times$ weight $= \left(\dfrac{35}{30} \times 100\right) \times 7$
$= 816.66...$
Crisps index number $\times$ weight $= \left(\dfrac{25}{18} \times 100\right) \times 4$
$= 555.55...$
Weighted index number
$= \dfrac{470.58... + 7308.20... + 816.66... + 555.55...}{4 + 85 + 7 + 4}$
$= 91.5$ (1 d.p.)
This means spending has decreased by $100 - 91.5 = 8.5\%$.

2) a)

Year	2014	2015	2016	2017
% change	1.5%	0.0%	0.7%	2.7%
Index	101.5	100	100.7	102.7

 b) 2016 bill: $£444 \times 1.007 = £447.108 \approx £447.11$
2017 bill: $£447.108 \times 1.027 = £459.179... \approx £459.18$

Page 67 — Summary Statistics — Rates of Change

1) a) Crude death rate $= \dfrac{3820}{130\,000} \times 1000$
$= 29.38... = 29.4$ (3 s.f.)
Crude birth rate $= \dfrac{5670}{130\,000} \times 1000$
$= 43.61... = 43.6$ (3 s.f.)

 b) $4.56 = \dfrac{number\ of\ unemployed\ people}{130\,000} \times 1000$
$\Rightarrow$ number of unemployed people $= 592.8$

Page 68 — Summary Statistics — Rates of Change

1) a) <18: $\dfrac{0.02}{1000} \times 110 = 0.0022$
18-29: $\dfrac{8}{1000} \times 280 = 2.24$

$30\text{-}60: \dfrac{12}{1000} \times 260 = 3.12$

$>60: \dfrac{56}{1000} \times 350 = 19.6$

Standardised rate:
$0.0022 + 2.24 + 3.12 + 19.6 = 24.9622$

b) Crude rate for this town: $0.02 + 8 + 12 + 56 = 76.02$
So both rates are significantly lower for this town than Portlidge, but the difference is less after standardising.

Page 69 — Estimating Population Characteristics

1) **a)** $30 \div 200 = 0.15$
$0.15 \times 1\,000\,000 = 150\,000$ tourists

b) £750

c) The interquartile range of the sample is $250 - 50 = 200$ miles, so an estimate for the interquartile range of the population is also 200 miles.

Page 70 — Estimating Population Sizes

1) $\dfrac{10}{20} = \dfrac{30}{N} \Rightarrow N = \dfrac{30 \times 20}{10} = 60$ frogs

Section Five — Analysing and Interpreting Diagrams

Page 72 — Scatter Diagrams — Correlation

1) **a)** Zero correlation (or weak positive correlation)

b) Weak negative correlation

c) Strong positive correlation

d) Strong positive correlation

Page 73 — Scatter Diagrams — Using Lines of Best Fit

1) **a)** $\overline{x} = (80 + 49 + 38 + 58 + 68 + 72 + 46 + 70 + 59) \div 9$
$= 60$
$\overline{y} = 20 + 18 + 6 + 12 + 18 + 14 + 14 + 15 + 18) \div 9$
$= 15$
Double mean point = (60, 15)

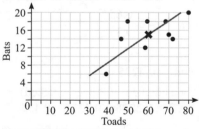

You could have put bats on the x-axis and toads on the y-axis, as long as your points and trend line are right.

b) Accept 10, 11 or 12 bats

c) 180 is far beyond the range of the data ($38 \leq x \leq 80$) and extrapolating is unreliable.
You could also mention that the correlation doesn't look very strong.

Page 74 — Scatter Diagrams — Regression Lines

1) **a)** The line goes through, e.g. (45, 430) and (135, 360).
gradient $= \dfrac{430 - 360}{45 - 135} = -\dfrac{7}{9}$
y-intercept $= 430 - \left(-\dfrac{7}{9} \times 45\right) = 465$
So the line has equation $y = 465 - \dfrac{7}{9}x$

b) For every minute that passes, the height of the water in the tank decreases by $^7/_9$ of a centimetre.

c) For $x = 100$, $y = 465 - \left(\dfrac{7}{9} \times 100\right) = 387$ cm (3 s.f.)

Page 75 – Spearman's Rank Correlation Coefficient

1) **a)** The ranks and differences are in the table below.

	A	B	C	D	E	F	G	H
Lewis	5	1	8	6	4	2	3	7
Dee	1	7	3	4	8	6	2	5
d	4	−6	5	2	−4	−4	1	2
d^2	16	36	25	4	16	16	1	4

$\sum d^2 = 16 + 36 + 25 + 4 + 16 + 16 + 1 + 4 = 118$
$r_s = 1 - \dfrac{6 \times 118}{8(8^2 - 1)} = -0.405$ (3 d.p.)

b) There is moderately strong negative correlation, so their tastes are quite different.

Page 76 — Interpreting Correlation Coefficients

1) **a)** There is very weak negative correlation.

b) E.g. He could be correct. If the SRCC was close to −1 then it would show strong negative association. This wouldn't be detected by Pearson's PMCC if the association is non-linear.

Page 77 — Time Series

1) **a)** For 2015 Q1-Q4, $(13 + 12 + 14 + 18) \div 4 = 14.25$
By similar calculations, the other moving averages are:
14.75, 16, 16 and 16.25.

b)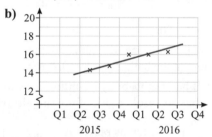

Page 78 — Time Series

1) **a)**

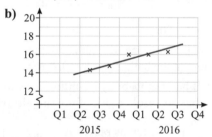

b) Square points on the graph, plotted at $y = 202.5, 197.5, 190, 192.5, 197.5, 195, 197.5, 195, 192.5$

c) Thicker line on the graph.

d) From the trend line, average seasonal effect for Q4 $= [(210 - 197) + (230 - 195) + (220 - 192)] \div 3$
$= £25.33$ (nearest whole pence)

e) $190 + 25.33 = £215.33$ (nearest whole pence)
It's okay if your answers for parts d) and e) are slightly different — your trend line probably won't match up exactly with the one we've drawn here.

Answers

Section Six — Probability

Page 80 — Probability

1) a) even chance – 0.5

b) impossible – 0

c) certain – 1

2) HHH, HHT, HTH, THH, HTT, THT, TTH, TTT

Page 81 — Probability

1) P(pink poodle winning)

$$= \frac{\text{Total number of pink poodles}}{\text{Total number of poodles}} = \frac{5}{8}$$

(or 0.625, or 62.5%).

Page 82 — Relative Frequency and Risk

1) a) Total number of spins: $69 + 98 + 83 = 250$

Relative frequency of magenta $= \frac{69}{250} = 0.276$

Relative frequency of silver $= \frac{98}{250} = 0.392$

Relative frequency of turquoise $= \frac{83}{250} = 0.332$

b) By using a larger number of trials (spins). The more trials there are, the more accurate the probability is likely to be.

Page 83 — Relative Frequency and Risk

1) a) Relative frequency $= \frac{\text{Number of times it happened}}{\text{Number of trials}}$

$$= \frac{32}{40} = \frac{4}{5} = 0.8 = 80\%$$

b) The absolute risk of missing the ball is 1 – the probability they hit the ball: $1 - 0.8 = 0.2$ (or 20%)

c) Tennis player B has a probability of hitting the ball of $60\% = 0.6$, so has an absolute risk of missing the ball of 0.4 (or 40%).

Relative risk $= \frac{\text{risk for tennis player A}}{\text{risk for tennis player B}} = \frac{0.2}{0.4} = \frac{1}{2}$

So tennis player A is half as likely to miss the ball as tennis player B.

Page 84 — Expected and Actual Frequencies

1) Expected frequency

= number of trials × probability of outcome

$$= 24 \times \frac{1}{6} = 4$$

2) First, work out the probability of the spinner landing on blue:

$$P(\text{blue}) = \frac{\text{number of blue sides}}{\text{total number of sides}} = \frac{1}{5}$$

Then you can work out the expected frequency:

Number of trials × probability of outcome

$$= 200 \times \frac{1}{5} = 40 \text{ times}$$

Page 85 — Sample Space Diagrams

1)

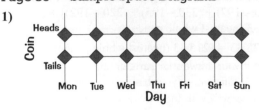

Page 86 — Venn Diagrams and Two-Way Tables

1)

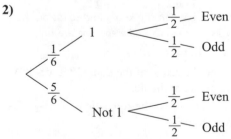

Page 87 — Venn Diagrams and Two-Way Tables

1) a) P(student in choir and football team) = 0.1

b) P(student not in football team) = 0.3 + 0.4 = 0.7

Page 88 — The Addition Law

1) P(odd number or six) = P(odd number) + P(six)

$$= \frac{1}{2} + \frac{1}{6} = \frac{4}{6} = \frac{2}{3}$$

2) P(diamond or king) = P(diamond) + P(king)

$$- P(\text{diamond and king}) = \frac{13}{52} + \frac{4}{52} - \frac{1}{52} = \frac{16}{52} = \frac{4}{13}$$

Page 89 — Independent Events

1) P(6 on 1st roll and even number on 2nd roll)

$$= P(6) \times P(\text{even number}) = \frac{1}{6} \times \frac{1}{2} = \frac{1}{12}$$

2) P(late at least once) = 1 – P(not late at all)

$$= 1 - [P(\text{not late}) \times P(\text{not late}) \times P(\text{not late}) \times P(\text{not late})$$
$$\times P(\text{not late})]$$

$$= 1 - \left[\frac{2}{3} \times \frac{2}{3} \times \frac{2}{3} \times \frac{2}{3} \times \frac{2}{3}\right]$$

$$= 1 - \frac{32}{243} = \frac{211}{243}$$

Page 90 — Tree Diagrams

1) a)

```
                                    0.65 ─ Chicken   0.65 × 0.65
                    Chicken <                        = 0.4225
              0.65          0.35 ─ Beef              0.65 × 0.35
                                                     = 0.2275
        <
              0.35                  0.65 ─ Chicken   0.35 × 0.65
                    Beef <                           = 0.2275
                            0.35 ─ Beef              0.35 × 0.35
                                                     = 0.1225
```

P(both chicken) = 0.4225

b) P(one beef, one chicken) = P(beef, chicken) + P(chicken, beef) = 0.2275 + 0.2275 = 0.455

2)

```
                                1/2 ─ Even
                    1  <
              1/6        1/2 ─ Odd
        <
              5/6                1/2 ─ Even
                    Not 1 <
                            1/2 ─ Odd
```

P(rolling 1 then rolling even) $= \frac{1}{6} \times \frac{1}{2} = \frac{1}{12}$

Page 91 — Conditional Probability

1) P(no dog | cat)

$$= \frac{\text{Number of households with cats but no dog}}{\text{Number of households with cats}} = \frac{5}{9}$$

Answers

2) a) P(male | fez)

$$= \frac{\text{Number of males preferring fezzes}}{\text{Number of people preferring fezzes}} = \frac{20}{32} = \frac{5}{8}$$

b) P(fez | male)

$$= \frac{\text{Number of males preferring fezzes}}{\text{Number of males}} = \frac{20}{75} = \frac{4}{15}$$

Page 92 — Conditional Probability

1) a) First, draw a tree diagram:

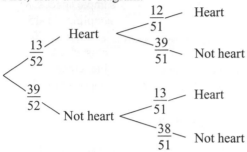

$$\text{P(both hearts)} = \frac{13}{52} \times \frac{12}{51} = \frac{156}{2652} = \frac{1}{17}$$

b) P(1st card is a heart | 2nd card is a heart)
= P(both hearts) ÷ P(2nd card is a heart)

You know P(both hearts) from part a), so you need to find P(2nd card is a heart).

The event '2nd card is a heart' can occur in two ways — both cards are hearts or 1st card not heart, 2nd card heart. You already have the probability for both hearts so you need to work out P(not heart, heart) using fractions from the tree diagram:

$$\text{P(not heart, heart)} = \frac{39}{52} \times \frac{13}{51} = \frac{507}{2652} = \frac{13}{68}$$

So $\text{P(2nd card is a heart)} = \frac{1}{17} + \frac{13}{68} = \frac{1}{4}$

Now put everything into the formula for the General Multiplication Law:

P(1st card is a heart | 2nd card is a heart)
= P(both hearts) ÷ P(2nd card is a heart)
$$= \frac{1}{17} \div \frac{1}{4} = \frac{4}{17}$$

You could just say that P(2nd card is a heart) = $\frac{1}{4}$ by explaining that if the first card isn't given, then the second card is equally likely to be any of the four suits.

Section Seven — Probability Distributions

Page 94 — The Binomial Distribution

1) a) E.g. the probability of any patient having a cold is independent of any other having a cold, or the probability of any patient having a cold is the same as for any other patient.

b) 20% of patients have a cold so let p = P(patient has a cold) = 0.2 and q = P(patient doesn't have a cold) = 0.8. Then the number of patients with a cold in the waiting room can be modelled by B(2, 0.2).
$(p + q)^2 = p^2 + 2pq + q^2$
P(0 patients with a cold) = q^2 (since this has no p term)
$= 0.8^2 = 0.64$

Page 95 — The Binomial Distribution

1) a) Let p = P(pass) = 0.4 and q = P(fail) = 0.6. Then the number of people who pass each day can be modelled by B(9, 0.4). You need the expansion of $(p + q)^9$. Using the nCr button, the numbers in the ninth row of Pascal's triangle are 1, 9, 36, 84, 126, 126, 84, 36, 9, 1 and so $(p + q)^9 = p^9 + 9p^8q + 36p^7q^2 + 84p^6q^3 + 126p^5q^4 + 126p^4q^5 + 84p^3q^6 + 36p^2q^7 + 9pq^8 + q^9$.
P(three or fewer passes)
= P(0 pass) + P(1 pass) + P(2 pass) + P(3 pass)
$= q^9 + 9pq^8 + 36p^2q^7 + 84p^3q^6$
$= 0.6^9 + (9 \times 0.4 \times 0.6^8) + (36 \times 0.4^2 \times 0.6^7) + (84 \times 0.4^3 \times 0.6^6) = 0.4826$ (4 d.p.)

b) You'd expect $9 \times 0.4 = 3.6$ people to pass.

Page 96 — The Normal Distribution

1) Draw a sketch of the normal distribution to help:

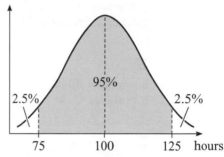

2.5% of the data is below 75 and so, by the symmetry of the distribution, 2.5% is above 125. This leaves 95% of the data within the interval (75, 125). For a normal distribution, you expect 95% of the data to be within 2 standard deviations of the mean, so the interval (75, 125) is the same as the interval $(100 - 2\sigma, 100 + 2\sigma)$. Hence, $100 + 2\sigma = 125 \Rightarrow 2\sigma = 125 - 100 = 25$
$\Rightarrow \sigma = 25 \div 2 = 12.5$ hours

Page 97 — Quality Assurance

1) a), b)

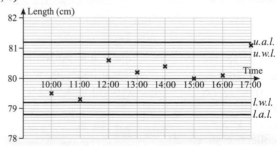

The target value is 80 cm so the warning limits should be at $80 - (2 \times 0.4) = 79.2$ cm (labelled *l.w.l.*) and $80 + (2 \times 0.4) = 80.8$ cm (labelled *u.w.l.*). The action limits should be at $80 - (3 \times 0.4) = 78.8$ cm (labelled *l.a.l.*) and $80 + (3 \times 0.4) = 81.2$ cm (labelled *u.a.l.*).

c) There is a sample mean between the upper warning limit and the upper action limit so a further sample should be immediately taken. If the mean of this sample is also above the upper warning limit then production should be stopped.

d) Sample means are more consistent than actual data values, so the standard deviation of the lengths will be greater than 0.4.

Index